a b c d e f g h i j k

# The Art of
# Royal Icing

## Eddie Spence MBE

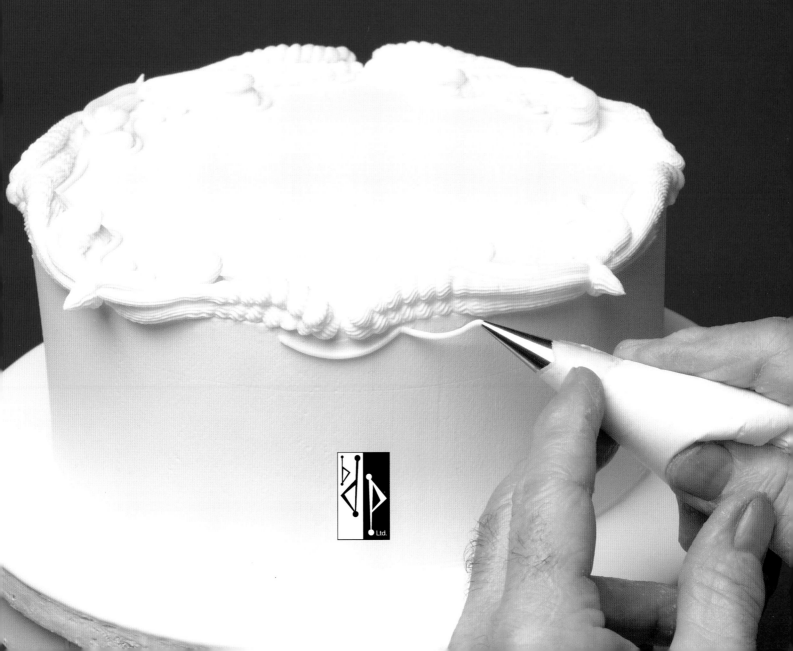

First published in March 2010
by B. Dutton Publishing Limited,
The Grange, Hones Yard,
Farnham, Surrey,
GU9 8BB.

Reprinted in October 2010, July 2011,
May 2012 and June 2013.

Copyright: Eddie Spence 2010

ISBN-13: 978-1-905113-15-6

Special edition ISBN-13: 978-1-905113-16-3

Publisher: Beverley Dutton

Editor: Jenny Stewart

Art Director/Designer: Sarah Ryan

Deputy Editor: Jenny Royle

Graphic Designer: Zena Manicom

Publishing Assistant: Louise Pepé

Photography: Alister Thorpe

Printed in China

# Foreword

I was so delighted and truly honoured to be asked to write this foreword to Eddie's long-awaited book.

He has been a valued friend over many years and a like-minded colleague. His input and dedication within our industry has been astounding and a credit to him.

His enthusiasm never wanes; he always holds his audiences and students spellbound and in awe of his skill with a piping tube to produce stunning work with such ease. Chattering away, creating a masterpiece, whilst we all hold our breath, attempting the same!

Eddie is a kind and considerate person who always makes his students feel at ease and has time for everyone.

This beautiful book shows Eddie's immense skill, uniqueness and individuality within its pages. Those of us who have had the good fortune to attend one of his classes, or meet him, will recognise his distinctive work and his endearing quality.

I am sure the book will be a huge success and enjoyed by one and all.

**Paddi Clark**
November 2009

Some 30 years ago I was lucky enough to be introduced to the art of cake decorating and sugarcraft. It was an optional lesson that was tagged onto a Friday afternoon. It was purely a voluntary thing, and many of my friends really could not be bothered to turn up.

Thankfully, I took the course and found an exciting and totally unique area to cooking that I never knew existed. We royal iced cakes, made pastillage and real marzipan.

The skills and knowledge gained have never left me, even now; time permitting I love to play around.

A couple of years ago I decided to brush up on my skills and went to work with Eddie at Squires Kitchen. I was a little nervous, if I'm being honest, not really sure what to expect. We had a fabulous couple of days; he is not only a wonderful teacher, but also a very kind and gentle man.

I have found in life you meet a lot of people who are very good at their chosen career. Occasionally, very occasionally, you come across a real master. This happened to me when I met Eddie. I have no hesitation in saying that, bar none, he is the best confectioner, baker and cake decorator I have ever met in my life. His attention to fine detail, coupled with his vast knowledge, make me wonder if I will ever meet anybody like him again.

This book showcases all of Eddie's wonderful skills and will be a book that professional and amateur cooks refer to for many years to come. I feel incredibly privileged to have not only met Eddie, but worked with him.

If I could be half as good as him, I would be very happy indeed.

**Phil Vickery**
December 2009

*This book is dedicated to my darling wife, Betty.*

# Acknowledgements

I would like to say a very special thank you to my son, Paul, his lovely wife, Jackie, and their two sons, Christopher and Joshua. They have always been such a great support to me.

Especial thanks to Beverley and Robert for their encouragement and for giving me the opportunity to publish my work.

Many, many thanks to my lovely friends and colleagues, Jenny Stewart and Sarah Ryan. Without their aid, I could not have compiled the many years of work that have been put together to make this book.

Thank you to Joan Mooney for the loan of her photograph album.

# Introduction

Having taught royal icing for fifty years, I have been asked on many occasions to write a book specifically on royal icing.

By writing this book my aim is to teach beginners and advanced students all the techniques they need, from simple line work to finer, more advanced royal icing, right up to exhibition standard. These techniques are presented in a series of royal icing tutorials in its various forms. All diagrams, templates and step-by-step work are in simple form to make the learning process easy-to-follow and fun.

As you work through the methods in this book you can start off practising on plaques, cake tops and dummy cakes, which will give you the confidence to attempt more advanced designs. Once you have mastered the techniques there are several cake designs at the back of the book that you can follow to get quick results. These designs can be altered for various types of cake to make it suitable for the occasion. Once you have practised the techniques using the tutorials, you can start to use the principles of working with royal icing to design your own cakes, incorporating your own style and personality into your work.

I would not have been able to write this book without my family. My son Paul, his wife Jackie, and their two sons Christopher and Joshua have always been such a great support to me and I am extremely proud to be Paul's father. My wonderful brother, George, who likes to be referred to as my much younger brother (only by two years!) goes on holiday with me every year; we have been to some of the most beautiful places that I would never have seen without him. He has a heart of gold and is always there on the end of the phone, no matter what the time or problem. My youngest brother, William, who really is much younger than me (sixteen years), has given me a huge amount of help and guidance over the years; his knowledge is never ending and he never falters. It is always special being with my brothers and I am very proud of what they have achieved, particularly considering where we all started. The support, help and endless love they have all given me pulled me through the very sad time in my life when we lost my darling wife, Betty.

This book has given me the opportunity to share my love of royal icing with all my students and friends, as well as introducing it to those who are new to the art. I hope you enjoy the book and that it will inspire you to create your own work of art in royal icing.

*Eddie Spence M. B. E.*

# *Contents*

# From the Royal Mile to a Royal Honour

## A Biography of Eddie Spence

Eddie collecting his MBE in 2000.

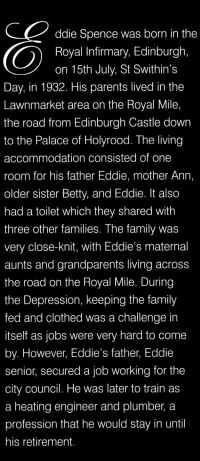

Eddie Spence was born in the Royal Infirmary, Edinburgh, on 15th July, St Swithin's Day, in 1932. His parents lived in the Lawnmarket area on the Royal Mile, the road from Edinburgh Castle down to the Palace of Holyrood. The living accommodation consisted of one room for his father Eddie, mother Ann, older sister Betty, and Eddie. It also had a toilet which they shared with three other families. The family was very close-knit, with Eddie's maternal aunts and grandparents living across the road on the Royal Mile. During the Depression, keeping the family fed and clothed was a challenge in itself as jobs were very hard to come by. However, Eddie's father, Eddie senior, secured a job working for the city council. He was later to train as a heating engineer and plumber, a profession that he would stay in until his retirement.

Two-and-a-half years after Eddie was born, his younger brother, George, was born. The family moved to better accommodation in the West Port of Edinburgh where they had a living room/bedroom, a kitchen and their own private toilet. Eddie can distinctly recall life at the new house: "Our mum used to bathe us in the deep sink in the kitchen and the three children slept in the same bed, head to toe. Although this was a modest lifestyle, our parents were extremely loving and we all enjoyed a very happy upbringing." Eddie remembers his mother keeping the house spotless and his father painting and decorating the house on a regular basis. Although the living conditions were cramped by today's standards, they had more than most families around them.

At the age of five, Eddie attended Castle Hill Primary School, the local state school. He remembers, "Although everyone was poor, everyone was the same so there was a great sense of community."

On 1st September 1939, Eddie's father decided to play the trumpet in the territorial army band, and joined the Royal Army Service Corps, a decision which was to have huge consequences. The next day, World War II broke out and he was sent to England to train before being posted to France. "He was one of the lucky ones who survived Dunkirk," recalls Eddie. "He was saved by the Navy, managed to escape the beaches and returned safely to England." He was only wounded once during his whole time serving in the army: after he had returned from Dunkirk, he put his kitbag on the rack on the coach on the way to Edinburgh, then when he got his bag down, his helmet fell down and hit him on the head! Happily, he returned home safely to his wife and three children.

Eddie was twelve when the war ended in 1945. He was a very introverted child who was always drawing, so he chose to go to Darrock Technical School where he excelled in artistic subjects such as woodwork, technical drawing and the sciences. He studied there for two years before leaving to work in a bakery.

An advertisement for Mackie's bakery published in The Scotsman, 1967.

Eddie's career started at Mackie's bakery, J & W Mackie & Son Limited, in Prince's Street, on his fourteenth birthday. He started in the store department weighing out all the ingredients required for the bakery. "All apprentices started off in the store department, mainly because it got you accustomed to the ingredients used. We also had to deliver coffees, teas and sugars to all the restaurants in the building." Mackie's itself was a large bakery and catering establishment boasting a royal warrant: the sign above the door read, 'By appointment to the King'. They provided catering services for the festival club and Edinburgh Palace and were well known for their Scotch shortbread.

That same year, Eddie started going to night classes in the bakery school in Torphichen Street, then moved to the School of Bakery and Catering which was originally Castle Hill primary school that Eddie had attended as a boy. He took courses four nights a week: flour confectionery, bread making, cake decoration, and bakery science combined with bakery management and bacteriology.

Although he devoted most of his time to his work, Eddie was also a keen sportsman: he ran with the Edinburgh Harriers, swam and dived with the Grove Swimming Club, and also loved cycling. By this time, Eddie and his family had moved to the outskirts of the city to a house with three bedrooms (and a private bathroom!).

Eddie's youngest brother, William, was born sixteen years after Eddie, just after the war. Each of the four siblings chose very different career paths but they were all highly successful in their vocations. Eddie's sister, Betty, worked for the Scotsman Paper publications at the age of sixteen and worked her way to the top of the advertising department for the firm. She then moved to Glasgow where she was an important figure in advertising for Scottish Television. His brother, George, worked for John Menzies, and moved very quickly up to management level, progressing up to director.

1953 A four-tier wedding cake using commercial decorations and favours. The approximate price at that time was around £15, which would have been around 1½ weeks' wages. The height of the bottom tier alone would be around 15cm (6"), then next would be 13cm (5"), 11.5cm (4½"), and the top two tiers 10cm (4") each.

Left: 1947 The Queen and Prince Philip's wedding cake made by Bert Paterson, John Thompson, Margaret Maclaren and Eddie. Above: Commercial cakes from Mackie's made during the 1950s, decorated by Eddie and the team. Eddie would have been in his early 20s when these were produced.

William became a director of Boots the Chemist and is now international retail director for the Body Shop. Eddie puts his family's achievements down to his upbringing. "Our father always said, 'A fair day's work for a fair day's wage. Whatever I may do, let me do it now because I'll never pass this way again.' We were very lucky throughout our childhood to have such loving and caring parents."

In the years following the war, young men were conscripted into the army if they didn't have an apprenticeship. Being in the trade, Eddie was exempt until the age of 21. However, weighing under eight stone, being just on the minimum height requirement for the army (five feet two inches), and suffering from ulcers due to his nervous disposition, Eddie was exempt from joining up. That year, he was put in charge of the wedding cake room at Mackie's, having entered several competitions previously and won a handful of medals and cups with the

help of his manager and chairman of the Master Bakers Association, Bert Paterson, and the assistant manager, John Thompson.

As Head Confectioner, Eddie helped Mackie's to enter baking exhibitions up and down the country, mainly with John Thompson and the rest of the bakery. As a team, they won the British Open Confectionery Trophy, the Fleming Trophy, the MacAdam Shield, and many other medals and accolades.

Bert Paterson and John Thompson were both well-known figures in the industry and well-respected judges for bakery competitions. "When you have tutors like John and Bert, their inspiration and encouragement helps your profession enormously. As a team, we produced four large window displays every year, and had the largest windows in the whole of Princes Street." They decorated windows during the Edinburgh Festival

1954/5 Two cakes from a window display in Mackie's.

and, using the famous Edinburgh Floral Clock in West Princes Street Gardens as a design, replicated the clock in icing for a display. They also made a cuckoo in a house made from wood but decorated in sugar which struck on the hour. Later, they made a castle which was prefabricated in wood, iced and placed on a turntable. "When the cuckoo came out, we had a Ferrograph tape recorder with a loop tape which played 'by the left, quick march' in the distance. The turntable came round, a toy horse with a flag appeared followed by a pipe major and a full accompaniment of pipes and drums coming round on the turntable, the music getting louder as they came round. During the festival, the children waited for the pipe music and cuckoo display every half-hour." A few years later, Eddie and his team came up with the idea of putting a magic eye in the window so that the children could put their hand over the eye to activate the mechanism and start the bagpipes. However, the attraction proved to be

rather more popular than expected! "This wasn't such a good idea in the end because, as the Ferrograph was underneath the window, it was overworked and blew up!" Needless to say, a new motor had to be bought and Eddie's bosses weren't pleased. A fan was added under the window and the display timed for every fifteen minutes to keep the crowds entertained.

Eddie and his team decorated window displays for Christmas, Easter and Halloween every year. This involved a great deal of work but dressed windows were always a good way to attract customers. Other than these special windows, there were displays inside the shop. One of the displays in the spiral staircase up to the tearooms consisted of a six-tier wedding cake. "In the early days, most wedding cakes were white, but I had a great idea: when George Dunbar, a supplier of novelty bakery products, came up with coloured favours for wedding cakes, I thought it would be brilliant to decorate

1952 Decorated shortbread for the Scottish table at the British Confectioners' Association exhibition. The shortbread was decorated by Eddie with artwork painted by Mr. Vaughan.

1953 'For Auld Lang Syne' cake decorated for the Dusseldorf competition which Eddie helped to design and decorate with Bert Paterson.

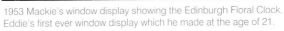

Booklet from the 1953 International Confectionery Fair in Dusseldorf, Germany with details of the British entrants.

1953 Mackie's window display showing the Edinburgh Floral Clock, Eddie's first ever window display which he made at the age of 21.

Photography: A G Ingram Ltd.

Left: 1962 (Left to right) John Thompson and Bert Paterson, Eddie's deputy manager and manager respectively. The cake shown here was a team effort for Sir Hugh Fraser (2nd Baronet) and Patricia Bowie's wedding. Right: Commercial wedding cakes from Mackie's made during the 1950s, decorated by Eddie and the team.

Photography: Norward Inglis

1956 Examples of commercial birthday cakes.

the six-tier wedding cake in different colours. All the colours were very pale and delicate, going from blue to pink, followed by pale lilac, cream, ivory and peach so that each tier was a different colour." In theory, it was a good idea to show different coloured cakes, but in practice, customers started asking for their cakes in different colours too. "It drove the bakery team up the wall because they had to ice cakes in so many colours! Within three months, I had re-decorated the cakes with white icing and coloured favours." In a typical week, Eddie and his team were turning around fifteen to thirty wedding cakes a week, sometimes more. They were especially busy before 1st April and 1st September because these were the dates that the Inland Revenue sent out tax rebates.

At the age of 21, Eddie was to meet the love of his life, Betty, at the local ice skating rink. "It was love at first sight. I will always recall how Betty's lovely legs and fabulous figure caught my eye and my heart simply followed. From that moment, we were

inseparable." At the age of 23, Eddie married his beloved Betty and in the same year, he was asked to start teaching in the bakery school. "With the job at Mackie's came a flat where Betty and I lived for around four years, rent-free. They looked after me very well." Despite his years of experience in the industry and high achievements, Eddie lacked self-confidence: "When I was asked to teach at Edinburgh bakery school, I was still very introverted and didn't think I had the knowledge or expertise to be a teacher at such a young age. I was very lucky at college as I was taken under the wing of William ('Willy') Tait, our head of department. He was a brilliant technician and a wonderful friend. Willy was the test baker for the Co-op flour mills so was very knowledgeable in the science of baking and a superb cake decorator.

"My wife, Betty, said that Willy Tait wouldn't have asked me if he didn't think I had the aptitude for the job. 'Anyway,' she said, 'if you don't like it or don't fit in, you can always resign

from the position.' But I loved the position and it was nice to be called Mr. Spence in the classroom instead of Eddie." Eddie started teaching all aspects of baking and, when one of the cake artistry teachers suffered from ill health, Eddie was asked to take over the position. Despite his initial doubts, he had uncovered a talent and passion for teaching, saying, "I was very lucky to have a job that I loved to do."

The Scottish equivalent to the London City & Guilds certification was still not recognised, so with seven years' training as a baker's apprentice and two years of teaching bakery skills, Eddie started to teach the art of cake decoration to City & Guilds standards. "Because I didn't have the City & Guilds certificate, I had to bring in an art teacher to teach aspects of art and design theory whilst I taught the technical and practical side of cake decorating. However, as the art teacher had no knowledge of cake decorating, I was, in fact, teaching him!" He was so determined to achieve the very best standards for himself and his class

13

Photography: Norward Inglis

Left: 1955 Edinburgh Floral Clock in royal icing. The design was taken from the Floral Clock in Princes Street gardens and was shown during the Edinburgh Festival. Each flower was piped individually and the design also incorporated a little house with a cuckoo. After this, a castle made in sugar complemented the window which was synchronised with an electric clock in the cake. Right: 1969 Celebration cake for Peart's bakery in Derby.

that the students went to Eddie's home every Sunday for six weeks before the examination, going through past City & Guilds papers together. Eddie sat the City & Guilds exam with his students and, not surprisingly, achieved a first class pass with distinction. As a testament of his teaching skills, all of the students except one passed with merit or credit grades. (The other student was too nervous to sit the exam.) After this, Eddie started teaching City & Guilds qualifications at Edinburgh's School of Baking, followed by Napier College.

Eddie worked at Mackie's for 23 years during which time he was promoted to Head Confectioner and Deputy Under-Manager. The bakery was then bought out by United Biscuits for whom Eddie worked for nine months as Head Confectioner and Improver. He soon found that he wasn't able to use his talent as a cake artist in such a large firm, spending his time supervising others rather than taking on the hands-

on work that he had excelled in at Mackie's. It was time for a change.

By this time, Eddie and Betty had three children: a daughter, Debra, and two sons, Derek and Paul. They all moved down to a bakery in Derby owned by a personal friend, Mr. Martin. At Mackie's, they used to train bakery managers' and master bakers' sons and Eddie became good friends with many of them. Mr. Martin had been one such trainee; when he found out that Eddie was unsettled in his job, he offered him the position as Head Confectioner at his bakery. Eddie went there by himself at first and remembers his arrival vividly: "I arrived in the February in bitter cold – the worst weather ever seen in Derby – to this lovely, large mansion house which was owned by Mr. Martin."

Eddie's wife and three children were amazed when they saw Bearwardcote House. They moved into an annexe three storeys tall. "The master bedroom was larger than the flat we had after we

got married. The children loved it and used the bed alcove as a stage!"

Having had only a couple of weeks to settle in, the bakery manager asked Eddie to enter the East Midlands Exhibition in Leicester. His skills did not go unnoticed and he was awarded with several medals and cups as well as the East Midlands trophy. After the exhibition, Eddie was asked to teach at Kedlestone Road College and then moved down to Wilmorton College, teaching cake artistry on a part-time basis. He stayed in Derby for around nine years altogether then, when Mr. Martin sold the business, the new owners employed Eddie as Assistant to the Bakery Manager. He ran the bakery in the manager's absence as well as the cake artistry room (where there were fifteen members of staff). Eddie was assisted by two "brilliant" women, Sue Brannon and Sue Haresnape, who helped Eddie with several demonstrations in Derby and the surrounding area.

Photography: Hampshire Chronicle

Eddie teaching a class of students at Sparsholt College. He taught here from 1986 to 1995.

Photograph courtesy of Mary and Michael Ford

Gold State Coach made for The Queen's Silver Jubilee, 1979. Eddie worked on this project with Mary and Michael Ford. The coach was made from royal icing and modelling paste: it weighed a staggering 25.4kg (56lb) and measured 81cm (32") long and 53cm (21") high.

When the promotional opportunity came, Eddie was not keen to take over the position of Bakery Manager, so answered an advertisement in Baker and Confectioner magazine for a Tutorial Manager at Mary Ford's prestigious sugarcraft school in Bournemouth. He was accepted and went down to the south of England to get settled before bringing down his wife and children. Despite the upheaval, the children loved their new home: "They thought their prayers had been answered – they lived in lovely holiday resort. We even bought a beach hut on the seafront."

The first project that he did with Mary and Michael Ford and Michael's father was the Gold State Coach in icing to celebrate The Queen's Silver Jubilee. The piece was made from royal icing and modelling paste: it weighed a staggering 25kg (56lb) and measured 81cm (32") long and 53cm (21") high. It was displayed at the *Sucre d'Art* exhibition at the Museum of Fine Arts in Paris.

At the time, Eddie had two assistant teachers and the team of three started work together with Michael Ford by making their own chocolates (a great success), then Easter eggs, Christmas novelties, and other imaginative confections. They began demonstrating to the public, which encouraged people to come to the day and evening classes that they started. By a stroke of luck the bakery students' movement was holding its biannual conference in Bournemouth that year. The school held demonstrations during that week and, in some cases, in the morning, afternoon and evening. That helped the weekend courses to fill up and the classes were extremely successful.

Royal icing was the most popular method of cake decorating at the time, but Eddie and the other tutors also started to teach chocolate work at Easter time. Always one to use his initiative, Eddie came up with an idea for his students. "I had a little trick that

I used to do to make a chocolate bowl. I would give each of the students a balloon to blow up, dip it up to halfway into melted chocolate, bob it up and down to take off the excess chocolate then place it upside down into a container to allow it to dry. You then gave it a second coating of tempered chocolate, and allowed it to dry again. Using piping chocolate (chocolate with a touch of glycerine added) you could pipe shells and scrolls onto the chocolate. To finish off the bowl you would then pipe a base and, while the chocolate was still soft, place the balloon into it and let it dry. Then, by taking a pin and making a small hole at the knot of the balloon, you would let the balloon down very gradually, leaving a lovely chocolate bowl which could be used as an edible trifle dish (filled with cold jelly and fruit), or turned into a basket with chocolate flowers. There were many uses for the bowl and I had been demonstrating this technique for several years." In theory this appeared to be an easy thing to

Left: 1960 Princess Margaret's wedding cake. Above: Eddie teaching at Squires Kitchen's International School of Cake Decorating and Sugarcraft in Farnham.

do, but during one class, Eddie soon became aware of the pitfalls first-hand! "Round the horseshoe-shaped table, I had three students for one bowl of tempered chocolate. There were nine students on one table and three on another. I gave them a balloon each and they started to dip them into the chocolate. All of a sudden, BANG! I was covered in chocolate! The student whose balloon had burst was not touched at all, but the student on her left was speckled with chocolate! My tie and collar were covered with chocolate; it was even on the ceiling. All of a sudden, another balloon which hadn't been tied properly blew up and stuck to a student's chin, giving him a distinctive Van Dyck-style beard!" Once they had tidied up, the students asked Eddie to go through the techniques again. Thinking that the first incident had been caused by the student's long nails, Eddie confidently proceeded to demonstrate the technique again, ensuring the balloon was tied tightly. "I dipped the balloon in to the chocolate, bobbed it up and

down and… BANG! I was covered in chocolate again! The moral of the story is, don't buy balloons that are made of synthetic materials instead of rubber as the warmth of the chocolate expands the air in the balloon, causing it to burst. Nevertheless, all the rubber balloons survived!" Even the experts have to learn on the job sometimes.

Eddie joined the British Sugarcraft Guild at its inauguration in 1981, demonstrating and judging for the members before being made president of the association from 1992 to 1995. As part of his work for the BSG, Eddie opened many exhibitions, judged competitions, and demonstrated in Australia, Sweden, and the USA among other countries.

As a result of his close association with the Guild, Eddie was asked by Beverley and Robert Dutton to be a judge at Squires Kitchen's annual cake decorating and sugarcraft exhibition around 16 years ago. After meeting him, they asked Eddie

Above: Eddie working on the wedding cake for Prince Charles and Lady Diana.
Right: the finished cake on display at Buckingham Palace.

to become a regular tutor at their prestigious International School of Cake Decorating and Sugarcraft in Farnham. "It was an honour and a privilege to do this for them. They were very welcoming to my good wife, Betty, and myself, and have been lovely friends ever since." His classes are still extremely popular with students from all over the world and he continues to judge at the Squires Kitchen exhibition every year.

Over the course of his career, Eddie has decorated several cakes for the Royal family and other high-profile figures. While he was working at Mackie's, Eddie decorated wedding cakes for Princess Margaret (Eddie's first royal wedding cake) and Sir Hugh Fraser, working in partnership with John Thompson. At Mary Ford's, Eddie designed a wedding cake for Prince Charles and Lady Diana (one of twenty-three cakes, one of which was the official cake made by the Royal Navy) and decorated it with Mary and Michael Ford. He also designed Prince

Andrew and Sarah Ferguson's cake and cake stand for their wedding in 1986 and decorated the cake with Mark Bennett. He then had the privilege, with the Bournemouth Sugarcraft Guild, to decorate a cake for The Queen's Golden Wedding Anniversary in 1997. "I made the cake with the help of my good friends at the British Sugarcraft Guild: Pat Grey, Val Davis, Les Williams, Josie Percy (who made the floral display for the cake top), Janet McCreedy (who made the cakes), and Jean Riggs (who painted the palaces on the plaques for the top tier). Pat's husband, Bill Grey, made the special boxes and stand, and my very good neighbours Trisha and Andy loaned me their van to take the cake to the palace. Without their support, hard work and enthusiasm it would have been very difficult. We made a great team and it was an honour and a wonderful experience. I am sure everybody was proud to have helped with such an important task."

Eddie taking Prince Charles & Lady Diana's cake to Buckingham Palace in a Rolls Royce.

Photography: Janet McCreedy

The Queen's golden wedding anniversary cake. Extra cutting cake was made for the celebrations and the cake was donated to the Leonard Cheshire Foundation, a charity based in Scotland, for their golden jubilee.

Images courtesy of British Ceremonial Arts Limited

Eddie collecting his MBE 'for services to the Sugarcraft Guild and Industry' from The Queen in 2000.

Eddie collecting his MBE in 2000 with his son, Paul, and daughter-in-law, Jackie.

Eddie with his beloved wife, Betty.

Sadly, Eddie's beloved wife Betty died from a heart attack in October 1999. "It was one of the saddest days of my life because without her, I wouldn't be in the position I am today." Just a few days later, Eddie received a letter from Buckingham Palace to say that he had been nominated for the 2000 Honours List to receive an MBE for Services to The Sugarcraft Guild and Industry. "At first, I was not going to accept it, but my son, Paul, said that Betty knew all about my friends in the trade who had put my name forward for the honour. He said that she would have wanted me to accept the MBE so I took him and his wife, Jackie, to Buckingham Palace for the ceremony on Tuesday 24th October 2000. I have never been so nervous in all my life – I felt like a little boy and had to be excused nine times before I went in to get my medal!" Receiving the MBE was a well-deserved honour for Eddie, and Betty would most certainly have been proud.

After working with Mary and Michael Ford for eight years, Eddie was asked to teach full-time at Sparsholt College in Hampshire. He taught cake artistry, bread making, flour confectionery, use of colour, design, calligraphy, and the art of making sugar flowers. He also taught a class of handicapped children from Lankhill School in Winchester and students from Peter Symonds Sixth Form College. Three times a year he went to King Alfred's College in Winchester to teach Japanese students in Shoei College – a part of the main college – British styles of cake artistry such as Swiss rolls, gâteaux, tortes, chocolate novelties and Valentine's cakes. In addition to his classes for students, Eddie demonstrated to cake

artistry tutors, including members of the British Sugarcraft Guild, and professional bakers and chefs. He decorated display work for the college open day, and helped the head of department, Elizabeth Redwood, organise craft weekends such as embroidery and patchwork. Elizabeth, a former student of Eddie's at Mary Ford's, appointed Eddie as a full-time tutor, one of 32 lecturers under her management.

Eddie has made several appearances on television during his career, featuring on programmes in Ireland, Australia, and in the UK. His most recent appearance was on ITV1's This Morning programme with resident chef, Phil Vickery, and presenters Fern Britton and Phillip Schofield. "I was very thankful for the opportunity to work with Phil Vickery on such a prestigious show. He is a very talented chef to whom I had the privilege of teaching some of my skills in royal icing." After the show had been aired, Eddie became something of a celebrity: later that day he was in a supermarket when he noticed two ladies staring at him. "They approached me and said, 'Are you Eddie who was on the television this morning?' This happened four times that day!"

With a career spanning over six decades, an MBE to his name, numerous accolades and having taught countless students, Eddie Spence is one of the most well-known and respected figures in the industry. He still teaches at Eastleigh College three days and one evening per week, and at Squires Kitchen on a regular basis. "I still love teaching, demonstrating and judging. I always say, 'If you love what you do, you never have to work'."

# Preparation & Basics

# Equipment and Edibles

Most of the exercises in this book only require a few basic tools and edibles for practising different techniques in royal icing. As you progress to making your own cake tops (plaques) and cake projects, it is worth checking that you have everything you need before you start.

If you are new to royal icing you will find that you can start piping with only a handful items in your workbox, so I have given a list of what you will need within each tutorial. As you become more advanced you can build up your tools when you need them. I have accumulated the following basic items over the years and always have them to hand before starting on a project.

## Equipment

### 1 Cake drums (boards), hardboards and cards

Always use a 15mm thick cake drum (often referred to as a cake board) under the base of a cake and a thinner (4mm) hardboard under cakes that are to be stacked or tiered (never place one tier directly on top of another).

### 2 Cake tins (not pictured)

Make sure the sides are at 90° to the base (not sloping inwards or outwards).

### 3 Cellophane

### 4 Cling film

### 5 Cocktail sticks

### 6 Compass

This is extremely useful if you are creating or resizing templates, particularly where you are dividing a cake top into equal portions (e.g. for oriental string work).

### 7 Corkscrew

### 8 Dowels

If you are stacking or using pillars on a multi-tiered cake, you will need to support the lower tiers with dowelling rods. I recommend using plastic cake dowels as they are more hygienic than wooden ones.

### 9 Desk lamp

Choose a lamp that can be angled towards your work and fit it with a 40W bulb.

### 10 Fine scissors

### 11 Flower cutters: daisy and primrose

### 12 Greaseproof paper or piping bags

You can either buy ready-made piping bags or make your own from greaseproof paper (see page 43).

### 13 Icing nail

These are available in different sizes depending on the size of flower you wish to create.

### 14 Icing ruler (straight edge)

### 15 Kitchen cloths

### 16 Large serrated knife

Choose a knife with a blade at least 35cm (14") long so that it is easy to trim large cakes flat.

### 17 Masking tape

Make sure the masking tape you use is soft tack so it can be removed easily.

### 18 Measuring jug

Use a plastic jug as they are thinner than glass so are easier to use.

### 19 Mixer/mixing bowl

Use a stainless steel bowl if possible and ensure it is sterile before use.

### 20 Modelling tool no. 2: blade and shell (PME)

### 21 Non-stick board (large)

### 22 Non-slip mat

Always place a piece of non-slip mat under your work board to prevent it from moving as you work. This is also very useful for transporting cakes so that they don't move around in their boxes.

### 23 Non-stick rolling pin (large)

### 24 Paintbrushes

I recommend using good quality artists' brushes in nos. 1, 2 and 3 round (for painting) and flat brushes (for dusting). Keep a set of brushes solely for sugarcraft use.

### 25 Palette knives

You will need different palette knives for different purposes: large and small, straight and cranked palette knives are available from sugarcraft suppliers (see page 320).

### 26 Paper and pencil

### 27 Paring knife

### 28 Pillars

Plaster and plastic pillars and separators are available in many different styles and sizes. Always use plastic cake dowels in conjunction with pillars to prevent them from sinking into the cake. (Instructions for dowelling a cake are given on pages 46 to 47).

### 29 Piping nozzles

For best results, always use professional piping nozzles: I recommend using nozzles from PME and Bekenal. Always make sure the nozzles are clean before using them and refrain from using nozzles with a seam. The sizes you need will depend on the work you wish to create but for most piping work I would recommend having nos. 0, 1, 1.5, 2 and 3 plain; 42, 43, 44 rope; 56, 57, 58, 59 petal; 50, 51, 52 leaf; 31 ribbon; and 55 chrysanthemum.

### 30 Plunger cutters: blossoms

### 31 Ruler

### 32 Scriber

### 33 Side scrapers

### 34 Sieve

### 35 Small pots for coloured icing

### 36 Sugar shaker

### 37 Tea strainer

If you are making your own royal icing (see recipes on pages 28 to 29), you can use a tea strainer to strain the egg white.

### 38 Tea towel

### 39 Turntable

A tilting turntable is useful for working on the sides of cakes and if you are creating extension work (see pages 184 to 191).

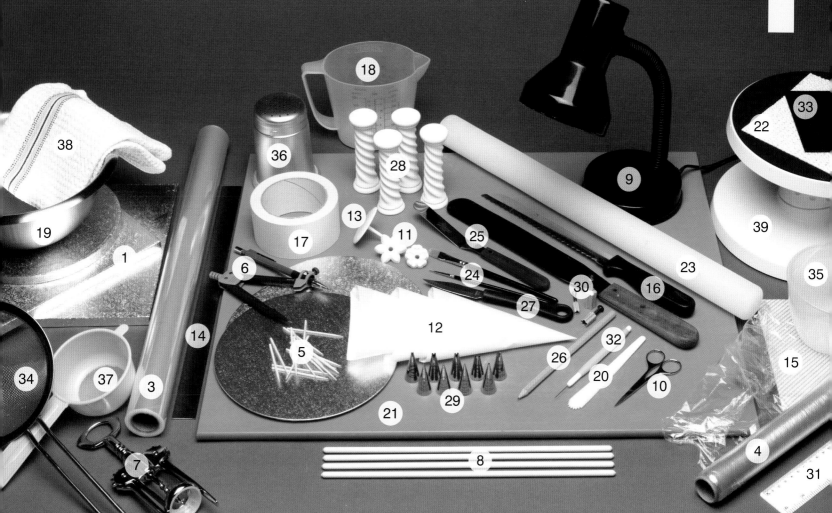

# Edibles

**1 Apricot glaze**

Apricot glaze or pureé is neutral in flavour and colour and is high in natural pectins (so it is less likely to go mouldy).

**2 Clear alcohol (e.g. gin or vodka)**

**3 Egg white (albumen)**

An ingredient in royal icing. The egg white is not cooked so you may prefer to use dried albumen (see Important Note on page 30).

**4 Fortified and pure albumen**

Dried albumen (egg white) is used as an ingredient in royal icing and is available from sugarcraft suppliers (see page 320).

**5 Glycerine**

An ingredient which is added to royal icing to make it set softer.

**6 Icing sugar in shaker**

Always dust the work board and rolling pin with icing sugar before rolling out marzipan, sugarpaste, modelling paste or flower paste to prevent sticking.

**7 Lemon juice (citric acid) or white vinegar (acetic acid)**

Either of these can be used in royal icing recipes where fresh egg white is used to add strength to the icing.

**8 Marzipan**

Always use a good quality marzipan with an almond content of at least 23.5%.

**9 SK Professional Dust Food Colours (see opposite)**

**10 SK Professional Liquid Food Colours (see opposite)**

**11 Sugarpaste**

Sugarpaste is useful if you are short of time as it is much quicker to cover a cake with sugarpaste than royal icing (full instructions are given on pages 40 to 41). Once the cake is covered you can add piped decorations onto the cake in royal icing.

**12 White vegetable fat**

This is used to grease cellophane when making off-pieces such as run-outs.

## Instant mix icings

A range of instant mix icing sugars is available from Squires Kitchen. If you prefer not to make your own, these can save time and will produce consistent results. SK Instant Mix Royal Icing, Run-out Icing and Extension Icing are suitable for different purposes and are quick to prepare: simply add water following the instructions on the pack and mix.

## Food colourings

Any colours that you use for all royal icing work should be liquid dyes that don't contain glucose or glycerides. Squires Kitchen Professional Liquid Food Colours are ideal for this purpose: they can be used to colour the icing, to paint on detail, and in an airbrush. It is always useful to have a selection of colours to hand: I use Rose, Cyclamen, Holly/Ivy and Vine most frequently, particularly for floral designs. To achieve a skin tone, use a small amount of Chestnut with a touch of Cyclamen.

If you require a high-strength or dark colour, you can use a combination of liquid and dust colours to deepen the colour. Using too much liquid colour for darker shades will alter the consistency of the icing, so the dust colour balances this out.

Edible paint, including edible metallic paint, can also be used to add detail or colour to finished pieces (see instructions for gilding on page 47). By mixing metallic dust colours with confectioners' glaze you can create a glossy finish.

Dust colours can be added to clear alcohol to make a quick-drying paint and are also ideal for use with or without stencils to create soft backgrounds.

Paste colours are only really used for colouring roll-out pastes such as sugarpaste and marzipan so are not required in royal icing work. However, if you are covering a cake with sugarpaste or making a cake top plaque, this can be coloured as required using paste food colours.

*For more information on how to use food colourings see page 45.*

25

# Recipes

## Rich fruitcake

**A good fruit cake should:**

- have square 'shoulders' and sides and a slightly rounded top;

- have a good bloom (gloss) on top and good colour;

- have a clean cut, a pleasant aroma and a rich (but not overpowering) flavour;

- be moist but not wet;

- have an even distribution of fruit;

- be evenly baked on the top, sides and base.

I recommend the following recipe for an 18cm (7") round cake. If you are having difficulty achieving good results, suggestions for troubleshooting start on page 312. To adjust the recipe for different shapes and sizes, see page 29.

## Ingredients

340g (12oz) currants

130g (4½oz) sultanas

130g (4½oz) raisins

85g (3oz) cherries

55g (2oz) peel

55g (2oz) ground almonds

215g (7½oz) plain flour

5ml (¾tsp) ground cinnamon

3ml (½tsp) mixed spice

170g (6oz) butter

170g (6oz) soft dark brown sugar

170ml (6fl oz) eggs (approximately 3 x large) at room temperature

18ml (1tbsp) black treacle

85ml (3fl oz) brandy, rum, cherry brandy (or other liqueur of your choice) for soaking fruit

## Preparation and baking

1 Clean the fruit in lukewarm water. Strain and leave to dry on a clean tea towel.

2 Soak the fruit in alcohol and leave for 2 days. Prepare the batter mixture following your chosen method (see below).

3 Line the base and sides of a cake tin with greaseproof paper and preheat the oven to 170°C/325°F/gas mark 3.

4 Once the mixture is in the tin, place it in the centre of a baking tray and tie a piece of corrugated cardboard around the outside of the tin. The height of the cardboard should be at least 2.5cm (1") greater than the top of the tin. Cover the top with another piece of corrugated cardboard.

5 Place the tray complete with cake tin and cardboard into a preheated oven, reduce the temperature to 150°C/300°F/gas mark 2 and bake for the suggested time (see page 29). About 45 minutes before the cake is ready, remove the cardboard cover from the top of the cake and finish baking.

6 After baking let the cake rest for approximately 3 hours. Spray a little alcohol on top: this will accelerate the maturing process of the cake.

## Method 1: sugar batter

1 Cream the sugar, butter and treacle together.

2 Add the eggs in at least 6 stages, scraping down the sides of the bowl each time. If the batter starts to curdle, add a little flour and beat until the curdle disappears.

3 Fold in the rest of the dry ingredients.

4 Add the fruit and mix by hand. Do not use a mixer as this will cause the fruit to break up and bleed.

5 Place the mixture into the tin. Do not put the scrapings from the side of the bowl on top of the cake as this will result in the surface of the cake having no fruit content. Level the mixture with damp (not wet) hands.

6 Bake in a preheated oven, following the instructions above.

## Method 2: flour batter

1 Mix the sugar and eggs and whisk together.

2 Add the mixed spice, ground cinnamon and almonds to the flour. Cream the butter with an equal amount of the flour mixture. Mix in the treacle.

3 Add the sugar and egg mixture to the butter and flour mixture in around 5 stages, blending well at each stage.

4 Blend any remaining flour into the batter, ensuring it is smooth and free from lumps.

5 Fold in the fruit by hand until it is well mixed and evenly distributed.

6 Place the mixture into the tin. Do not scrape the sides of the bowl as this will result in the surface of the cake having no fruit content. Level the mixture.

7 Bake in a preheated oven, following the instructions above.

*Tip* Most people use the sugar batter method but I have found the flour batter method works well for exhibition-standard cakes. It does take practice to get this method right but produces good results.

## Portion guide

You can calculate the approximate number of portions that you will get from any size cake easily if you work in inches. Based on one serving of rich fruitcake measuring 1½" x ½" or 1" square, use the following simple methods:

- For a square or oblong cake, multiply the length by the width,

  e.g. for an 8" square, 8 x 8 = 64 servings, for an 8" x 6" oblong, 8 x 6 = 48 servings.

- For a round cake multiply the diameter by itself then subtract 20%,

  e.g. for an 8" round, (8 x 8) – 20% = 51.2, so approximately 50 servings.

- For a hexagonal cake, measure the shape point-to-point, multiply this number by itself then subtract 25%,

  e.g. for an 8" hexagon (point-to-point), (8 x 8) – 25% = 48 servings.

If you are unsure about calculating the number of portions or you have an unusually shaped cake, draw the shape of the cake onto paper then draw a grid of 1½" x ½" boxes over the top. Count the number of full boxes to give the approximate number of portions (do not count any that are cut off round the edge). Depending on how the cake cuts you may have to make slightly larger pieces but the guide above allows for this.

## How to cut a cake

To cut a cake into portions, cut across the centre first then cut parallel lines approximately ½" apart. Once you have worked across the cake, cut perpendicular lines 1½" apart, again starting in the centre and working outwards towards the edges.

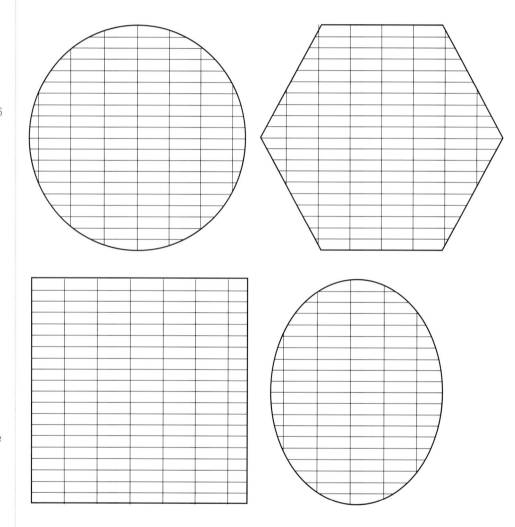

# Size chart

Use the recipe on page 26 in the following quantities to make cakes in different shapes and sizes:

| Round | 15cm (6") | 18cm (7") | 20cm (8") | 23cm (9") | 25cm (10") | 28cm (11") | 30cm (12") | 32cm (13") |
|---|---|---|---|---|---|---|---|---|
| Square | 13cm (5") | 15cm (6") | 18cm (7") | 20cm (8") | 23cm (9") | 25cm (10") | 28cm (11") | 30cm (12") |
| Butter | 85g (3oz) | 140g (5oz) | 200g (7oz) | 285g (10oz) | 340g (12oz) | 510g (1lb 2oz) | 595g (1lb 5oz) | 795g (1lb 12oz) |
| Soft dark brown sugar | 85g (3oz) | 140g (5oz) | 200g (7oz) | 285g (10oz) | 340g (12oz) | 510g (1lb 2oz) | 595g (1lb 5oz) | 795g (1lb 12oz) |
| Eggs | 85ml (3fl oz) | 140ml (5fl oz) | 200ml (7fl oz) | 285ml (10fl oz) | 340ml (12fl oz) | 510ml (19fl oz) | 595ml (1pt 2fl oz) | 795ml (1pt 9fl oz) |
| Plain flour | 100g (3½oz) | 175g (6¼oz) | 215g (9oz) | 340g (12oz) | 425g (15oz) | 595g (1lb 5oz) | 680g (1lb 8oz) | 850g (1lb 14oz) |
| Chopped glacé cherries | 45g (1½oz) | 70g (2½oz) | 85g (3oz) | 115g (4oz) | 170g (6oz) | 225g (8oz) | 285g (10oz) | 340g (12oz) |
| Currants | 130g (4½oz) | 225g (8oz) | 340g (12oz) | 455g (1lb) | 625g (1lb 6oz) | 795g (1lb 12oz) | 1.13kg (2lb 8oz) | 1.36kg (3lb) |
| Sultanas | 70g (2½oz) | 100g (3½oz) | 140g (5oz) | 200g (7oz) | 280g (10oz) | 340g (12oz) | 395g (14oz) | 510g (1lb 2oz) |
| Raisins | 70g (2½oz) | 100g (3½oz) | 140g (5oz) | 200g (7oz) | 280g (10oz) | 340g (12oz) | 395g (14oz) | 510g (1lb 2oz) |
| Mixed peel | 30g (1oz) | 60g (2oz) | 70g (2½oz) | 85g (3oz) | 115g (4oz) | 140g (5oz) | 170g (6oz) | 200g (7oz) |
| Ground almonds | 45g (1½oz) | 45g (1½oz) | 70g (2½oz) | 85g (3oz) | 115g (4oz) | 140g (5oz) | 170g (6oz) | 200g (7oz) |
| Mixed spice | ¼tsp | ¼tsp | ½tsp | ¾tsp | 1tsp | 1¼tsp | 1½tsp | 1¾tsp |
| Ground cinnamon | ½tsp | ½tsp | ¾tsp | 1tsp | 1¼tsp | 2tsp | 2½tsp | 2¾tsp |
| Black treacle | 1½tsp | 2tsp | 1tbsp | 1¼tbsp | 1½tbsp | 2tbsp | 2tbsp | 2½tbsp |
| Brandy, rum or cherry brandy | 50ml (1¾fl oz) | 85ml (3fl oz) | 100ml (3½fl oz) | 155ml (5½fl oz) | 210ml (7½fl oz) | 315ml (11fl oz) | 370ml (13fl oz) | 485ml (17fl oz) |
| Approx. baking time | 1¾ hours | 2¼ hours | 3 hours | 3½ hours | 4½ hours | 5¼ hours | 5¾ hours | 6 hours |

# Royal icing

I have two recipes for royal icing, one of which uses dried albumen, the other fresh eggs. If you are unsure about using raw eggs in icing, dried albumen is a good substitute.

Important Note: The Food Standards Agency recommends using only pasteurised egg in any food that will not be cooked (or only lightly cooked).

If you decide to use fresh egg white always use eggs bearing the Lion mark, which guarantees that they have been produced to the highest standards of food safety. All Lion Quality eggs come from British hens vaccinated against salmonella, are fully traceable and have a 'best before' date on the shell as a guarantee of freshness.

Eggs can carry bacteria, so always wash your hands before and after handling eggs. Cracked or dirty eggs should not be used. Good hygiene should always be practised when preparing any food. For more information and advice, contact the Food Standards Agency or the British Egg Information Service.

## Recipe 1 (using dried albumen)

### Ingredients

15g (½oz) dried albumen (fortified or pure*), sieved

85ml (3fl oz) previously boiled, lukewarm water

455g (1lb) icing sugar

*If you are making the icing for run-outs or off-pieces, use pure dried albumen (or fresh eggs, see recipe 2) as this is more stable.

Reconstitute the albumen in the water, following the instructions on the packet. Make up the royal icing following one of the methods below and allow to stand (overnight if possible) for best results.

## Recipe 2 (using fresh eggs)

### Ingredients

90g (3oz) free range egg white (equivalent to 3 medium eggs)*

455g (1lb) icing sugar

5-7 drops lemon juice or 4-5 drops white vinegar

*Separate the egg whites the day before then cover and leave in the fridge. The egg whites will strengthen overnight. Always sieve the egg white through a fine tea strainer or sieve.

## Tip

Royal icing should not be too aerated: it should be stiff enough to hold its shape and yet feel soft when piped. When exposed to the atmosphere it will set very hard and brittle. When making icing for coating cakes, 1 or 2 teaspoons of glycerine may be added to the recipe which will cause the icing to set much softer.

The first essential element in the preparation of royal icing is to ensure that all utensils are clean and free from grease. Grease prevents adequate aeration of the sugar and results in icing which is heavy in character and difficult to pipe.

## Hand beating: wooden spatula

1 Beat the reconstituted albumen or fresh egg whites with $2/3$ of the sifted sugar until white and thick (approximately 10 minutes of continuous beating). The more beating that is done at this stage, the less beating it will need in the next.

**2** Add the remaining sugar and a few drops of lemon juice or white vinegar if using fresh egg white. Beat to off-peak consistency (i.e. the tips of the peaks bend over).

**3** Keep covered with a clean, damp cloth to prevent the icing from skinning over.

## Mixing by machine

For best results use double the ingredients in the recipe.

**1** Place the reconstituted albumen or egg whites into the bowl of a mixer. Stir in the sifted icing sugar, place the bowl into the machine and beat as slowly as possible. Beat for approximately 10 minutes until the icing is stiff enough to hold its shape. The length of time it takes to mix the icing to the correct consistency will depend on the speed of your mixer. This usually takes around 10 minutes but can take up to 20.

**2** When you have achieved the correct consistency, make a note of how long it took to mix so that you can refer to it next time.

*Tip*

It is not likely that icing made by hand will be over-mixed. However, when mixed in a machine, care must be taken to ensure that the icing is not over-beaten. This would result in icing of a fluffy nature which, if used in coating, would cause a bubbly or rough surface instead of a smooth one. If over-beaten icing was used for piping, it would cause frequent breaks in the piping thread due to the air pockets in the sugar. To check that the consistency of the icing is correct, lift a spoonful out of the bowl: the icing should form a peak that bends slightly.

## How much icing?

The quantity of marzipan and royal icing (or sugarpaste) that you will need for a cake is easy to calculate. Weigh the fruitcake when baked: you will need approximately half the weight as a guide for the marzipan and the same again for the royal icing,

e.g. if a 20cm (8") round cake weighs 1.76kg (3lb 14oz), you will need 880g (1lb 15¼oz) of marzipan and 880g (1lb 15¼oz) of royal icing or sugarpaste.

For quick reference or in case you are using a sponge cake mix, this table gives the approximate quantities of marzipan/royal icing/sugarpaste required for the most common shapes and sizes.

| Cake size | | Marzipan/icing for round | | Marzipan/icing for square | |
|---|---|---|---|---|---|
| 12.5cm | (5") | 340g | 12oz | 440g | 15½oz |
| 15cm | (6") | 480g | 1lb 1oz | 625g | 1lb 6oz |
| 17.5cm | (7") | 650g | 1lb 7oz | 850g | 1lb 14oz |
| 20.5cm | (8") | 880g | 1lb 15oz | 1.14kg | 2lb 8oz |
| 23cm | (9") | 1.14kg | 2lb 8oz | 1.42kg | 3lb 2oz |
| 25.5cm | (10") | 1.42kg | 3lb 2oz | 1.87kg | 4lb 2oz |
| 28cm | (11") | 1.75kg | 3lb 14oz | 2.44kg | 5lb 6oz |
| 30.5cm | (12") | 2.1kg | 4lb 10oz | 2.72kg | 6lb |

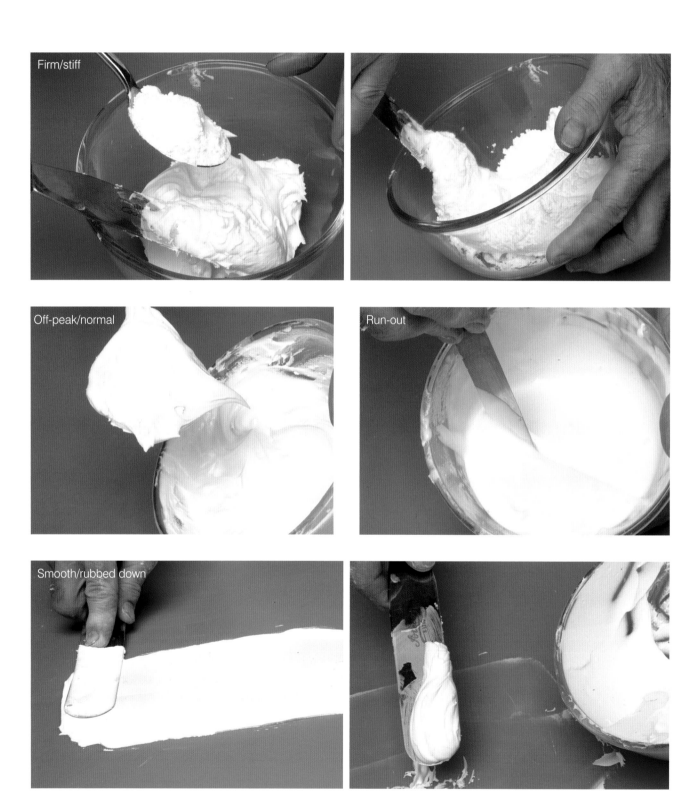

Firm/stiff

Off-peak/normal

Run-out

Smooth/rubbed down

# Types of royal icing

You will find that you need slightly different consistencies of icing for different purposes. Always prepare the icing as normal (following one of the recipes overleaf), then alter it as needed.

| Consistency | Method | Uses |
|---|---|---|
| Firm/stiff | Add 1 heaped tablespoon of icing sugar to every 175g (6oz) of sieved royal icing and stir (do not beat). If you only require a small amount of icing, add 1 heaped teaspoon of sieved icing sugar per 90g (3oz) of royal icing. If the icing is too stiff (indicated by wrinkles in the icing), dip an artists' brush in cold water and add a drop to the icing. The consistency should allow a slight flow without losing its shape. | This consistency is suitable for piping hair, fur and feathers and for piping flowers onto nails. The icing will not collapse or lose its shape. |
| Off-peak/normal | Take the icing straight from the bowl and transfer the amount needed into a separate bowl. Beat until it is at off-peak consistency. To test this, make peaks with a palette knife, spoon or spatula: the tips of the peaks should bend over. | This consistency is suitable for drop line and extension work, scrolls, filigree and pressure piping. |
| Smooth/rubbed down | 'Rub down' (i.e. paddle) some icing on a non-stick board or similar using a palette knife. This expels the air bubbles, making the texture smooth. If necessary, add a few drops of cold water. | This type of icing is suitable for covering cakes and for pressure piping small figures. |
| Guttering | Prepare the icing as for run-out work (see below) but add slightly less cold water: when you cut into the icing, it should flow together after 16 seconds. This stiffer consistency ensures the icing holds its shape on a curve. | Suitable for run-outs that will dry on a radius curve, rather than flat. |
| Run-out | Paddle the icing as for the smooth consistency to eliminate any air bubbles. Add cold water (preferably from the fridge) until the consistency is such that when you cut into the icing, it flows together on the count of 10 (after approximately 10 seconds). | This icing is suitable for all run-outs, e.g. block lettering and collars. |

*Instructions on how to colour royal icing are given on page 45.*

# Techniques

Apart from learning how to make royal icing (see recipes on pages 30 to 31), there are several other basic techniques that you will need to practise before you can decorate cakes with royal icing. The methods described here are presented in the way that I would teach them, but you may have learnt or developed your own ways of covering a cake with marzipan or making a piping bag, for example. If your preferred methods work for you, keep using them, otherwise you should find these techniques easy to follow.

## *Covering a rich fruitcake with marzipan*

### You will need:

#### Materials

Rich fruitcake

Apricot glaze

SK Marzipan, half the weight of the cake (see page 31)

Icing sugar in shaker

#### Equipment

Cake tin, same size and shape as the cake

Cake cards, same size and shape as the cake

Large, serrated knife

Large palette knife

Non-stick board

Non-stick rolling pin

Small, sharp knife

Paper template, e.g. till roll

Ruler

To create a smooth edge when cutting, dip the knife in just-boiled water, wipe dry, then use a sawing action to cut cleanly through the cake.

1 In order to create a flat, level surface for the covering you will need to trim the top of the cake flat. The easiest way to do this is to place one or two cake cards into the tin in which the cake was baked (this will raise the cake up to the required level), place the cake back in the tin and use a large serrated knife to trim the top of the cake level with the tin. Remove from the tin and use little pieces of marzipan to fill in any holes in the sides of the cake.

2 Bring some apricot jam to the boil and leave it in the microwave while you roll out the marzipan. Boiling the jam prevents mould spore from forming in the jam and using it whilst hot will kill any bacteria on the cake. Apricot jam is naturally high in pectins, which will also help to prevent mould.

3 Knead the marzipan on a non-stick board dusted with icing sugar until it is soft and pliable. If the marzipan is too firm to work with, heat it very gently in the microwave on the defrost setting for two to three minutes. Roll out the marzipan on a non-stick board dusted with icing sugar to a thickness of approximately 7mm (¼"). Using a small, sharp knife, cut out a piece the same shape but slightly bigger than the top of the cake.

4 Reheat the apricot jam for a few seconds in the microwave and place on a heatproof surface using heatproof gloves (the jam will be very hot). Using a large palette knife, spread a thin layer of apricot glaze over the top of the cake. Place the cake upside down onto the marzipan and trim the marzipan to size. Turn the cake back round the right way so that the marzipan covering is on top. Place on a cake drum.

## Round cakes

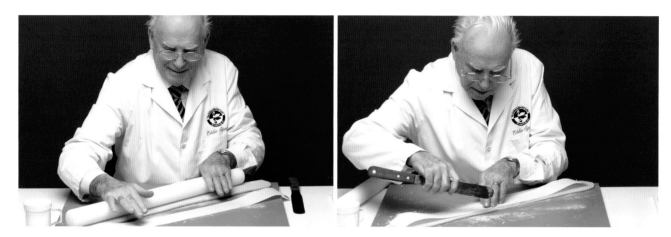

5  Take a length of paper (till roll is ideal), wrap it round the cake and cut to size. Trim to the height of the top of the marzipan covering. Roll out a long sausage of marzipan to the length of the paper template. Using the heal of your hand, flatten out the marzipan, then roll over with a rolling pin to a thickness of approximately 4mm ($^1/_8$") and cut the marzipan to size. Make sure that you keep the marzipan dusted with a little icing sugar to prevent it from sticking to the board.

6  Reheat the apricot glaze again and spread a thin layer onto the marzipan strip. Carefully place the side of the cake onto this and roll to the other end of the strip to cover the sides. Trim neatly at the join and smooth it closed with your fingertip.

7  Allow the marzipan covering to dry overnight. If you are making a wedding cake with two or more tiers, leave the marzipan to dry for two or three days to ensure it is firm enough to support the upper tiers.

## Square cakes

(continued from page 35)

5 Roll out some marzipan to a thickness of approximately 4mm (¹/₈"). Measure the height and side of the cake. Cut an oblong: the height should measure 4 times the height of the cake; the width should be as long as the side of the cake + 1.3cm (½"). Keep the marzipan dusted with a little icing sugar to make sure it doesn't stick.

6 Reheat the apricot glaze again and spread a thin layer over the marzipan, leaving the top quarter uncovered. Place the side of the cake onto the bottom of the marzipan and cut to size.

7 Turn the cake 90° and cover the next side in the same way, increasing the length of the strip by 4mm (¹/₈") to allow for the thickness of the existing marzipan covering. Repeat again to cover the third side.

8 Spread hot apricot glaze over the last section of marzipan and place the cake on top to cover the fourth side. The marzipan will need to be 8mm (¼") longer than the cake side to allow for the marzipan coating on each side.

9 Allow the marzipan covering to dry overnight. If you are making a wedding cake with 2 or more tiers, leave the marzipan to dry for 2 or 3 days to ensure it is firm enough to support the upper tiers.

The same principles of covering the sides of a square cake apply to any shape with flat sides such as a hexagon or octagon. To ensure the corners are straight, cut towards the opposite point of the shape rather than in line with the cake sides. Ensure the marzipan is only 4mm (¹/₈") thick on all the sides.

# Covering a rich fruitcake with royal icing

Make sure you allow plenty of time for icing the cake. Ideally, you should coat the top in the morning, coat the sides of a round cake in the evening or 2 opposite sides of a square cake in the evening and the remaining opposite sides the following morning. Repeat this procedure for applying a second coat, starting with the top of the cake when the sides are dry. For general celebration cakes, 2 coats should be enough; if you are making a wedding cake, you should apply 3 to 4 coats for a finer finish.

## You will need:

### Materials

Rich fruitcake, coated with marzipan (see pages 34 to 37)

Royal icing, half the weight of the cake (see page 31)*

### Equipment

Cake drum

Turntable

Palette knife

Straight edge

Desk lamp

Side scraper (plain or comb)

1 Place the cake on a cake drum the same shape and approximately 7.5cm-10cm (3"-4") bigger than the cake (depending on the overall design) then onto a turntable. Mix up enough royal icing to a smooth consistency for coating the cake. Rub (paddle) the icing on a clean surface with a palette knife to eliminate any air bubbles.

2 Start by coating the top of the cake. Use a palette knife to spread a thin, even coat of icing over the cake top then use a straight edge to level it off. Hold the straight edge at both ends and pull it towards you to create an even finish. Neaten off the edges using a palette knife. Place under a desk lamp at a distance of around 25cm (10") and leave to dry, ideally for several hours.

* Ensure you include glycerine in the recipe for coating cakes (see page 30).

3 Use the palette knife to apply icing to the sides of the cake. For round cakes, apply an even coating all the way round the sides. For square cakes, coat two opposite sides first. For hexagonal or octagonal cakes, cover alternate sides first (i.e. 1, 3, 5, 7). Use a side scraper (plain or comb) to level off the icing round the cake sides, neaten any rough edges with a palette knife and allow to dry.

4 For square, hexagonal or octagonal cakes, cover the remaining sides and allow to dry.

5 Apply a second coat of icing in the same way as before: top followed by sides. When coating hexagonal or octagonal cakes, start with the top again, followed by the second set of alternate sides (2, 4, 6, 8), then the first set (1, 3, 5, 7). This helps to keep the sides even. Allow to dry completely.

6 If you are making a wedding cake or competition piece, apply 3 or 4 thin coats of icing altogether. This will allow you to achieve a very smooth, fine finish.

7 To coat the board on which the cake is placed, you can either pipe an outline around the edge and flood in the area around the cake (see instructions for making run-outs on page 145), or reduce some of the rubbed-down icing to guttering consistency (see page 33), coat the board with a palette knife and knock the board against the work surface to level off the icing. Leave to dry overnight. When dry, the cake is ready to decorate.

# Covering a rich fruitcake with sugarpaste

If you are short of time or do not have the confidence to cover a cake with royal icing you can use sugarpaste (rolled fondant) instead. The decoration can be piped on in the same way as for a royal iced cake; the main difference to note is that the top corner is rounded, not square, so this may not be suitable for collars or panel designs.

## You will need:

### Materials

Rich fruitcake

SK Marzipan, half the weight of the cake (see page 31)

Icing sugar in shaker

Apricot glaze

Sugarpaste, half the weight of the cake (see page 31)

Clear alcohol (e.g. gin or vodka)

### Equipment

Large, serrated knife

Cake drums, same size and slightly bigger than the cake

Non-stick board

Non-stick rolling pin

Palette knife

Pastry brush

Spare cake board, large

Smoother

Mini cakes can be coated with sugarpaste in the same way as for larger cakes. Design ideas can be seen on pages 266 to 283.

1 Trim the top of the cake flat (in the same way as for covering a cake with marzipan, see page 35). Invert it onto the centre of a cake drum and fill in any holes with small pieces of marzipan.

2 Roll out the marzipan to a thickness of approximately 4mm (¹/₈"). Use the rolling pin to roughly measure the paste, ensuring it is big enough to cover the top and sides of the cake.

3 Boil the apricot jam in a microwave (see page 35) and spread a thin layer over the cake using a palette knife. Carefully fold the marzipan over the rolling pin and lift it onto the cake. Gently smooth the paste down the sides of the cake, lifting it with one hand and smoothing it with the palm of the other.

4 Use a smoother to create a neat, smooth finish. Trim neatly around the base of the cake and allow to dry, preferably overnight.

5   Just before covering the cake with sugarpaste, brush the marzipan surface and edge of the cake drum with clear alcohol using a pastry brush. Make sure the whole surface is covered but do not use too much otherwise the marzipan will become sticky.

6   Roll out the sugarpaste on a non-stick board dusted with icing sugar. When the paste is approximately 4mm-5mm ($^1/_8$"-$^3/_{16}$") thick and large enough to cover the cake and board all-in-one, slide a large cake board underneath it. Position the large board over the cake and carefully slide the sugarpaste into position. This method prevents the sugarpate from stretching and tearing; alternatively you can use a rolling pin to lift the paste.

7   Use one hand to lift the paste from the edge and the palm of the other hand to ease the paste down the side of the cake. Take care not to pull the paste downwards as this will cause it to tear. Bring the paste to the edge of the cake drum and smooth over the cake and board with a smoother. Trim neatly with a palette knife then polish the surface with a smooth pad of sugarpaste wrapped in cling film.

8   Allow the sugarpaste to firm, preferably overnight, to reduce the risk of marking the paste. Once you have finished decorating the cake, trim the cake drum edge with 15mm width ribbon in a co-ordinating colour and secure in place with a non-toxic glue stick or double-sided tape. Overlap the ends slightly and make sure the join is at the back.

# Plaques (cake tops)

Plaques are a great way to save time as they can be made in advance. They are also ideal for practising your skills on before you work directly on a cake.

## You will need:

### Materials

Sugarpaste

Icing sugar in sugar shaker

### Equipment

Non-stick board

Non-stick rolling pin

Large, round template, e.g. cake tin

Small, sharp knife

Waxed paper or cellophane

Spare cake cards

1  Roll out the sugarpaste on a non-stick board dusted with icing sugar to a thickness of no more than 4mm (1/8"). Use a round template to cut out a circle the same size as the cake or gateau; the tin in which the cake was baked is ideal.

2  Carefully transfer the plaque to a sheet of waxed paper or cellophane dusted with icing sugar to allow easy release and place on a cake card to keep it flat.

3  Decorate the plaque with your chosen design (suggestions are given on pages 192 to 213). When the decorated plaque is dry, slide a thin cake card underneath the plaque to release it from the paper, then place on top of a buttercreamed gateau or cake.

To hide the join around the edge, pipe buttercream shells around the outside. For gateaux, stick toasted almonds, chocolate vermicelli or toasted coconut around the sides for a very quick finish.

Plaques can also be stuck down onto a marzipan-covered cake by moistening the top with clear alcohol (e.g. gin or vodka). Brush the sides of the cake with clear alcohol, cover the cake with sugarpaste, then use the cake tin to cut out a circle the same size as the plaque from the top. Dampen the marzipan top with clear alcohol then slip the decorated plaque into position. This method saves time and is ideal where a cake can only be covered a day or two before it is required (e.g. if you are using a sponge cake).

# Making and filling a piping bag

Piping bags are easy to make, but if you are short of time you can purchase them ready-made from your sugarcraft supplier. I use the following method:

1 Take a 76cm x 46cm (30" x 18") sheet of greaseproof paper. Fold the sheet over but do not make a crease. Using a large, sharp knife, cut the sheet in half. Fold the sheet again to give ¼ size and cut: this will give the required size for a large bag (no. 3 nozzle or larger). To make a small bag (for a no. 2 nozzle or smaller), fold in half again and cut.

2 Fold the paper on the diagonal but not point-to-point: there should be a strip on either side of the triangle. This will give you an overlap so that, when the bag is made, you will have 3 layers of paper between your hand and the icing (on the fold) which gives the bag strength.

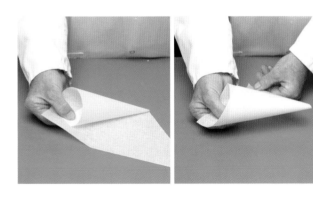

3 Bring one side of the bag round to create a point in the middle of the long side. The fold over should be 4cm-5cm (1½"-2") below the pointed side of the paper (at the top). Hold this in position then bring the other side round in the same way.

4 Fold in the corners of the bag then make 2 small tears or cuts and fold in to hold the bag in place. This will stop the bag from opening. Do not use staples.

When filling a piping bag with royal icing, make sure you do not use too much icing. Aim to half-fill the bag each time.

1 Cut 1.3cm (½") off the end of the bag and place the nozzle into the bag so that it protrudes 1.3cm (½") out of the bottom.

2 Make a circle with your index finger and thumb and drop the bag into it so you are holding it halfway up. Using a small palette knife, place no more than a heaped teaspoon of icing into the bag, so that it is only half-filled.

3 To close the bag, flatten the top, fold in the corners like an envelope then tuck the point in by 1.3cm (½"). Fold in the sides ('shoulders'), then fold it over again so that it is sealed at the top. You are now ready to pipe.

Keeping the nozzle against a damp cloth while you are working prevents the icing at the tip from drying out. Always clean your nozzles thoroughly after use to keep them in good condition: leave them in hot soapy water for a few hours for the sugar to dissolve.

# Colouring royal icing

Food colours are available in three main forms: dusts, liquids and pastes. Their different uses are explained on page 25.

You should only use liquid food colours for most royal icing work, particularly run-outs. Paste colours contain either glucose, glycerine or glycerides; these are hygroscopic and will absorb moisture from the atmosphere, causing the royal icing to soften and run. This causes run-outs to disintegrate when they are removed from the cellophane. The other advantage of using liquid dyes is that you can control the amount of colour used, then you can repeat the same method to achieve the same colour again.

1 Weigh out the required amount of royal icing and place into a small bowl. Using a pipette, add a few drops of colour and mix into the icing with a palette knife.

2 Repeat until the desired colour is achieved, then make a note of how much icing and colour was used.

3 If you wish to create a strong colour, too much liquid can cause icing to become too fluid. Use the handle of a teaspoon to add small amounts of the corresponding dust food colour at a time to strengthen the colour without altering the consistency of the icing.

4 Cover the bowl with cling film and allow the colour to develop for at least 30 minutes. Beat again before use.

# Dowelling a cake

If you are making a cake with more than one tier you will need to dowel the lower tiers to prevent the cake from sinking. This applies to stacked cakes and those will pillars. If you are making a stacked design, remember that each cake must be placed on a thin cake board (usually of the same size so that it cannot be seen) in order for the dowels to be supported.

## You will need:

Paper, pencil and scissors for template

Plastic dowelling rods

Pillars (if required)

Compass

Scriber

Craft knife

Cutting board

1 Make a paper template the same shape and size of the cake drum or board to be used on the tier above. This will ensure the pillars are supported by the board above.

2 For cakes with 4 pillars, fold the shape into quarters (corner to corner for a square). If you wish to use 3 pillars (e.g. for a heart-shaped cake), fold the template into quarters, fold this in half, then fold each half into the centre. This will divide it into 6, so use alternate sections to divide it equally into thirds. For a stacked cake (i.e. no pillars), use 4 dowels for the lower tiers where more support is needed and 3 for the upper tiers.

3 Unfold the template and place it centrally on top of the cake. If you are using pillars, place a pillar on one of the dividing lines, inside the border design on the cake. Mark the inner and outer points of the base of the pillar on the template and remove from the cake. Halfway between these 2 points, mark the central point of the pillar. Use a compass to take this measurement from the centre, then mark on each quarter or third of the template.

4 Place the template on top of the cake and make a pinprick with a scriber on the 3 or 4 points. If the cake features a centre design,

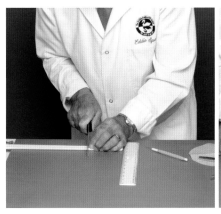 

mark the central point as well while the template is in place. Remove the template.

5 Using a sterilised corkscrew, carefully make a hole in the icing, only down to the marzipan (not into the cake itself). Make the other 2 or 3 holes for the dowels.

6 Push a plastic dowel down into the cake until it touches the board at the base. Mark the dowel level with the surface of the icing. Repeat with the other holes, using a new dowel each time. Remove the dowels and place on a cutting board.

7a If you are using flat pillars (with no hole) or if you are making a stacked cake, cut the dowels to the highest point of all the markings. This ensures the cake will be level and will not tilt. Reinsert the dowels into the cake.

7b If the pillars are hollow, place them in position over the dowels and mark level with the top of the pillars. Remove the pillars and dowels and cut all four dowels to the level of the highest point. Re-insert into the cake and place the pillars in position over the dowels.

7c If you are using plaster pillars with a shallow hole in the base, measure the depth of the hole using a spare dowel. Check that the holes in the pillars are all the same depth. Mark the dowels to the height of the cake then add on the depth of the pillar hole and cut all four to this height (the highest mark on all four dowels if they differ). Reinsert the dowels into the cake and place the pillars into position.

*Tip*

Make sure all the dowels are sterile before they are inserted into the cake by wiping with clear alcohol or submerging in boiling water.

# Gilding

Piped decoration and lettering can be gilded with edible metallic paint or dust colour mixed with clear alcohol.

1 Using a soft brush, apply the edible paint or dust mixed with clear alcohol (e.g. gin or vodka) to the piece that is to be gilded. Allow to dry then add another coat if required to intensify the colour.

2 To clean paintbrushes after gilding, gently rub liquid soap into the brush before washing thoroughly with warm water. If you put the brush straight into water, the gum in the gold paint will harden and will ruin the brush.

47

# Pressure Piping

Pressure piping looks so beautiful and delicate, yet often people are reluctant to try it. The beauty of pressure piping is that it can be instantaneous and it dries quickly because there is no added water in the icing.

The exercises show you how to develop your pressure piping skills using the simplest of techniques. Once you have mastered the basic piped shapes, you really can pipe almost anything – a little practice is all it takes!

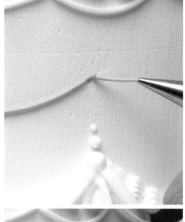

## *Tips* for successful pressure piping

- Practise piping on spare boards or plaques until you gain confidence in the technique. You can then pipe directly onto a cake.

- The consistency of the icing is very important: always use rubbed-down icing for a smooth finish when pressure piping. Where you wish to add texture or definition, you can use the icing fresh or beaten to stiff-peak consistency. Where you require the icing to be stiffer and hold its shape (e.g. for hair), add a teaspoon of sieved icing sugar to every 90g (3oz) of icing.

- To help when pressure piping, only use very fine nozzles (such as a no. 0 or 00) for fine detail such as tiny dots. For larger flowers and figures, use larger nozzles: this will save you getting sore fingers as you don't need to use as much pressure with larger nozzles.

- You can use fine ribbon nozzles for details such as belts, bows and horses' reins.

## Materials

Royal icing, rubbed down (see page 33)

## Equipment

Piping bags

Plain piping nozzles, ranging from no. 0 to 2 (depending on the design)

No. ST50 small leaf nozzle (optional)

Fine artists' brush

Surface on which to pipe (e.g. spare board, card, plaque or cake top)

Scriber (for some designs)

# Basic natural shapes

All forms, such as flowers and animals, derive from these six shapes:

A: Circle

B: Oval

C: Pear

D: Crescent

E: Reverse 'S' scroll

F: 'S' scroll

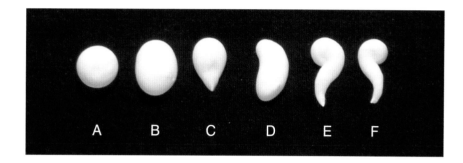

The size of the shapes depends on the individual requirements of the design. The patterns should balance with the size of the cake tiers pro rata, i.e. the top tier will feature the smallest designs and the bottom tier the largest designs.

# Floral designs

## Round flowers

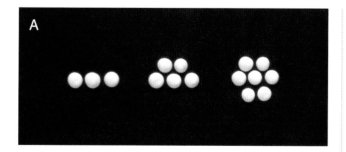

**A:** To pipe a simple 'dot' daisy, use a no. 1 or 1.5 nozzle.

1 Pressure pipe a dot and take the take-off point to the side of the dot so that it disappears, avoiding an unwanted point.

2 Pipe a dot on either side in the same way, then add two dots above and two dots below the central dot.

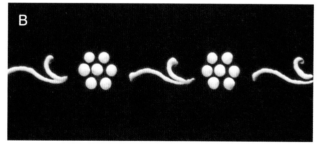

**B:** For a simple daisy design, use a no. 1 nozzle.

1 When piping repetition work, mark the centre dot all the way round the cake, ensuring the dots are evenly spaced.

2 Next, pipe a dot on either side of the centre to complete the second stage and repeat all around the cake.

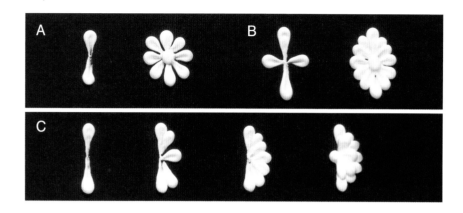

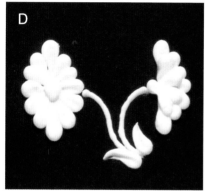

**3** For the third stage, pipe two dots above and below the central dot and repeat around the cake.

**4** When the daisies are complete, scratch pipe S and C scrolls between the daisies by keeping the nozzle on the surface of the cake (see page 69 for more scratched scroll designs).

## Pear- and oval-shaped flowers

**A:** The more elaborate daisy derives from the pear shape. To pipe this design, use a no. 1 nozzle.

**1** Make a dot, stop piping and pull the nozzle through the centre of the dot to leave a dimple. This creates a petal.

**2** Pipe another petal in reverse underneath the first so that they meet in the centre.

**3** Add 2 more petals on the horizontal, then 4 diagonally. Pipe a dot in the centre to finish.

**B:** To pipe an oval-shaped flower, use a no. 1 nozzle.

**1** Pipe the top petal first, as with the round flower, but this time ease off the pressure as you come up through the petal, making it elongated. Pipe another petal beneath the first.

**2** Pipe 2 horizontal petals, making them slightly shorter than the first pair.

**3** Pipe 2 petals on the diagonal in-between each pair of petals.

**4** To finish, pipe an oval dot in the centre of the flower

**C:** To make a daisy in profile, use a no. 1.5 nozzle.

**1** Pipe an up and down stroke for the first 2 petals, as for the oval-shaped flower.

**2** Pipe one short horizontal petal, then add 2 petals above and 2 petals below this one on the diagonal to fill in the gaps. There should be 7 petals altogether.

**3** Pipe 4 short petals on top to give the flower relief. Finish by adding a dot at the back for the seed box.

**D:** To create an offset daisy design, use a no. 1.5 nozzle.

**1** Pipe an oval daisy and a daisy in profile next to each other.

**2** Pipe a loose S and a C scroll for the stems of the flowers. To pipe the leaves at the base of the stems, pipe a dot, stop piping and then pull the tip out in a slight curve.

**E:** To create a symmetrical daisy design, use a no. 1.5 nozzle.

1 Pipe a drop line C scroll (see pages 62 to 79 for drop line work), then add a longer reverse C scroll beneath it. Pressure pipe a daisy in the centre.

2 Add as many leaves as required (see offset design opposite), ensuring the design is balanced.

## Heart-shaped flowers

**A:** To make a simple flower with 4 or 5 heart-shaped petals, use a no. 1 nozzle.

1 Make a dot and pull down slightly on the diagonal. Pipe another dot next to it and pull down onto the point of the first shape to make a heart.

2 For a simple 4-petal flower, add a horizontal heart on either side and 1 underneath, all joining at the central point.

3 For a 5-petal flower, start by piping a heart on the down stroke as before then work around the flower, keeping the petals close to each other. Finish the flower by piping a dot in the centre.

**B:** You can make a shamrock in the same way using a no. 1 nozzle.

Pipe 3 heart-shaped petals and add a short S scroll for the stem.

**C:** For a heart-shaped flower side design, use a no. 1 nozzle.

1 Scratch pipe a wavy line around the side of the cake using a no. 1 nozzle.

2 Pipe an S scroll in-between each curve, then pipe heart-shaped flowers at the ends of the S scrolls.

3 Add a few leaves on the stems as described above, but do not add too many as the design may become imbalanced.

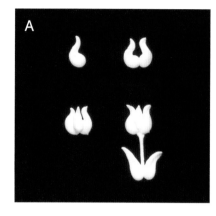

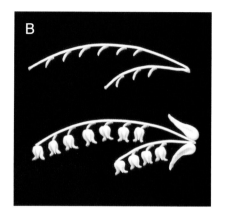

**D:** For an offset heart-shaped flower design, use a no. 1 or 1.5 nozzle.

1 Pipe a C scroll, a reverse C and another C to create the stems.

2 Pipe half-flowers (like shamrocks) at the ends of the stems then add a full flower in the centre of the scrolls.

3 Add leaves to the stems, keeping the design balanced.

## Bell-shaped flowers

These derive from the S scroll and include tulips, bluebells and lily-of-the-valley. These examples are all piped with a no. 1 nozzle.

**A:** Tulip

1 Pressure pipe an S scroll in an upward motion, making the base full and rounded.

2 Pipe a reverse S scroll next to the first one so the bases are touching.

3 Pipe a dot between them and pull up through the centre.

4 Pipe a straight stalk from the base of the flower head and add a leaf on either side (see instructions for the daisy, page 52).

**B:** Lily-of-the-valley

1 Pipe 2 curved lines for the stems, one shorter than the other. Add several short lines from the stems to form the bracts.

2 Pipe a small, bell-shaped flower on the end of each bract in the same way as for the tulips. Exaggerate the point of each petal. Add 2 large leaves at the end of the stems.

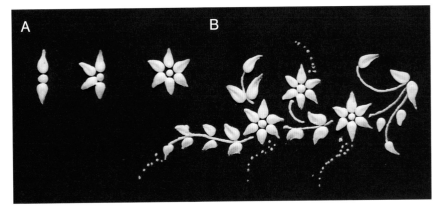

## C: Bluebell

This flower is very useful for filling in spaces between frills and other decorations on a sugarpasted cake.

1   Pipe a loose S scroll followed by a C scroll and a smaller S scroll for the stems. Add bracts in the same way as for the lily-of-the-valley.

2   Pipe in the flowers as before but make them more elongated. Add 2 leaves and a bulb at the base.

## Star-shaped flowers

A:  To pipe a star-shaped blossom, use a no. 1 nozzle.

1   Start by piping a dot in the centre. Pipe another dot above this and pull through in an upward motion, then repeat below the central dot in a downward motion.

2   Add 2 petals on the diagonal on one side.

3   Repeat step 2 on the other side to form a 6-petal flower.

B:  To create an offset star-shaped flower design, use a no. 1 nozzle.

1   Use a scriber to pinprick where the flowers will be positioned on the cake.

2   Pipe in the centre dots, then add the 6 petals to each flower, as described in A.

3   Scratch pipe curves to fill the space between the flowers, ensuring that there is a small gap between them. Pipe leaves on the stems.

4   To extend the design, pipe tiny dots to resemble ferns and fill out as required. This is useful as a space filler and helps to keep the design light.

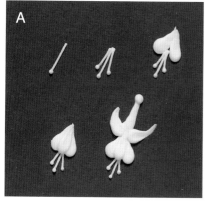

**C:** To pipe large or small daffodils, use a no. 1 and a no. 0 nozzle. A small leaf nozzle (ST50) is optional.

1 Using the no. 1 nozzle, pipe a dot in the middle and add 6 petals around it in a star shape.

2 Prepare a bag of stiff royal icing with a no. 1 nozzle for the trumpet. Pipe a circle around the centre dot, then continue piping round the circle, getting higher and higher. Ease off the pressure at the top to give a smooth finish.

3 Using a no. 0 nozzle, pipe a wavy line on top of the trumpet around the circle.

4 To make the leaves, use either a small leaf nozzle or cut a V with a 45° angle at the tip of a piping bag, as shown. Holding the bag to the side of the V, pipe long leaf shapes, starting at the base and tailing off at the tip. Pipe a few long leaves and some smaller ones.

5 Add stems beneath the flowers using the no. 1 nozzle.

6 To pipe a daffodil in profile, pipe a central dot. Add a petal above and below this, then add 2 diagonal petals on one side only. Pipe the trumpet as before on the side, then pipe 2 petals on top of the trumpet.

7 For the closed bud, pipe a teardrop but keep it as a half-rounded shape and do not pull through.

8 Using a no. 0 nozzle, add short tufts of grass at the base of the flowers.

## Teardrop-shaped flowers

**A:** To pipe the fuchsia you will need no. 0 and no. 1 nozzles (or no. 2 for a bigger flower).

1 Using a no. 0 nozzle, pipe 3 stamens by pressure piping a short line with a dot on the end. Pipe a line on the diagonal followed by 1 on either side in a triangular shape.

2 Using a no. 1 nozzle (or a no. 2 for a larger flower), pipe a dot and pull through to a point just above the stamens to make a bulbous petal. Repeat on the opposite side of the stamens to meet the same point. Pipe a third petal on top and taper down to the same point to form the skirt.

3 Add a curved teardrop shape on either side to give the fuchsia its shape.

4 To make the seed box, pipe a dot, ease off and pull through to form a teardrop. Add a dot on the end.

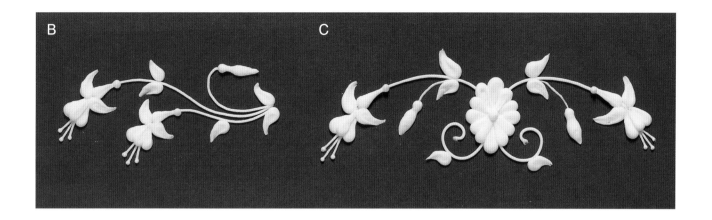

5 To pipe a bud, start with a small dot, ease off the pressure, then increase the pressure and make a long teardrop.

B: To make a small scratch-piped fuchsia design you will need no. 0 and no. 1 nozzles.

1 Scratch pipe S and C scrolls onto the side or top of the cake for the stems.

2 Pipe a flower at the end of each stem as before, starting with the stamens, followed by the skirt, petals and finally the seed box. Add a bud and leaves using a no. 1 nozzle.

C: To make a symmetrical fuchsia design for the top or sides of a cake you will need a no. 0 nozzle and a no. 1 or 2 nozzle (depending on the size of the design).

1 Mark out the spacing on the side or top of the cake using a scriber. Mark a central dot for each flower.

2 Scratch pipe the scrolls to link the flowers, then add the stamens, skirt, petals and seed box for the 2 flowers, as before.

3 Pipe an oval daisy in the centre using a no. 1 or 2 nozzle and add an oval dot in the centre (see page 52). Using a no. 0 nozzle pipe a few dots on top of the flower centre.

4 Add a bud on either side of the daisy and add leaves on the stems.

More elaborate floral designs can be used to balance lettering on cake tops (see page 204).

# Side and centre designs

These designs use the simple pressure piping techniques described in this chapter. The examples shown here can be used as space fillers on the top or sides of cakes.

**A:** Circular design/wreath

For this particular design you will need a no. 1 piping nozzle and a round cutter (the size will depend on the size of the cake).

1 Place a round cutter on the cake and scratch pipe as far round the circle as required.

2 Pipe in a series of simple blossoms and leaves around the circle, piping in opposites to ensure the design is evenly balanced. As you work up the wreath, reduce the size of the flowers each time to achieve harmony in your design.

3 To create the bow, pipe heart-shaped petals into the centre, then run two parallel lines downwards for each ribbon tie. Finish with an oval in the centre.

4 Simple monograms or single letters can be piped in the centre: this is an excellent way to personalise a wedding cake. For lettering, see pages 128 to 135.

**B:** Trellis work

You will need no. 1 and 2 nozzles to create a trellis design.

1 Starting with a no. 1 nozzle, drop line S and C scrolls to form a horn shape, then fill in the trellis work by drop lining vertical then curved horizontal lines (loose C scrolls) between the scrolls. (See pages 62 to 79 for more information on drop line work.)

2 Pressure pipe a cluster of small daisies and leaves with small scrolls for the flower stalks. Add as much or as little detail as is required.

3 Take a no. 2 nozzle and over pipe on top of the initial scrolls with a rope action (see pages 83 to 84). Start off with a very slight movement then make the rope thicker as you work along the scroll. Taper the line to a point at the end.

### C: Daisy side design

For a small daisy side design, use a no. 1 nozzle. This design is useful for filling in the space above a frill.

1 Pipe a small 6-petal daisy in the centre of the cake side. Leave a gap of 1 petal length, then add another daisy on either side on the diagonal.

2 Pipe a C and reverse C scroll at the top, then an S and reverse S on either side. Add a few leaves along the stems.

### D: Double heart design

This is a useful design for a wedding cake and you can pipe initials onto the hearts for a personal touch. Use a no. 1 and either 1.5 or 2 nozzle.

1 Pipe the hearts first using a no. 1.5 or 2 nozzle (see page 53).

2 Using a no. 1 nozzle, drop line the stems from the top of the hearts, joining them at a single point. Add curved leaves along the stems and finish with a few dots to balance the design.

3 If you wish, drop line the initials of the recipients on top of the hearts (see lettering on pages 128 to 135).

### E: Corner design

This basic shape fits perfectly into the corner of a cake, so can be used on the top or sides of a square, hexagonal or octagonal cake. Use a no. 1 and no. 1.5 or 2 nozzle.

1 Using a no. 1 nozzle, pipe a series of scroll stems on the horizontal, all joining at 1 point. Do the same with a series of vertical stems, joining at the same point.

2 Pipe a large flower on top of the joining point of the stems with a no. 1.5 or 2 nozzle. I have chosen a 12-petal flower with a pointed centre. To create this, pipe the petals in opposite pairs then use a bag of stiff royal icing to pipe pull-ups in the centre, starting in a ring around the base and working towards the centre. Pull the bag upwards as you pipe then take off the pressure to create a point.

# Combining
# Drop Line Work
## with Pressure Piping

Once you have perfected the basics of pressure piping, the next key skill to learn is drop line work. As the name suggests, lines are 'dropped' onto the cake surface to create a range of effects. This technique can be used to decorate the edge of plaques, cake sides, and for extension work (see pages 184 to 191).

This tutorial describes ways in which drop line work can be used and demonstrates how this can be combined with pressure piping.

# *Tips*
# for successful drop line work

● Always use freshly beaten icing to off-peak consistency (see page 33).

● Never use the icing for more than 20 minutes at any given time. This is because when the icing is beaten, air bubbles are incorporated into the mixture. When left in a warm atmosphere (or in your hand when holding a piping bag), the air expands, making the icing very 'short'. This means that when you are piping, the icing has a tendency to break, so piping long lines is difficult. Every time you use icing from the bowl, it must be beaten afresh to ensure a good consistency is achieved.

● Hold the piping bag with your index finger straight down the front and apply pressure from the thumb only. Use your other hand to steady the piping hand but not to apply pressure.

● When creating drop line work, make sure the nozzle is at least 4cm (1½") above the piping surface (e.g. cake or plaque).

● When piping a repetitive pattern on the top or sides of a cake, make a paper template for the cake, divide into sections then mark these divisions onto the cake with a scriber before you start piping. This will ensure that the pattern is even.

## Materials

Royal icing, made to off-peak consistency (see page 33)

SK Professional Liquid Food Colours of your choice (depending on the design)

## Equipment

Piping bags

Plain piping nozzles, ranging from no. 0 to 3 (depending on the design)

Surface on which to pipe (e.g. spare board, card, plaque or cake)

Greaseproof paper (to make cake templates)

Scriber

Fine artists' brush

# Basic drop line exercises

These first examples show basic shape and form exercises in drop line work which can be used to make exquisite designs.

You will need to use a plain nozzle (size will depend on the project but you can practise with a no. 1 or 1.5). All designs can be piped freehand, or divisions can be marked into the cake using a scriber to ensure the pattern is even.

*Tip*

Practise piping scrolls in varying sizes by adjusting the height of the nozzle as you pipe. The higher you hold the nozzle, the larger the curve will be.

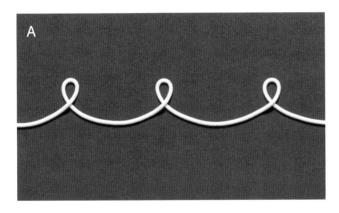

**A:** Pipe a steady curve with 1 loop. Keep the pressure constant throughout.

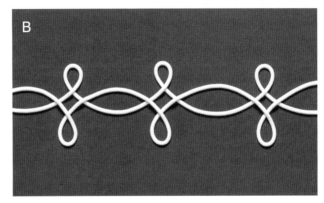

**B:** Pipe the first stage (as above) and add reversed loops. Keep the pressure constant throughout.

**C:** Pipe a pattern of 3 loops – small, large, small – in which the rhythm changes but the pressure remains constant. Add pressure piped reverse teardrops and dots to the pattern. This achieves a basic design using a combination of drop line work and pressure piping.

**D:** Pipe 1 large loop in a continuous rhythm followed by the small, large, small loop pattern (left) running in parallel.

**E:** For this design you will need to measure divisions of 4cm (1½") between each section. (This may be larger or smaller, depending on the size of the cake.) Pipe a tight curl, starting with a C scroll on the upper stroke, retaining the height of the piping nozzle, then dropping it down as you work towards the end. Add an S and reverse S scroll at the base of the line as if they are from the same stem. To balance the design, pipe a teardrop and dot in the centre of each scroll pattern.

For the fleur-de-lys, point the end of the nozzle away from you and push the icing away to create the central part. Add a teardrop with a downward curve on either side followed by a dot in the middle.

# *Drop line scrolls*

The lines of scroll work should appear to flow into one another. Secondary lines should flow alongside other scrolls and should be tapered onto the top of the primary scrolls so that they appear to disappear into the stem of the natural curve. Tapering lines is an important technique to master, especially for larger designs where a number of lines overlap.

**A:** Symmetrical scroll design

1 Drop a straight vertical line around which you will pipe the scrolls.

2 Drop line an S scroll on one side of the line and a reverse S on the other size.

3 Pipe C and reverse C scrolls in the gap at the bottom, keeping the curls quite tight by holding the nozzle fairly close to the surface.

4 Pipe a small S and reverse S at the top.

5 Pipe a dot at the bottom and 6 dots around it to make a flower. Add a single dot at the top then add a few leaves on the scrolls to finish.

## B: Asymmetrical scroll design

**1** Pipe a reverse S scroll, ensuring the lower part of the scroll is larger than the top. This will give the design balance and stability.

**2** Pipe a C scroll inside the S, tapering the line down to the base of the first scroll so that they flow seamlessly together.

**3** Pipe a reverse C scroll along the base of the reverse S.

**4** Pipe an outward S scroll, leave a gap, then finish the line on top of the other scrolls.

**5** Pressure pipe a flower, such as a daisy, at the base of the scroll to hide the join of the lines (see pages 51 to 57 for pressure piped flowers). Add a few leaves but not so many as to break up the lines of the design.

## C: Drop line side design

Dropped lines are particularly useful as side designs as they can fall from the sides of a cake.

**1** Divide the cake proportionately using a ruler/template and scriber.

**2** Drop line the first shallow curve, then add a slightly deeper curve underneath, joining the ends together. Repeat along the side of the cake.

**3** Pipe a stem for a shamrock above each set of curves, joining it at the same point on one side.

**4** Pipe dots at the joins of the dropped lines, then add a shamrock and leaves on each stem (see page 53). Add a straight dropped line between each set of curves and pipe leaves down both sides.

**5** To finish, you can add pressure piped wavy lines between the curves. You will need to use a small nozzle such as a no. 0.

# Built~up line work

Built-up line work, also known as '3-2-1 line work' can be piped using nozzle nos. 3, 2 and 1. I prefer to use nos. 2, 1 and 0 so have described this exercise using these sizes, but choose whichever suits you.

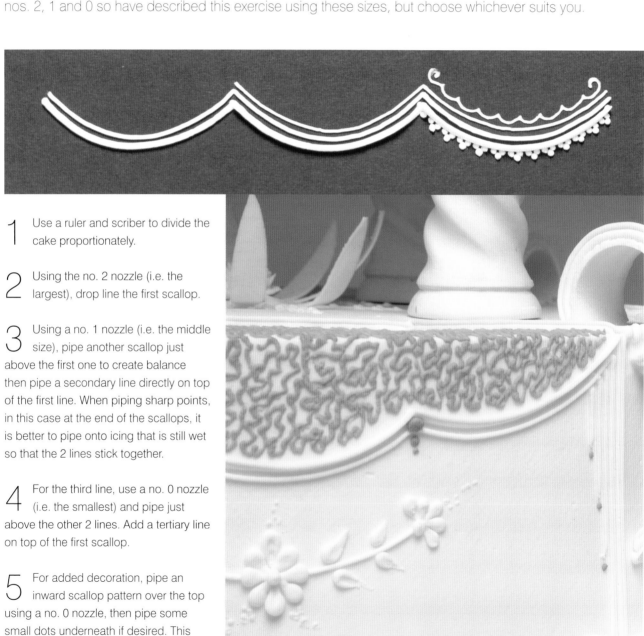

1 Use a ruler and scriber to divide the cake proportionately.

2 Using the no. 2 nozzle (i.e. the largest), drop line the first scallop.

3 Using a no. 1 nozzle (i.e. the middle size), pipe another scallop just above the first one to create balance then pipe a secondary line directly on top of the first line. When piping sharp points, in this case at the end of the scallops, it is better to pipe onto icing that is still wet so that the 2 lines stick together.

4 For the third line, use a no. 0 nozzle (i.e. the smallest) and pipe just above the other 2 lines. Add a tertiary line on top of the first scallop.

5 For added decoration, pipe an inward scallop pattern over the top using a no. 0 nozzle, then pipe some small dots underneath if desired. This makes the design look more like lace.

# Scratched scrolls

These designs can all be used as space fillers alongside drop line work. Practise each one using either a no. 0 or 1 nozzle.

**A:** Inward scallop. Always pipe scrolls on an inward curve in order to achieve sharp points.

**B:** Simple interlinking S scrolls.

**C:** Series of interlinked S scrolls.

**D:** Series of linked C scrolls.

**E:** Teardrop and dot design.

**F:** Teardrop and dot (as in design E) with a C and reverse C to create a fleur-de-lys.

**G:** C scroll, S scroll, reverse C and reverse S.

**H:** Scallop piped with a rope action/ running bead, getting smaller towards the point.

**I:** Double scallop design, i.e. scallop piped with a rope action (as in design H) with further C scroll added.

**J:** Interlinked S scrolls piped using a rope action.

**K:** S, C and reverse C piped using a rope action with a dot to finish.

**L:** Dot daisy – 3 dots with 2 above and 2 below – with an S scroll stem and C scroll leaf.

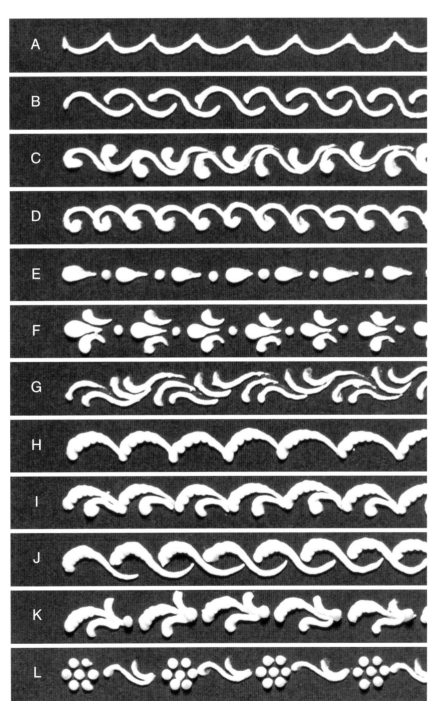

# Combining pressure piping, scratch piping and drop line work

Side designs and borders can be piped using a combination of techniques. These designs can also be piped onto ribbon which can be attached to the cake after it has been decorated.

When piping repetitive patterns such as borders, pipe one stage at a time all the way around the cake (or along the ribbon) as this helps to keep your work consistent.

## A: Daisy border design

In addition to the basic materials and equipment, you will need SK Daffodil and Holly/Ivy Professional Liquid Food Colours and a small palette knife for this design.

1 Place some off-peak royal icing into a piping bag with a no. 2 nozzle. Using a ruler as a guide, drop line 2 parallel lines.

2 Pressure pipe a daisy between the lines, just above the centre. Following the angle of the petal on the diagonal, leave the length of 1 petal then pipe in the diagonal petal of the next flower just below and to one side of the first daisy. Do the same on the opposite side, then fill in all the petals on all 3 flowers, ensuring you leave space between the horizontal lines. Pipe a yellow dot in the centre of each.

3 Scratch pipe a C and reverse C on either side of the top daisy. I have used green icing for the stems but you may prefer to use white or a different colour to complement the cake.

4 Using icing that is the same colour as the cake covering, pipe a tiny spot at the centre point between each set of daisies as a guide. Pipe an S scroll on either side of the point for the stems, then join the daisies up with short lines.

5 Add leaves on the S and C scrolls, keeping them minimal so as not to break up the design.

6 Carefully lift off the centre spots of icing with a palette knife or similar.

7 Fill in the spaces just above the horizontal lines of the design with simple scratch piped designs (see suggestions on page 69). Add a running bead at the base to add weight (see opposite).

## B: Running bead

1 Place some off-peak royal icing into a piping bag with a plain nozzle of your choice. The size of the nozzle will depend on the size of the cake.

2 Drop line a straight line across the cake or plaque.

3 To pipe the running bead, squeeze gently, stop, then lay down the tip to create a little pearl. Once you get into the rhythm of the piping you can speed up, which will help to keep the beads the same size.

4 Scratch pipe a simple design beneath the running bead for added decoration (see page 69).

## C: Violet border design

In addition to the basic materials and equipment, you will need SK Daffodil, Holly/Ivy and Violet Professional Liquid Food Colours for this design.

1 Wrap a strip of greaseproof paper around the cake and fold in half as many times as required to give 2.5cm-4cm (1"-1½") sections. Mark each section on the cake using a tiny spot of icing in the same colour as the cake covering or a scriber. This method is easier than working freehand and ensures the pattern is constant.

2 Using a rope action, pipe a fairly large scallop pattern along the top and bottom. Each scallop should be as wide as the sections marked earlier.

3 Pipe purple teardrops to create the violets, giving each flower 5 petals and making the lower petal slightly larger than the others. Pipe 3 violets in each part of the design and add yellow centres. Use the scallops to set the distance between the flowers: every set of flowers fits between 3 scallops.

4 Scratch pipe S and C scrolls around the flowers for the stems and add leaves.

### D: Drop line oval border design

In addition to the basic materials and equipment, you will need SK Daffodil, Holly/Ivy and Violet Professional Liquid Food Colours for this design.

1 Drop line a straight horizontal line. Pressure pipe a series of dots approximately 2.5cm (1") away from the line at 2.5cm (1") intervals. Drop line another straight line on the other side of the dots at the same distance as before.

2 Drop line an S scroll starting at 1 dot, crossing through the next dot and finishing at the next. Pipe another S scroll from the middle point of the last scroll and so on until you have a wavy line going all the way around the cake.

3 Pipe 8 teardrops inside each almond shape to create an oval daisy (see page 52). Add an oval centre in purple to accentuate the shape of the flower. Pipe leaves at the points of the scallops.

4 Lighten the edges by scratch piping 3 small scallops to every 2.5cm (1") large scallop.

### E: Bunches of grapes border design

I have drop-lined this design using a no. 2 nozzle, but you can scratch pipe it if you are piping onto the side of a cake.

1 Drop line 2 horizontal lines, using a ruler as a guide for the width.

2 Drop line 1 long, continuous S curve between the lines, then pipe shallower S curves onto the lower curve of the long line. Blend this line into the first to hide the join. If you are left with a pull-off point, use a damp artists' brush to level off the line.

3 To pipe a bunch of grapes, hold the nozzle at a 45° angle. Pipe 1 dot, then 2 dots below, 3 below, 3 larger below then 4, 3 and 2. You can pipe the grapes as separate dots or, once you gain confidence, in one continuous motion as running beads.

4 To pipe the leaves, cut a V shape in the tip of a piping bag (see page 56), hold the bag at a 45° angle and pipe the leaves out to one side. This will also hide the join between the grapes and the stalk.

5 Using a no. 1 or 0 nozzle, pipe in the tendrils using either drop line work or scratch piping.

6 Finish the decoration by scratch piping a double scallop above and below the edges (see page 69).

## F: Circular design

Drop line circles are only suitable for cake top work: if you are piping a curve onto the side of a cake, you can either scratch pipe the design or pipe the complete design onto a plaque which can then be attached to the side of a cake.

When drop lining a circle, it is better to stand up as you are working so that you are piping directly over the top of the cake (or plaque). You can move your body in a circular motion as you pipe which helps to create an even, circular line. If you are right-handed it is easier to pipe clockwise, if you are left-handed pipe anti-clockwise.

For this design you will need a round cutter or a set of dividers (similar to a compass but with no pencil) and stiff-peak icing.

1 Place a round cutter onto the cake surface or scribe a circle using a set of dividers.

2 Prepare a bag of stiff-peak royal icing with a no. 1.5 nozzle. Start at the bottom of the circle on the surface of the cake, then lift and hold the nozzle at least 4cm (1½") above the surface of the cake. Carefully drop a line just outside the cutter or directly onto the scribed line, keeping the pressure constant as you work round the circle.

3 Ease off the pressure and bring the nozzle down at the end to hide the join – this will take some practice so it is worth piping a few circles onto a spare board first.

F

4 To decorate the circle, add pressure piped leaves (see page 52) on either side of the piped line.

5 Mark the centre of the circle with a tiny dot of icing. Drop horizontal and vertical lines inside the circle through the central point, starting approximately 2cm (¾") away from the edge.

6 Mark 4 points between the lines, each one approximately 1.3cm (½") from the centre, and make a dot. Drop line S and reverse S scrolls on either side of each straight line, keeping the nozzle a little lower on the drop as you pipe from a large curve to a small curve. This helps to create a tight curve.

7 Using a no. 1 nozzle, start on the inside of each S scroll and pipe a reverse C scroll. Keep the nozzle fairly low to maintain a tight curve. Repeat on each side of the pattern.

8 Pipe a small dot at the end of each straight line to hide the finishing points. Pipe a larger dot to hide the joins between the S and C scrolls.

9 Using a no. 2 nozzle, pipe a large dot in the centre, then use a no. 1.5 nozzle to pipe pull-out petals out from this dot. Start with the petals around the outside and work inwards, easing off the pressure as you pull out of each petal to make a point. You should end up with a rounded flower resembling a dahlia.

### G: Heart design

The same principles apply to hearts as to circles, i.e. a dropped line design can only be piped flat, whereas scratch piped designs can be piped directly onto the side of a cake. This design is an example of scratch piping and you can use any colour to complement the cake.

For this design you will need a heart cutter and SK Bluebell, Daffodil and Holly/Ivy Liquid Food Colours.

1 Place a heart cutter onto the cake surface. Use the same colour icing as the cake covering and scratch pipe the heart shape onto the cake with a no. 0 nozzle.

2 Pipe a 6-petal forget-me-not (in the same way as a daisy) at the top of the heart. Leave the length of 1 petal between flowers and continue to pipe round the heart. Always pipe the first pair of petals following the line of the heart and add the flowers in opposites to ensure the design is symmetrical.

3 To make the design a little more interesting, miss out a couple of flowers around the sides of the heart. Add in 2 large daisies on 1 side and 1 on the other (see page 52). At this stage, you may also wish to add a monogram or greeting in the middle of the heart (see pages 130 to 135).

4 Pipe yellow centres on the forget-me-nots and pull-ups in the centre of the daisies to resemble stamens.

5 Using a no. 1 nozzle, pipe leaves between the flowers at a slight angle, following the line of the heart and forming a lozenge shape. Add further scratch piped stems and leaves by the daisies.

### H: Oval design

This design can be used on the centre of an oval or oblong cake. With a little practice, this design can be piped directly onto the surface of a cake, but always mark the start and finish points of the scrolls with a scriber before you start.

1 Using a small piping bag fitted with a no. 2 nozzle, pipe the straight lines first, then add the large, outer S and reverse S scrolls.

2 Pipe the inner scrolls, then add the leaves with the same nozzle.

3 Pipe a dahlia flower in the centre using freshly beaten royal icing in a piping bag fitted with a no. 2 nozzle (see circular design on page 73). If required, the flower can be piped in colour, for example, pipe the first set of petals in dark pink, lighten the icing with white and pipe the second stage, then continue adding white to create paler tones as you reach the centre.

# Freestanding designs

These piped designs can be used for the top and sides of sugarpasted or royal iced cakes. They are ideal for wedding and anniversary cakes, either attached to the top edge, standing up on the board, or as a side design on the cake. They can also be used to make cake top decorations, either as a part or whole of the overall design.

Scrolls are used in many of the designs here: further instructions on piping scrolls are given on pages 80 to 93.

## Preparation

As these designs are piped as off-pieces rather than directly onto a cake, you will need to prepare the templates (on page 286) under a sheet of cellophane greased with white vegetable fat as follows:

1 Draw the template onto paper and secure to a flat surface (such as a non-stick board) with masking tape.

2 Cut a piece of cellophane that is bigger than the template and secure over the top with masking tape. If using cellophane from a roll, keep the outer side uppermost so that the edges do not curve upwards.

3 Lightly grease the cellophane with white vegetable fat so that the finished piece can be removed easily when dry.

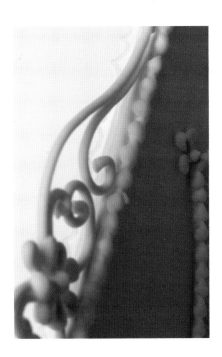

*Tip*

In order for freestanding pieces to hold their shape, the piped lines must always touch each other within a framework.

## A: Engrailed scallop design

Engrailing is a heraldic term for this type of semi-circle pattern. This design can be used as a cake top edge decoration for a square, hexagonal or octagonal cake.

1 Prepare the template under a sheet of greased cellophane and place some freshly beaten off-peak icing into a piping bag with a no. 1.5 nozzle.

2 Outline the design first, then add in the scrolls and fleurs-de-lys.

3 Pipe dots around the edge of the scallops. This adds decoration and also helps to strengthen the piece.

## B: Scroll design

This design can be used as a freestanding top edge design on a square, hexagonal or octagonal cake. To make pieces for a round cake, pipe the design over a curve with the same radius as the cake, such as the cake tin in which the cake was baked, a piece of guttering, or a piece of corrugated card. If you use card, carefully measure the diameter and circumference of the cake and secure the ends of the card to a flat surface, ensuring you use the same measurements.

1 Secure the template to a flat or curved surface (as required) with a sheet of greased cellophane over the top. Place some royal icing into a piping bag with a no. 2 nozzle.

2 Drop line the straight line across the bottom first. Next, start from the inside curve on the left-hand side and pipe the S scroll, then repeat on the other side. Make sure the 2 S scrolls just touch the edge of the straight line.

3 Pipe in the smaller scrolls, making sure that the end of the line disappears on top of the first (i.e. the larger scroll).

4 Finish off the design by pressure piping a flower in the centre (see pages 51 to 57). If required, the flower can be piped separately (as an additional off-piece) and attached in place when dry.

**C:** Oblong design

This piece can be used as a top decoration or side design, and can also be used to make square, hexagonal or octagonal boxes.

1 Pipe the straight lines with a no. 2 nozzle using the drop line technique.

2 Pipe in the scrolls and flower in the same way as for the scroll design, opposite.

3 This piece can be stabilised and strengthened with running beads along the sides and top. The bottom edge can be strengthened when the dried piece is stuck to the board or cake surface.

B

Variation

Using a section of the design you can pipe a scroll piece to be used as a corner or side piece for the base of the cake. Pipe with a no. 2 nozzle.

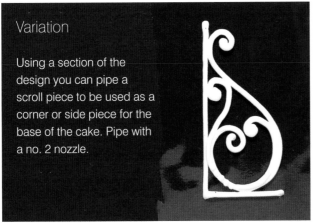

# Piped baskets

There are many ways to make baskets to decorate cakes: they can be piped directly onto the side of a cake or made from modelling paste and textured with a patterned rolling pin then filled with sugar flowers, for example. I have found an easy method to make piped baskets using a patty bun tin or an inverted plastic egg container greased with white vegetable fat.

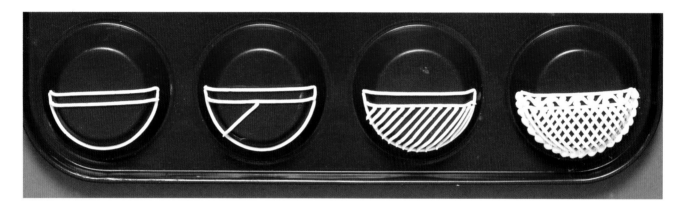

## To pipe a basket you will need:

### Materials

Soft and stiff peak royal icing (see page 33)

White vegetable fat

### Equipment

Piping bag

No. 2 plain piping nozzle

Patty tin or plastic egg container

Desk lamp

1 Grease the underside of the tin/container with white vegetable fat.

2 Prepare a bag of soft peak royal icing with a no. 2 nozzle. Drop a curved line around the lower half of the bun/egg shape, then add 2 horizontal lines across the centre to outline the basket.

3 Pipe a line at a 45° angle from the lower horizontal line to the curve across the middle of the basket. Fill in the rest of the basket with parallel lines, ensuring the ends always touch the outline. The lines should be a little more than the width of the nozzle tip apart. Do the same on the opposite diagonal, again starting from the middle, to complete the trellis.

4 Fill in the gap at the top with a scroll design or dots and finish by piping a running bead around the base to strengthen the piece.

5 When you have piped as many baskets as required, place under a desk lamp and leave to dry for at least a few hours, preferably overnight.

6 To remove the baskets when dry, place back under a lamp for a few moments to melt the white fat. Ease the baskets off with your fingers or a palette knife.

7 Secure the baskets to the cake with stiff royal icing before filling with sugar flowers (see opposite).

# Filling the basket

There are 2 methods for filling piped baskets, the second one being quicker. Choose whichever method suits you.

## Method 1

In addition to the materials and equipment required to pipe a basket you will need SK Holly/Ivy Professional Liquid Food Colour and the colour of your choice for the buds, piped blossoms in your chosen colour (see page 125) and a pair of fine scissors.

1   Colour some stiff royal icing with Holly/Ivy Liquid Food Colour and place in a piping bag with no nozzle. Snip the tip of the bag into a V shape, no greater than 45°.

2   Pipe along the top edge of the basket inwardly to fill the top part only. Do not pipe inside the basket.

3   Place pre-piped flowers on top of the leaves (or pipe them directly into the basket if preferred) and add a few leaves around them. Pipe in some buds in the same colour as the flowers to finish the design.

4   If required, you can add a handle to the basket (see Method 2).

## Method 2

In addition to the materials and equipment required to pipe a basket you will need SK Holly/Ivy Professional Liquid Food Colour and the colour of your choice for the flowers.

1   Prepare a piping bag with no nozzle. Fill 2 more piping bags with stiff royal icing in different colours (I have used blue and white), snip off the tip of each one and pipe each colour inside opposite sides of the empty bag. Each line of colour should be around 7mm (½") thick.

2   Cut a V into the tip of the bag and test the colours to make sure you are happy with the effect. Pipe in a circular motion (anticlockwise if you are right-handed, clockwise if you are left-handed) to create roses in the basket.

3   Pipe little buds on either side of the flowers, then add some leaves to finish (see Method 1 for instructions).

4   If required, pipe a handle over the basket using a rope action (see page 83) and add a bow on one side. You can also add further scroll decoration at the base.

# Scrolls

A scroll is a natural form which has been used through the centuries in many art forms, in heraldic coats of arms, and extensively in the interiors of old houses. The most important point to learn when developing piped scrolls is that the shape of a scroll is based on the leaf form: starting off fine, getting thicker in the middle, then tapering off at the end. When adding secondary or tertiary scrolls onto the base scroll, all the scrolls should meet up at the end as you would imagine the leaves forming on a stalk or stem. When piping scrolls, always avoid 'dog's legs', i.e. squaring off, and keep to nicely rounded shapes to create S and C scrolls.

# *Tips* for piping scrolls

- Always make sure the royal icing you are using is freshly beaten to slightly off-peak consistency (as with drop line and extension work, see pages 63 and 185).

- Make sure the end of the nozzle you are using is kept clean, especially if you are using rope nozzles, in order to achieve good definition in your piping.

- The exercises here are shown using a no. 43 rope nozzle, although once you have practised your technique you can use different nozzles depending on the cake you are decorating.

- When piping scrolls, always start with the largest curve and finish off with the smaller curves if feasible. This is because it is easier to make small curves when 'dropping off' at the end of the line.

## Materials

Royal icing, made to off-peak consistency (see page 33)

SK Professional Liquid Food Colours of your choice (depending on the design)

## Equipment

Piping bags

No. 43 and 44 rope nozzles and plain piping nozzles, ranging from no. 1 to 3 (for over piping)

Surface on which to pipe (e.g. spare board, card, plaque or cake)

# Basic scrolls

## A: The S scroll

Keep the bag at an acute angle to the cake surface – slightly less than 45° – and pipe a curve, rotating your wrist to create the shape. Taper at the end.

## B: The C scroll

Keep the angle of the piping bag at 45° or less as you pipe. With the nozzle pointing towards the centre, start at the top, pipe round the scroll, then taper to finish. Imagine the tail is continuous to achieve a smooth, tapered point. To achieve a rounded curve, start in the centre of an imaginary circle and come almost all the way round the circle before tapering off to the side.

## C: S and C scrolls together

1 Pipe an S scroll, ensuring the curves at the top and bottom are equidistant from each other.

2 Pipe the C scroll, starting in the centre of an imaginary circle, then come up to the S scroll stem and taper to finish. This forms the basic structure of a scroll.

# Developing the rope

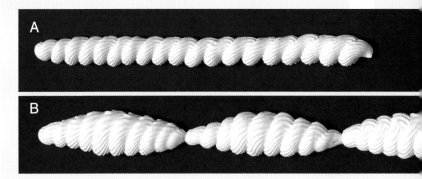

The next stage in scroll techniques is to develop your skills in piping using a rope action.

## A: Basic rope action

Hold the piping bag at an angle of less than 45° to the cake, squeeze the bag and rotate the nozzle, keeping a continuous pressure throughout to create a rope.

## B: Barrel scroll

The barrel scroll is thus named because it should have a natural curve from every angle. It is worth picturing this when piping barrel scrolls in order to achieve the desired effect. There are 3 basic methods for piping a barrel scroll; these all create the same result, so find which one suits you best. If you are piping onto a cake, you may wish to use a paper template or ruler to ensure that all the scrolls are the same size.

Method 1: Using a rope action, start by squeezing a fine line, then squeeze harder as you reach the centre. Decrease the pressure and taper the line to finish.

Method 2: Start with a fine line, then increase the size of the rotations (rather than increasing the pressure) and decrease to the end.

Method 3: Using a constant pressure, simply pipe back and forth (rather than in rotations) to achieve the barrel shape.

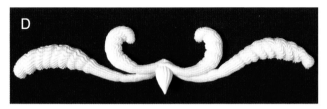

**C:** S and C scrolls (using the rope method)

1 Pipe the S scroll first, starting with a fine line, getting thicker at the top of the curve, and tapering at the end. To pipe a series of S scrolls, start each one on top of the end of the last.

2 To pipe the C scroll, start above the middle point of the S scroll, circle the nozzle anticlockwise to pipe the C shape then taper to a point on top of the S scroll.

**D:** Double S and C scroll (using the rope method)

1 To create a double scroll, pipe the first set as described (left) then add a reverse S and C scroll so that they join the first set in the centre. If you are right-handed, the hardest scroll to pipe is from right to left (the opposite is the case if you are left-handed). To make this easier, rotate the cake 45° away from your body so that you are piping towards yourself. Pipe the right-hand S scroll with anticlockwise rotations and the C scroll clockwise. Always pipe towards the centre of the scroll design.

2 Pipe a little pull-up in the centre to finish.

# Developing the C scroll

As you develop the C scroll design, pipe each stage all the way round the cake before proceeding onto the next. Piping in repetition will help you to work faster and will also give better definition and regularity to your work.

1 Start with a C shape and pipe a number of these scrolls in succession around the side or top of the cake.

2 Starting at the top of each C scroll, pipe a small S scroll. Pipe another small S scroll at the base.

3 Use a plain no. 2 nozzle to over pipe the design. Start at the top S scroll and pipe a reverse S using a rope action on each scroll. Pipe over the bottom S scroll in the same way and repeat around the cake.

4 Finish by over piping anticlockwise with a rope action onto the C scroll.

# Developing the S and C scroll

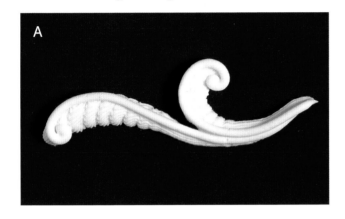

## A: Over piping scrolls

There are two methods for over piping the basic S and C scroll shape: the first is to continue piping using a rope action and taper the lines into the scrolls; the second is to over pipe coloured royal icing using the drop line technique (see pages 62 to 79). The S and C scroll shape is piped as before using a no. 43 rope nozzle and a no. 3 plain nozzle is used for the over piping in both methods here.

Method 1: Rotate the piping bag over the S scroll to create a rope effect, then lift the nozzle and drop the end of the line into place. This will give good definition. To over pipe the C scroll, start with a fine line, then get thicker in the middle as you reach the join, lift the bag and gradually pipe onto the edge of the scroll. The piped lines should all finish at one point on the same stem.

Method 2: Using the drop line technique, over pipe on the outside edge of the S scroll, tapering at the end. Repeat on the C scroll, then taper to the top edge of the scroll.

## B: Trellis work

These designs incorporate trellis work, which lightens the heaviness of the scroll. They are particularly useful on the corners of square cakes.

1 Pipe the S and C scrolls, either as a single or double design. When piping the C scroll, start on the diagonal rather than in the centre to make a simple C, again finishing at the same point as the S scroll.

2 Over pipe the scrolls with a rope action, tapering to the same point as before.

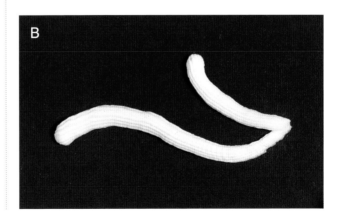

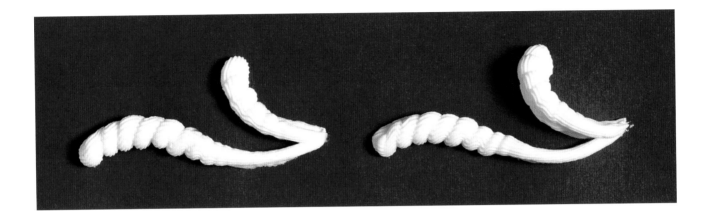

3 Over pipe the C scroll again to lift it higher.

4 To pipe the trellis, make the icing to a slightly stiffer consistency (add about two teaspoonfuls of icing sugar to a cup or so of icing) and colour if required. Place the freshly beaten icing in a piping bag with a no. 1 nozzle. Pipe straight, parallel lines at an angle, starting at the top of the scroll and

finishing at the base. Continue to the point where the scrolls meet. For a double scroll design, repeat on the opposite side, positioning the cake at an angle to make it easier to pipe.

5 Over pipe the trellis on the curve of the C scroll and continue to pipe parallel, curved lines down to the base of the scroll.

6 Once the trellis work is complete, over pipe the S and C scrolls with a no. 2 nozzle using a rope action. Alternatively, you can over pipe with a no. 3 nozzle and use a no. 1 nozzle to pipe a rope on top of the plain lines.

7 To hide the joins in the centre, pipe a small pull-up in white icing.

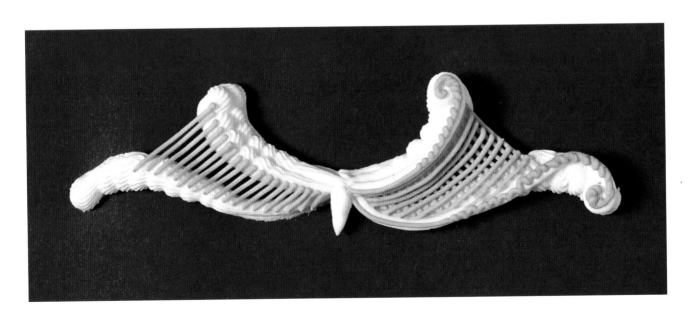

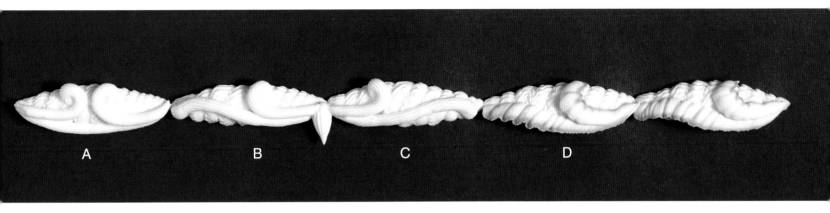

A          B          C          D

# Developing the barrel scroll

Whilst the basic shape of the barrel scroll remains the same, further embellishments can be added to suit the cake design.

### A: C scrolls

1 Using a rope nozzle, drop a line below the edge of the barrel.

2 Pipe a reverse C and a C scroll from the centre. This design can be used all the way round the cake.

### B: S and C scrolls

Pipe an S scroll on top of the barrel, then add a C scroll in the middle, tapered to the end. This can be continued round the cake.

### C: S and C scrolls reversed

Pipe a reverse S and C scroll as before then pipe a pull-up in the middle. This is useful for corner designs.

### D: Coloured over piping

For this design you will need a small petal nozzle.

1 Place a small petal nozzle in a piping bag. Fill another bag with coloured icing, snip off the end and pipe a line of icing up the inside of the first bag, level with the fine edge of the petal nozzle. Fill the other side of the piping bag with a contrasting colour (in this case, white).

2 Pipe a slight S scroll and a C scroll, remembering to keep the fine edge of the petal to the outer edge of the scroll when piping.

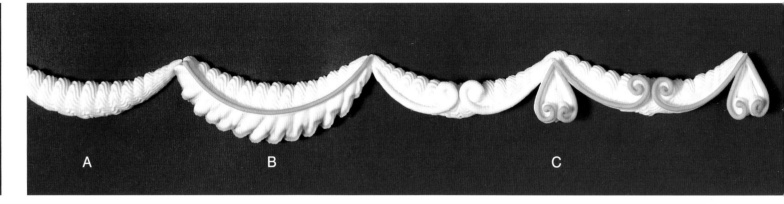

A　　　　B　　　　C

# Swags (flounces)

When piping swags around a cake, divide the cake proportionately so that the swags are of a suitable size for the cake. The design shown here is suitable for the top, side or base of a cake.

### A: Plain swag

Pipe the swags in the same way as for a barrel scroll but make a slight curve. Repeat around the cake.

### B: Coloured over piping, double swag

1 Drop a line 7mm (¼") from the base of each swag in your chosen colour using a no. 3 nozzle.

2 Using a petal nozzle with two colours of icing (see Developing the barrel scroll: D, page 87), pipe another swag underneath the line.

### C: Over piping, drop line work

1 Use a plain nozzle to pipe C and reverse C scrolls from the middle of each swag to the points.

2 Pipe a teardrop from the base upwards using a rope nozzle and over pipe reverse Cs onto the teardrops.

3 To define shape and form, it is feasible to over pipe in a colour with a no. 2 nozzle. Choose a colour to complement the cake design.

# Tip
## Keeping scroll work light

It is always important to keep piping work as light as possible so that it doesn't overpower the cake, but scrolls can be rather heavy. Drop line work used on the top and sides of a cake can create a gradual step down to the cake surface, as shown, thus lightening the design.

1 Pipe a series of barrel scrolls, as before.

2 Use the 3-2-1 method (see page 68) above and below the scrolls. (In some cases, just 2-1 line work is sufficient.)

# Running shells

To pipe a running shell around a cake, hold the bag at an acute angle to the top edge of the cake. As you pipe, the curves at the top and bottom should be equidistant from each other. When piping shells, ensure each one resembles an individual pearl. Shells can be piped with any size plain or rope nozzle, depending on the size of the cake.

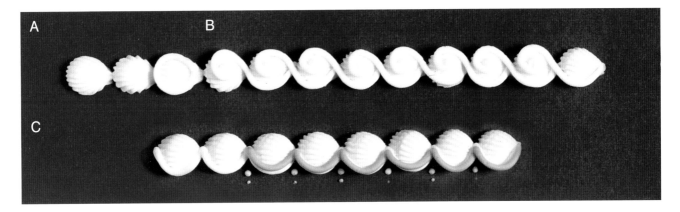

## A: Plain shell

1 Hold the bag at 45° to the cake surface, squeeze gently, stop, then bring to a point. The size of the shells will depend on the size of the cake.

2 Leave a little join-up in between the shells so that they maintain their definition when they are over piped. If the shells are piped correctly, you should be able to pipe a circle around the shell, as shown, without touching the shells on either side.

## B: Scroll design

1 Pipe a series of running shells, as described in A.

2 Over pipe each shell with a scroll using the drop line technique. Start in the middle of the shell and continue around the perimeter onto the base of the next shell and stop. This can be used as top or bottom edge decoration.

## C: Scallop design

1 Start at the edge of the shell and pipe along the bottom edge to emphasise the curve of the shell.

2 If you would like to add colour to the design, over pipe the scallops with coloured icing.

3 Add small dots between the shells to balance the design.

To alter the size of the shells, you can either change the size of the nozzle or apply more or less pressure to the piping bag as you work.

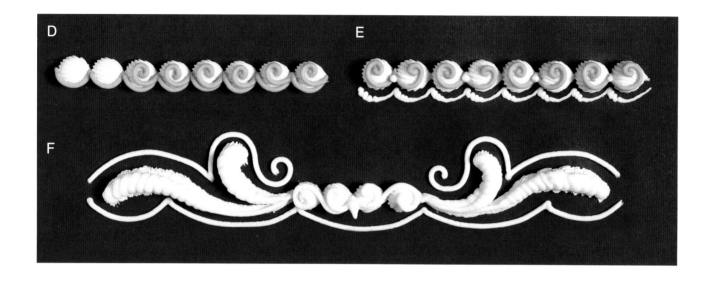

### D: C scrolls

1 Pipe the scallop design (C) in colour.

2 Over pipe C scrolls directly onto the shells with the same coloured icing.

### E: C and reverse C scrolls

Make sure you have an even number of shells before starting this design.

1 Follow the method for the C scroll design above, but this time pipe a C and reverse C on adjoining shells.

2 Finish with a white dot to hide the joins.

3 If required, scratch pipe a scalloped design above or below the shells to emphasise the shape (see page 69).

### F: Corner design

When piping S and C scrolls in reverse from the corners of a cake, the gap in between can be filled with shells if required. The designs in the centre can be varied using any of the over piping techniques described.

1 Pipe an S and reverse S scroll on either side of the corner then a C and reverse C scroll.

2 Add drop line work underneath and above to accentuate the shape of the scrolls and running shells in the middle with your chosen embellishment.

### G: Continuous scroll

1 Using a rope nozzle start on the top edge of the cake and pipe a rope and a dropped line over the edge to make a reverse S scroll, then stop.

2 Start on the edge of the cake again in the middle of the first scroll and pipe further reverse S scrolls in the same way.

3 Use a plain nozzle for the over piping. Starting just under the curve of each scroll, drop line a reverse S scroll and bring the line on top of the first scroll to finish at the same point.

4 Pipe a rope on top with the plain nozzle, this time starting at the beginning of the first set of scrolls.

# The pull~up (pear shape)

Before piping pull-ups on the side of a cake, it is feasible to cut a V shape into the scraper as you add the final coat of icing (see pages 38 to 39). This way you can create a ridge around the side of the cake at the required height which you can use as a guideline.

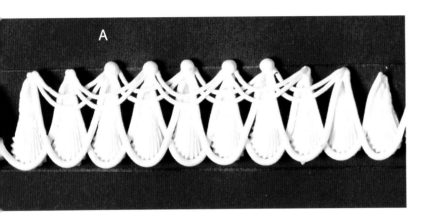

## A: Straight pull-ups

1 Using a no. 44 rope nozzle, squeeze icing onto the bottom of the cake (or ridge), pull up and stop. Repeat around the cake.

2 Place a no. 2 nozzle in a piping bag and fill with the same colour of icing. Drop lines between every other pull-up all round the cake, then come back on yourself and repeat on alternate pull-ups to overlap the first set of dropped lines.

3 To make this design finer, take a no. 1 nozzle and drop double lines up to the top of every other pull-up. Then work in reverse and pipe the same on alternate pull-ups to overlap the lines.

4 To hide the joins, pipe a bead at the top of each pull-up with a no. 1 nozzle.

## B: Curved pull-ups

1 Pipe soft S scrolls at an angle up the side of the cake with a rope nozzle.

2 Use a no. 3 plain nozzle to pipe an S scroll up to the top of each of the larger S scrolls. Using the same nozzle, pipe a rope design on top of the first set of scrolls, tapering at the top.

3 Make up a small bag of icing and cut a V in the tip (see page 56). Alternatively, you can use a leaf nozzle. Pipe a leaf in-between each pull-up, hiding the finished point. As you pipe, shake the bag back and forth slightly to create veins in the leaves, as shown.

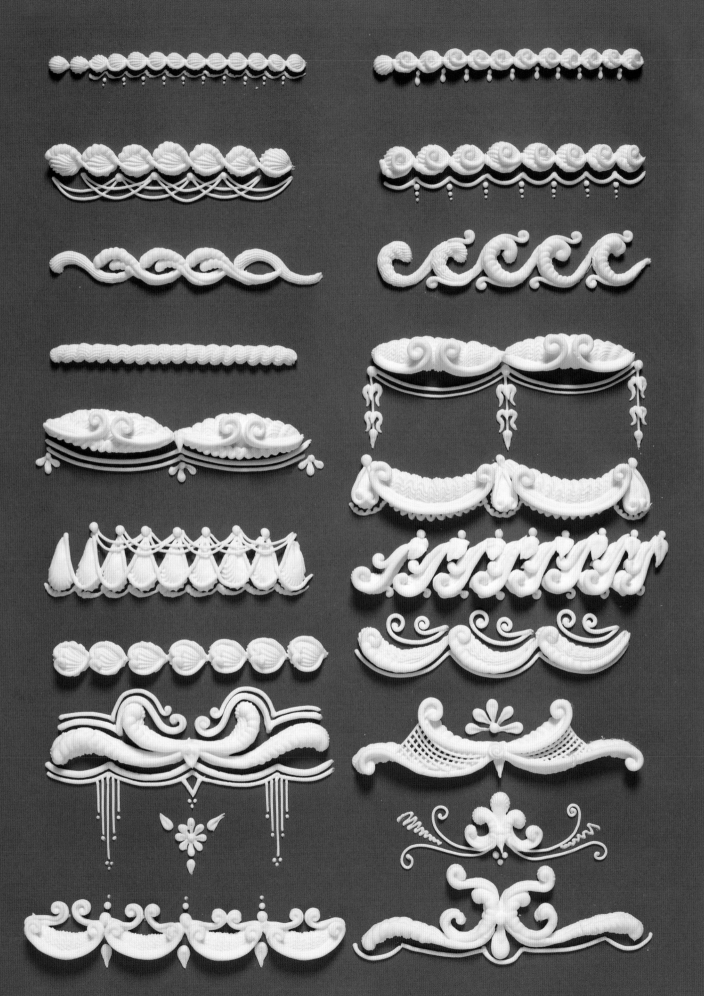

93

# Pressure Piped
## Figures & Motifs

When piping figures, you will usually need rubbed down or 'paddled' royal icing (see page 33). By rubbing down (paddling) the icing with a palette knife, the air is expelled which gives the icing a slight flow. This makes it easier to achieve a smooth finish when piping.

All of the designs shown here have been piped directly onto coloured card to clearly illustrate the techniques involved. However, when piping designs for a cake, I recommend making them as off-pieces where feasible, which can be positioned when dry. As you gain confidence you can pipe straight onto the cake.

# *Tips*
## for pressure piping figures and motifs

- When colouring icing, always use liquid colours so that the icing dries fully (see page 45).

- Many of the designs shown here can be made as off-pieces (see opposite). Simply pipe onto greased cellophane or waxed paper and allow to dry under a desk lamp in the same way as for run-outs (see pages 143 to 167).

- When piping figures and scenes, always start with the background and work to the foreground to help give perspective.

- In some cases, for example when piping faces, you may the need the icing to settle (lose its shape) when piped. If this is the case, rub down the icing a little more than usual or add a touch of cold water using an artists' brush.

- If you are making more than 1 of the same motif for a cake in colour, make sure the colours are controlled by weighing the icing and measuring the amount of colour used (see page 45). If the icing dries out or you run out, you can re-create the same colour again.

## Materials

Royal icing, rubbed down (see page 33)

SK Professional Liquid Food Colours (see each motif for requirements)

White vegetable fat

## Equipment

Piping bags

Nos. 1, 1.5, 2 plain piping nozzles

Fine scissors

Fine artists' brush

Desk lamp

Templates

Cellophane

Masking tape

Surface on which to pipe (e.g. spare board, card, plaque or cake)

# Preparation

If you are new to piping it is best to make these designs as off-pieces, meaning that they are piped off the cake and placed in position when dry (except where the design is particularly fine and delicate, such as the basic tree). Before piping the designs, prepare your templates in the following way:

1 Draw the designs onto a sheet of paper.

2 Secure the template to a flat surface such a non-stick board or spare cake drum using masking tape.

3 Cut a piece of cellophane to fit over the top of the template and secure in place with masking tape or dots of royal icing. If you are using a roll of cellophane, make sure you keep the outer side of the cellophane uppermost, otherwise the edges may curl up which may cause the icing to break.

4 Grease the cellophane with a thin film of white vegetable fat to ensure the pieces are easy to remove from the cellophane when dry. Do not rub the cellophane without the fat as this will cause static which will prevent drop line work from falling straight.

# Animals

A

**A:** Ducks (simple form)

1 Place some slightly rubbed-down orange (SK Nasturtium) royal icing into a piping bag with a no. 1 nozzle. Pipe the top of the beak followed by the lower part, giving it a slight curve to create a smile.

2 Pipe the back leg, making sure the top goes into the body.

3 Using white royal icing and a no. 1 nozzle, start by piping the head, then ease off the pressure down to the neck and increase it again as you pipe the body. Finally, ease off the pressure as you come to the tail and finish with a flick of the wrist.

4 Pipe the second leg and the webbed foot in orange. Add a wing by piping a small teardrop on the body, slightly curving the shape at the tip.

5 If desired, the body can be textured. Break the hard line at the chest with a fine artists' brush to give a feathery effect. Starting at the tail, brush in tiny feathers using a slightly curved action.

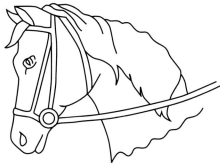

## B: Horse's head

In addition to the basic equipment you will also need a no. 30 fine ribbon nozzle.

1 Place a no. 1.5 nozzle into a piping bag and half-fill with stiff royal icing for the mane.

Where you require the icing to be stiff, always get into the habit of beating the icing to bring it back to off-peak consistency before use.

2 Rub down some royal icing with a palette knife and place in a piping bag. Cut a hole in the top of the bag to the size of a no. 2 nozzle. (You can use a no. 2 nozzle instead but cutting the hole gives you the option of making it bigger for larger parts of the design, should you need to.)

3 Pipe the horse's head, starting at the top behind the ear and working down to the neck using a back and forth motion. Take the icing down to the cheek and vibrate the piping bag on top of the icing to level it out and eliminate any streaks.

4 Using the same piping bag, add an oval for the horse's eye. Pipe in the ear behind the head by making a teardrop shape and pulling the tip of the bag through the icing to make a dimple. Pipe the horse's mouth.

5 Starting at the nose, pressure pipe the icing and increase the volume as you work up the head. Vibrate the icing to achieve a clean line. Continue to pipe over the forehead then round the eye and back down to the nose. Finally, build up the cheek by increasing the pressure, then decrease it again as you come back down to the ear.

6 Using a fine artists' brush, make a dimple for the nostril. Then, starting at the top of the head, pipe back and forth using stiff royal icing with a no. 1.5 nozzle to create the mane. Once you have piped halfway down, stop piping and brush through the icing to create a fine texture. Pipe the second stage of the mane and texture with a brush, as before. Rather than making straight brushstrokes, keep the texturing curved. Piping the mane in 2 stages will ensure that the icing is still wet when you are texturing it.

7 Starting at the top of the mane, pipe the forelock and texture with a brush.

8 Pipe inside the ear in the foreground using stiff royal icing and a no. 1.5 nozzle, then pipe the back end of the ear on top.

9 When dry, pipe the reins using a fine ribbon nozzle and stiff royal icing.

### C: Osprey

1. Start by piping the primary feathers on the wing in the background. Use a no. 1.5 or 2 nozzle and stiff royal icing to pipe each feather up one side and down the other. Texture with a fine artists' brush.

2. Pipe the secondary feathers using the running beads technique (see page 71). Brush through the centre of each bead to give a feathery effect. Pipe then texture 1 row of feathers at a time, overlapping each row over the last.

3. Pipe the top part of the wing as a running bead and texture with an artists' brush to create a downy appearance. Brush the outer edge smooth.

4. Pipe the leg in the background, using a slight roped action for the lower half of the leg (see page 83). This will give a knurled effect.

5. Pipe the tail using a back and forth motion and keeping an even pressure. Pipe 3 or 4 feathers at a time then texture with a brush.

6. Pipe the top of the beak and bring the tip down to a sharp point. Pipe the lower half of the beak and, while the icing is still wet, pull out the icing to a point with a fine brush.

7. Pipe the eye slightly larger than size. When you are over piping the eye at a later stage it will appear smaller.

**Tip** If preferred, the wing in the foreground could be piped onto greased cellophane beforehand, left to dry under a lamp and then stuck to the body when the body is still soft. You may have to support the wing in position until it is secure. This is useful for competition work as it gives perspective.

8 Pipe the top of the head and taper as you work down. Pipe the cheek underneath and continue back up to the head. Texture the surface with a brush. Pipe on top of the beak to create a raised join between the beak and head.

9 The next stage is piping the body. Start at the top and continue piping downwards, creating a slightly rounded shape for the body. Decrease the pressure as you reach the tail. Texture the body with a fine artists' brush and smooth out any imperfections in the icing.

10 Starting at the top of the second leg (in the foreground), use a rope action to create a knurled effect, as before. Pipe in the feet then texture both the feet the legs, starting at the bottom and working up.

11 Pipe the second wing, starting at the tip and using a back-and-forth motion to emulate feathers. Only pipe 2 or 3 feathers at a time and texture immediately with a fine brush so that the icing does not have time to skin over. Continue piping and texturing the feathers all the way down the wing.

12 Rub down some white royal icing and place in a piping bag. Snip off the tip to approximately the size of a no. 2 nozzle. Pipe the finishing touches on the wing and brush the ends into the shoulder.

# Easter figures

These piped figures are ideal decorations for an Easter cake: you can pipe them onto greased cellophane and place them onto a plaque well ahead of time and then simply place the plaque on top of the cake (see page 198 for a cake top design idea). Alternatively, you can use the figures to decorate Easter eggs or cupcakes.

You will need to prepare the templates (see overleaf) and the basic materials and equipment for pressure piping (see page 50); any extra items required are given for each figure.

## A: Female chick

1 Make up the royal icing to slightly off-peak consistency (just before it stiffens, so that there is a slight bend in the peaks). Colour some icing pink (using SK Rose Professional Liquid Food Colour) and start by piping the areas in the background. Pipe the inside of the hat then pipe from a third of the way up the bonnet and up around the edge with a rope action. The rope should get slightly smaller as you pipe down the bonnet.

2 Using orange (SK Nasturtium) icing, pipe the inside of the beak, then add the top of the beak and vibrate the nozzle in the icing to make it smooth. Add the bottom of the beak and, using a dampened artists' brush, brush out the peak at the back of the beak. If you lose definition on the inside of the beak, use the artists' brush to mark a dimple across the bottom part.

3 Using the rubbed-down white icing, pipe the eye.

4 Using a no. 2 nozzle (or snip off the end of the piping bag to the same size), pipe the chick using yellow (SK Daffodil) icing. Start by piping round the outer edge of the eye and fill in around the eye. Starting at the top, texture this icing with an artists' brush to resemble feathers. Pipe the cheek, making it fuller than before. Try to avoid any peaks; if you cannot get the icing smooth, you may find it easier if you rub down the icing slightly before placing it in the piping bag.

5 Using the pink icing, pipe with a rope action down from the top of the head and alongside the cheek. Using the same action, reduce the size of the rope as you pipe the rest of the bonnet (going towards the background).

If you find piping a rope difficult, you can pipe running beads instead.

6 Using the orange icing, pipe the foot in the background, starting inside the body with a rope action. Pipe the toe in the background and then add the next one on top and the third one on top again.

7 To pipe the body, take the yellow icing and pipe back and forth with a lifting action, ensuring the body stands higher than the cheek. Texture round the bottom edge of the body and around the tail to resemble feathers using an artists' brush. Turn the figure 90° (with the tail towards you) and pipe the wing approximately a third of the way up the body. Texture the top part of the wing to blend it into the body.

8 Pipe the second foot in orange and build up as before. Pipe the leg, starting inside the body using a rope action. Pipe a few yellow feathers between the leg and the body to hide the join.

9 Pressure pipe 2 daisies on the bonnet in white royal icing (see page 52). Add a yellow centre. Using stiff green (SK Holly/Ivy) royal icing, cut a 'V' at the tip of the bag to make an even point. Pipe little leaves onto the bonnet.

10 The bow is piped separately, so start on a spare area of greased cellophane. Pipe the centre part first then pipe each side. To pipe the ribbon ends, run the no. 1 nozzle down each side to a point to achieve a swallowtail effect. Leave to dry, then stick the bow to the bottom of the bonnet.

11 Place the chick on a spare board and leave under a desk lamp to dry. When dry, paint on the final details using a fine paintbrush and SK Black Liquid Food Colour.

### B: Male chick

1  Use the same colours as for the female chick and prepare some brown icing (using SK Bulrush Professional Liquid Food Colour) in a bag with a no. 2 nozzle, and rubbed-down blue (SK Bluebell) icing.

2  Using the rubbed-down blue icing, pipe the inside of the bonnet. Pipe the eye using the white icing. Add the inside of the beak using rubbed-down orange icing, then add the top part, stop and vibrate the tip of the nozzle to smooth the icing.

3  Pipe around the eye and down onto the top of the head with yellow icing, then texture immediately with a brush. Always add texture whilst the icing is still mellow. Pipe the cheek in yellow (do not texture) then pipe the wing in the background.

4  Pipe the walking stick in brown using a rope action. Pipe 2 yellow feathers over the top so that it looks like he is holding the stick.

5  Using slightly rubbed-down orange icing, pipe the foot and leg as before. Pipe the body, working back and forth and building it up in the centre to give a rounded effect. Ensure the body is higher than the cheek. Moisten an artists' brush and break up the lower edge of the body to create a feathery effect. Starting at the tail, texture the feathers using a slightly curved motion with the brush, following the curves of the chick's body.

6  Pipe some white icing back and forth for the hatband, then pipe the top of the hat in blue, vibrating the tip in the icing to achieve a smooth finish. Widen the hole at the tip of the bag slightly by snipping off a little more and pipe the brim of the hat. Tidy up the edge of the hat by piping a line of blue icing over the top.

7  Pipe the second foot, toes first, then add the leg and a few yellow feathers on top of the leg to blend it in. Rotate the chick 90° and pipe the wing in the same way as before, then texture to create feathers.

8  Pipe a white flower on top of the hat and add a couple of leaves, ensuring the icing adheres to the hat. Pipe the bow separately in the same way as before.

9  Allow to dry under a desk lamp. When dry, paint on the final details using a fine paintbrush and SK Black Liquid Food Colour.

## C: Ducks with hats

1 Pipe the top of the hats in blue, pink and yellow, then pipe in the ribbons using white royal icing. Pipe in the beaks, starting with the top, then add a finer line underneath on a slight curve to make it look like the ducks are smiling. Pipe the white of the eye. Pipe the back legs using slightly rubbed-down orange icing.

2 Take a bag of stiff, white icing, snip a fairly large hole in the bag and pipe from the top of the body down, using a back-and-forth motion. Immediately texture with a moistened artists' brush, breaking the line down the front first, then work across the bottom and up, making the marks smaller as you go up. Pipe in the head, then add the detail on the hats. Turn the board 90° and pipe the wings with a slight curve, then brush and texture the wings to blend them into the body.

3 Allow to dry under a desk lamp and then paint the detail onto the duck using a fine paintbrush and SK Black Liquid Food Colour.

## D: Lamb

1 Colour some royal icing black using a mixture of SK Black Liquid and Jet Black Dust Food Colour to prevent the consistency of the icing from changing (see page 45). Place into a piping bag and snip off the end.

2 Place some white royal icing in a bag and snip off the end or use a no. 2 nozzle. Start by piping the back ear, eye (slightly larger than the design), then the legs in the background. Pipe the body, using a circular motion to

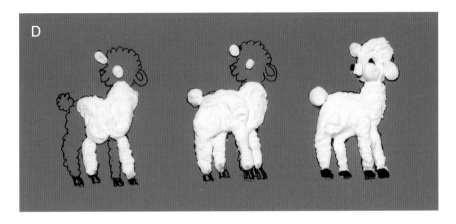

build up the icing and give the lamb a rounded stomach. Pipe the front leg in the foreground, then the tail and the rump. Make the rump higher than the front of the body. Add the back leg in the foreground. You can use an artists' brush to add detail to the lamb, particularly if some of the features have been lost by over piping onto the figure. Use the brush to define the shapes by undercutting the icing.

3 Using the black icing, pipe the background hoofs followed by the 2 in the foreground. Separate the hoofs using a brush.

4 Pipe round the forehead with the white icing and bring the icing out towards the nose. Pipe around the mouth, then build up the cheek. Pipe the inside of the ear, then pipe the ear on top of the head. Finally, add a black nose.

## E: Bird

1 Using white royal icing, pipe a curve starting at the shoulder and going right up to the tip of the wing. Add the feathers below this, then pipe in the secondary feathers and blend in with a brush. Allow to dry under a desk lamp.

2 Add a white eye and an orange beak. Using white royal icing, pipe round the forehead and add the cheek. Pipe a rounded body and taper to the tail. Pipe back under the body again to achieve a swallowtail. Texture the top of the head and the body with a brush (do not texture the cheek).

3 Turn the bird on its side and pipe the back wing using a back-and-forth motion. Pipe the body and ensure there is plenty of volume (if there isn't enough icing, the wing won't stick).

4 Stick the prepared wing into the body while the icing is still soft and pipe a little icing below the wing to hold it in place. Blend and texture this icing with a brush.

# Wedding motifs

These designs are all ideal for wedding cakes and favours and can also be used for other celebration cakes. Some can be piped as off-pieces on greased cellophane (such as the bell) whilst others should be piped directly onto a cake or plaque (such as the music motif).

You will need the basic materials and equipment for pressure piping (see page 50); any extra items required are given for each motif.

### A: Music motif

This design can be piped directly onto the top or sides of a cake. If it is for the sides, scratch pipe the design onto the cake surface (see page 69); for the top, drop line the design (see page 65).

1 Using a no. 1 piping nozzle and royal icing coloured as required, pipe 5 ledger lines in a slight S curve, bringing them a little closer at the end. Pipe a line at each end.

2 Add the treble clef, flat symbols, time signature, notes and bar lines. If you are piping a particular tune (such as the Wedding March), you can copy the notes from a manuscript if you have one.

3 Pressure pipe flowers and leaves around the design to balance it.

### B: Dove

1 Using a no. 1.5 or 2 nozzle (depending on the size required), squeeze a large dot and pull through to one side to make a teardrop shape.

2 Pipe 3 pull-ups at the point of the teardrop for the tail feathers.

3 Pipe a dot for the head at the bulbous end of the teardrop.

4 Starting at the shoulder, squeeze a bulb and take the wing through between the tail and the body.

5 Add the eyes and beak in your chosen colours and allow to dry under a desk lamp.

6 For added decoration, pressure pipe a tree branch in brown royal icing before piping the doves, then position the bodies on top and pipe the tail feathers over the top of the branch. Add a few simple leaves and flowers in your chosen colours.

### C: 3-dimensional bell

For this design you will need a no. 4 nozzle and either coloured sugar or SK Edible Gold Paint.

1 Place a no. 4 nozzle into a piping bag (or snip off the tip of the bag to the same size) and fill with slightly rubbed-down royal icing.

2 Pipe a bulb for the base of the bell onto greased cellophane. Keep a steady pressure and hold the bag approximately 4mm (1/8") from the surface. Once the base is complete, stop piping, lift the bag slightly then pipe steadily on top to create the bell shape. The easiest way to do this is to pipe from directly above, ensuring it is straight. Repeat to pipe as many bells as required.

3 Once you have piped the basic shape, you can sprinkle the bell with coloured sugar, which is ideal for matching colour schemes on a Christmas or wedding cake.

4 Place the bells under a desk lamp for approximately 30 minutes until they are firm enough to lift off the cellophane. Remove the bells from the cellophane, then scoop out the inside with the handle of an artists' brush or a cocktail stick, depending on the size of the bell.

5 Pipe in the clapper. When dry, the bells can be painted with SK Edible Gold Paint (if not covered with sugar).

6 To incorporate the bells into a design for a cake, you can add your own piped decoration such as piped flowers and leaves, as shown here.

# Christening designs

These designs are all perfect for christening cakes, cupcakes or cookies. You will need the basic materials and equipment for pressure piping (see page 50); any extra items required are given for each design.

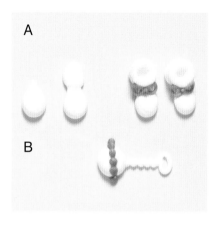

## A: Bootees

1 Place some slightly rubbed down white royal icing into a piping bag with a no. 2 nozzle. Pipe a large dot and, with the tip of the nozzle still in the icing, pull it up to make the dot rounded.

2 Pipe a second dot in the same way above the first. Pipe a wavy line in a circle on top of the second dot to form the ankle.

3 Pipe a bow between the 2 dots in the colour of your choice.

## B: Rattle

1 Pipe a large dot in the same way as for the first step of the bootees. Rather than pulling the nozzle out from the top, work to one side and continue to pipe a line in a slightly circular motion to form the handle.

2 Add a small loop at the end of the handle and a row of dots around the rattle in your chosen colour.

## C: Swan

1 Using white royal icing in a piping bag with a no. 1.5 or 2 nozzle, pipe a dot, bring the nozzle round in a circle, ease off the pressure, then increase the pressure as you come down to form a reverse S scroll.

2 Squeeze a large dot in the centre of the lower part of the S scroll, then taper off to the side to make the tail.

3 Using a smaller nozzle, start at the shoulder of the swan and pipe back and forth to create the wing.

4 Finally, add a beak and eye in your chosen colours.

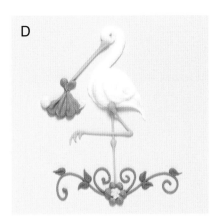

**D**

5 For the cygnets, simply pipe a small S scroll then a shorter teardrop and wing in the same way as before.

6 If you are working directly on a cake, pipe a pond scene for the ducks to swim in using coloured royal icing.

### D: Stork

1 Use the same techniques as for the swan but add a long beak and long legs. To make the knee joint, increase the pressure halfway along the legs to create a bulb before continuing down with an even pressure.

2 Use your chosen colour for the blanket and pressure pipe 2 small loops at the top and 4 at the bottom. Add a bulb for the baby's head and a little foot on the opposite side.

3 For added decoration, you can add a simple scroll design at the base.

# Christmas designs

These festive motifs have been piped using basic pressure piping techniques (see pages 48 to 61).

Before you start, prepare the templates under greased cellophane (see page 97) and fill the bags of icing required for the motifs you wish you pipe so that you can work efficiently.

## A: Basic tree

For this design you will need to prepare a bag of stiff royal icing in brown (SK Bulrush Professional Liquid Food Colour) and rubbed-down royal icing in white. This is best piped straight onto a cake as the fine branches may break if moved.

1  Use brown icing and a no. 1 nozzle to pipe the trunk. Start at the bottom and squeeze firmly, easing off the pressure as you reach the top. Pipe in the branches then add tiny branches at the ends using a no. 0 nozzle.

2  Using rubbed-down (paddled) white icing and a no. 1 nozzle (or cut the tip off a piping bag), pipe snow along the top edges of the branches. Add a line of snow at the base of the tree.

## B: Fir tree

For this design you will need to prepare bags of stiff royal icing in brown and green (SK Bulrush and Holly/Ivy Professional Liquid Food Colours) and rubbed-down royal icing in white. This design is also best piped straight onto a cake as the fine trunk may break if moved.

1  Pipe a straight line of brown icing for the trunk, starting at the bottom and tapering to a point at the top.

2  Half-fill a bag of green royal icing and snip off the tip to the size of a no. 1.5 nozzle. Turn the design upside down and pipe onto one side of the tree (the right if you are right-handed and vice versa), starting at the widest part. Pipe in a back and forth motion, getting progressively smaller as you reach the top of the tree.

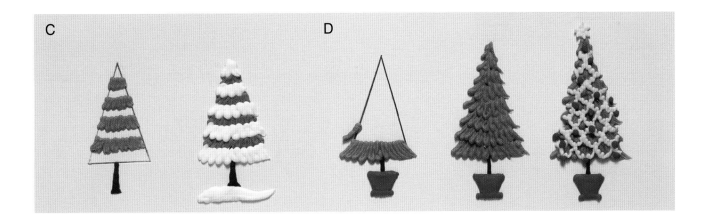

3 Turn the design 90° with the piped side away from you and pipe the other side of the tree. Again, start at the widest part and taper to the top, working with a back and forth motion.

4 Add a line of white rubbed-down icing along the base and pipe in 1 or 2 smaller trees to create perspective.

## C: Christmas tree, design 1

This design can be piped as an off-piece or directly onto a cake. You will need to prepare bags of stiff brown, green and white royal icing (SK Bulrush and Holly/Ivy Professional Liquid Food Colours).

1 If you are piping this as an off-piece, draw a tall, narrow triangle as a template and fix under a sheet of greased cellophane.

2 Pipe in the trunk using brown royal icing.

3 Using a back and forth motion, pipe 4 rows of green foliage across the tree, leaving gaps between each row.

4 Pipe stiff white royal icing in the same manner on top of the green, working from the bottom of the tree to the top. Add a line of snow at the base.

## D: Christmas tree, design 2

This design can also be piped as an off-piece or directly onto a cake. You will need to prepare bags of brown, green, yellow and red stiff icing (SK Bulrush, Holly/Ivy, Daffodil and Poinsettia Professional Liquid Food Colours) and red rubbed-down icing.

1 Prepare the same template under cellophane as for design 1 if you are piping the tree as an off-piece.

2 Pipe the trunk in brown, then add a red pot using slightly rubbed-down royal icing. Use a side-to-side motion to fill in the area.

3 Take the bag of green icing and, starting at the bottom corner of the tree, pipe a slight curve in an up and down motion. As you work across the tree, straighten up, then curve to the other side as you reach the other edge.

4 Start a second curve of green above the first so that the ends overlap the lower level of icing. Keep the bag lifted so the icing sits on top. Continue all the way to the top of the tree.

5 Use yellow icing in a bag with a no. 0 or 1 nozzle to pipe the tinsel. Start at the top of the tree and pipe down in a series of scallops. Alternatively, you could add candles on the tips of the branches. Add a small star on top.

6 Pipe baubles onto the tree in red royal icing. Allow to dry under a desk lamp if you have piped onto greased cellophane.

111

## E: Candles

The candles can be piped as off-pieces but the extra decoration on this design should be piped directly onto a cake or plaque. You will need to prepare bags of red, white, brown, dark green, light green and yellow stiff royal icing (SK Poinsettia, Bulrush, Holly/Ivy and Daffodil Professional Liquid Food Colours), and rubbed-down yellow and red icing. You will also need a no. 43 rope nozzle, SK Sunflower Professional Dust Food Colour, a no. 10 dusting brush and a few piped Christmas roses and buds (see page 127).

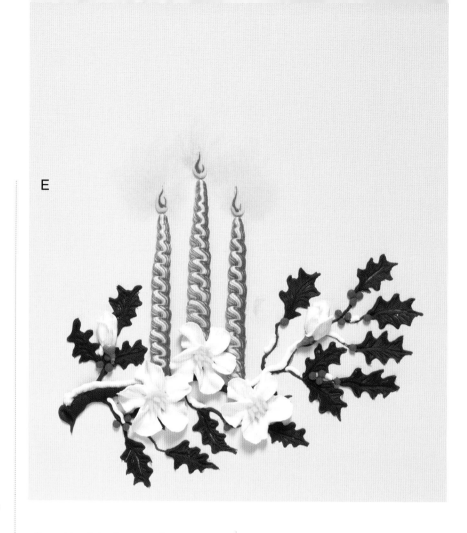

E

1 Take a medium sized piping bag, snip off approximately 1.3cm (½") at the tip and drop a no. 43 rope nozzle into the bag.

2 Make a narrow piping bag by making an extra half-turn in the greaseproof paper. Cut off approximately 7mm (¼") at the tip (roughly the size of a no. 4 nozzle) and fill with red royal icing.

3 Pick up the bag fitted with the rope nozzle and, where the paper overlaps inside, pipe a line of red icing from the tip and all the way up the side of the bag. Repeat on the opposite side inside the piping bag. Fill down the centre of the bag with stiff, white royal icing.

4 Using a rope action, start at the top of the candle, squeeze gently and then get wider as you work towards the bottom. Pipe a candle on

either side of the first one. If you are piping the candles as off-pieces, allow to dry and then secure in position on the cake with a dot of royal icing.

5 Using a dry artists' brush, dust an arc of Sunflower Professional Dust Food Colour above each candle on the cake surface to give a glowing effect.

6 Take a bag of rubbed-down yellow royal icing and pipe a teardrop for each flame. Take a small bag of rubbed-down red icing and, whilst the yellow icing is still soft, pipe an S scroll and a small C scroll on top of the yellow to resemble a flame.

7 Fill a piping bag with brown royal icing and cut a hole in the tip to approximately the size of a no. 2 nozzle. Pipe in the branches in

the same way as for the basic tree (see page 110). Dig the tip of the piping bag into the start of the branch and pull down to give it a hollow appearance.

8 Use dark green icing to pipe the outline of the holly leaves then brush through the icing with a fine paintbrush to create the veins (see brush embroidery techniques on pages 168 to 175).

9 Pipe red berries onto the holly then add white snow on top of the branches (as on the basic tree).

10 Stick the prepared Christmas roses in place with dots of royal icing (or pipe directly onto the cake) then use stiff yellow icing to pipe pull-ups for the stamens. Pipe a calyx onto the back of each bud using a small bag of light green icing.

## F: Christmas owl

For this design you will need dark brown, light brown, cream, red, green and orange royal icing (SK Bulrush, Chestnut, Poinsettia, Holly/Ivy and Nasturtium Professional Liquid Food Colours) as well as rubbed-down white and stiff white icing. You can make this as an off-piece (see template below).

1 Place some red royal icing into a piping bag. Use a no. 2 nozzle or snip off the tip of the bag to the same size. Pipe the hat.

2 Use light brown icing to pipe in the wings (follow the same method as for a dove, see page 106). Start with the large curve on the outside and work back and forth to fill in each wing.

3 Fill a bag with rubbed-down white icing and snip off the end to the size of a no. 2 nozzle. Pipe a raised bulb for the open eye, then pipe the closed eye with the light brown icing.

4 Use dark brown icing and a no. 1.5 nozzle to pipe the branch.

5 Use stiff light brown icing and a no. 0 nozzle to fill in the forehead area. Texture the icing with a damp artists' brush, starting at the bottom and working up.

6 Pipe the inside of the ear with cream icing and the outside with light brown. Add the tail in light brown.

7 Pipe a light brown horseshoe shape around the body then fill in the chest with stiff, white royal icing, keeping it plump. Texture as before, allowing the colours to blend.

8 Pipe a bobble on the hat in stiff white icing using a circular motion then pipe white and red stripes onto the stocking.

9 Snip off the tip of a small bag of orange royal icing to the size of a no. 1 nozzle and pipe in the feet and beak on top of the existing icing.

10 Fill around the eyes with cream icing in a circular motion then pull the icing out from the centre with a paintbrush.

11 Using rubbed-down white icing, fill in the hat and lightly texture with a brush.

12 Using an inward scallop motion, pipe in the holly then mark down the centre with a damp brush. Use red rubbed-down icing and a no. 1 nozzle to pipe in the berries.

13 Allow the owl to dry under a desk lamp. When dry, paint in the detail on the eyes, feet and hat.

## G: Father Christmas

For this design you will need stiff brown, green and white royal icing (SK Bulrush and Holly/Ivy Professional Liquid Food Colours), and rubbed-down black, red, flesh, orange and white (SK Black QFC and Poinsettia, Chestnut and Nasturtium Professional Liquid Food Colours). The nozzles you use will depend on the size of the motif you wish to create. You can make this as an off-piece (see template below).

1 Pipe in the eyes with rubbed-down white royal icing. Next, pipe flesh coloured icing onto the face, going around one eye, across the forehead and around the other eye, like a mask. Vibrate the bag slightly as you work to make the icing smooth.

2 Using rubbed-down red royal icing, pipe the hat, then pipe round the coat with an up-and-down motion, vibrating the tip of the bag to make the icing smooth.

Always pipe clothing in vertical lines rather than horizontal as this helps to create a more natural result.

3 Using rubbed-down black icing, pipe in the belt and boots, again vibrating the bag to smooth the icing. Add the gloves in green.

4 Using stiff white royal icing, pipe in the bobble on the hat, the cuffs on the sleeves, the trim on the coat and the top of the boots. Use the same icing to pipe in the beard, using an up-and-down motion. Leave a gap at the top.

5 Pipe the buckle on the belt using orange icing.

6 Using the flesh icing, pipe a teardrop for the nose.

7 Pipe the second stage of the beard with stiff white icing, then pipe round the hat in a circular motion. Add eyebrows, then pipe in the moustache with a pull-out on each side. Add a bobble on the coat.

8 Pipe a brown stem and add the green pine leaves. Using the same bag, pipe a thumb on top of the stalk. Add a line of snow at the bottom.

9 Allow the icing to dry, then paint in the eyes using Black QFC Liquid and the mouth with a little diluted Poinsettia Professional Liquid Food Colour.

## H: Robins

For this design you will need stiff bags of dark brown, light brown, red, orange, yellow and white (SK Bulrush, Poinsettia, Nasturtium and Sunflower Professional Liquid Food Colours) and a bag of rubbed-down white icing. You will also need some SK Black QFC Liquid.

1  Begin with the robin on the right-hand side. Pipe the tail in light brown using a back-and-forth motion. Pipe the eye with rubbed-down white icing, then pipe a line of stiff white icing down to the belly.

2  Pipe underneath the beak in light brown icing, then pipe a red breast in stiff icing. Use a dampened artists' brush to texture the icing, allowing the brown to blend into the red. This creates a feathered effect.

3  Pipe light brown icing from the forehead right down to the top of the tail. Again, texture with a fine paintbrush. Always start the texturing at the bottom and work up so that the feathers appear to overlap. In the same colour, pipe a line from the shoulder to the bottom of the wing, then go back and forth to get the primary feathers on the wing. Pipe 4 sets of running beads on top of the wing and texture to resemble the secondary feathers.

4  Pipe the second robin in the same way.

H

5  Pipe in the beaks on both robins using orange icing, keeping them thin. Add the legs in the same colour, but don't pipe the feet yet.

6  For the fences, use a back-and-forth motion in the direction of the wood grain. When the icing has dried slightly, use an artists' brush to paint in a few knots.

7  Using light brown icing, pipe the sides of the houses. Pipe the tree in dark brown icing. Add a dot of yellow in the windows of the houses.

8  Use well-rubbed-down royal icing for the snow (you will need a large piping bag for this). Pipe in the snow on the houses, starting with the outline then filling in and vibrating the tip to smooth the icing. If necessary, add a touch of cooled, boiled water to the icing to ensure that it has a smooth finish. Add snow to the fence, fence posts and fields then pipe a tiny amount onto the tree.

9  Using stiff green icing, cut a tiny V shape in the tip of the bag (see page 56). Pipe small leaves at the base of the fence post.

10  Take a bag of red royal icing and snip off the end. Pipe berries on top of the holly.

11  Allow the icing to dry, then paint the details onto the scene with Black QFC Liquid. Finally, once the snow has dried, pipe the birds' feet in orange.

# Piped Flowers
## using an Icing Nail

These piped flowers can be made as off-pieces (i.e. made separately from the cake) and stored ready for use. This means that you can make plenty of them well in advance and use them as a quick decoration for cakes, cupcakes, cookies and even desserts such as cheesecakes or gateaux. If the surface is moist (e.g. on a gateau), place the flowers in position just before serving, otherwise the sugar will dissolve.

More flower designs can be seen in the Pressure Piping and Pressure Piped Figures and Motifs chapters of this book.

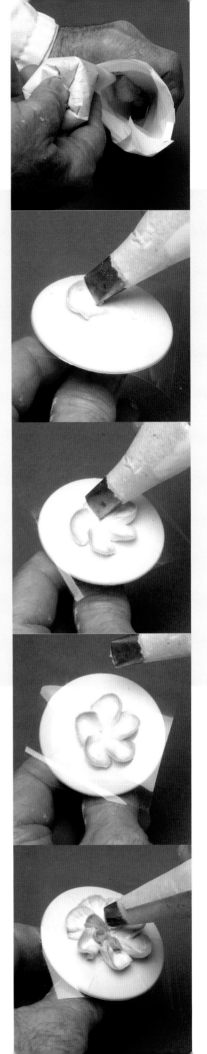

# $\mathcal{T}$ips
## for successful piped flowers

- When piping flowers it is very important to use freshly beaten royal icing. If it has been left overnight, put it back into the mixer and bring back to off-peak consistency.

- For every 175g (6oz) of royal icing, add 1 rounded tablespoon of sifted icing sugar. Lightly mix the sugar through the icing; do not beat the icing as this will incorporate air and the icing will dry too quickly. This will produce an icing that will stay firm and hold its shape as the dry sugar will help to accelerate the drying process.

- Where a petal nozzle is used the fine edge should always be on the outer edge of piped petals.

- Always pipe onto a small piece of greased cellophane or waxed paper when piping onto an icing nail. Use a dot of royal icing to hold the cellophane/waxed paper in place while you pipe, then carefully remove the flower and cellophane/waxed paper from the nail and leave to dry.

- When making coloured flowers always remember to use liquid food colours and not pastes as these will absorb moisture.

- If you are making the flowers in advance, allow to dry fully then store in a cake box in a cool, dry area. Do not use an airtight box as this will trap moisture.

## Preparation

For most or all of the flowers in this chapter you will need:

## Materials

Off-peak royal icing, stiffened with extra icing sugar (see above)

SK Professional Liquid Food Colours (see each flower for requirements)

White vegetable fat

## Equipment

Cellophane or waxed paper cut into squares

Icing nail

Piping bags

Piping nozzles (see each flower for requirements)

Desk lamp (optional)

# Daisy

The basic method is for a daisy but the colours used for the petals and flower centre can be changed to make different flowers.

In addition to the basic items you will need granulated sugar, SK Daffodil Professional Liquid Food Colour, a food-grade polythene bag, a no. 2 plain piping nozzle and a petal nozzle (size depends on the size of flower you wish to create).

1 Before you start piping, colour some granulated sugar yellow using SK Daffodil Liquid Food Colour (do not use paste colour). The easiest way to do this is to put some sugar into a food-grade polythene bag, put a few drops of colour into the bag and rub it through until the colour is evenly dispersed and all the sugar is coloured.

2 Take a small amount of freshly beaten royal icing and colour with SK Daffodil Liquid Food Colour. Place into a piping bag with a no. 2 piping nozzle and pipe a dot onto a sheet of cellophane or waxed paper (do not

grease). Make the size of the dots appropriate to the size of flower you wish to create.

3 Spread the yellow sugar onto a small tray or plate, level it off and dip the dots on cellophane into the sugar. Place under a lamp or leave overnight to dry completely.

4 Cut out squares of cellophane or waxed paper and place one at a time onto an icing nail, holding in place with a dot of royal icing. Take the appropriate size of petal nozzle for the size of flowers you wish to create. To pipe the daisies, hold the nozzle

at just under right angles to the icing nail with the thick part of the nozzle to the centre. Pipe out towards the edge, lift slightly then ease off the pressure towards the end to make a petal.

5 Turn the icing nail slightly and repeat the same method to make a 12-petal blossom. While the icing is still soft, place a yellow centre in the middle of the flower.

6 To pipe a half-daisy, place a square of cellophane or waxed paper on an icing nail. Start in the centre and work to the outside edge in the same way as before. Turn the icing

 You will be able to pipe quite quickly with a little practice so this is a great time-saving technique for decorating cakes.

nail as you work but this time, only pipe half the flower. Start again, this time piping on top of the first set of petals from the same central point. Pipe at least 1 petal less than in the first set and make them smaller.

7 To pipe a closed bud, place the cellophane on the icing nail, as before. Hold the nozzle perpendicular to the nail with the thick part of the nozzle in the centre. Squeeze the pressure in the middle and ease off towards the outer edge.

8 For an open bud, add a petal on either side and one on top.

 When you are confident, you can pipe the buds and half-flowers (i.e. those that don't require a centre) straight onto a cake.

# Sweet pea

In addition to the basic items you will need SK Cyclamen Professional Liquid Food Colour (or other liquid colour of your choice) and a large petal nozzle (around size 59).

1 To create a dark edge on the petals, fill a piping bag with a dark colour of royal icing, in this case deep pink. Cut 5mm (¼") off the tip of a narrow piping bag. Use the same liquid food colour to make a small bowl of pale pink icing.

2 Take a regular piping bag, cut 2cm (¾") off the tip and place a large petal nozzle into the bag. Where the narrow part of the nozzle is, pipe a line of deep pink icing up the inside of the bag, not quite to the top. Hold this bag with the line to the right-hand side and fill the bag with the pale pink icing.

3 Prepare a square of cellophane on an icing nail as before (hold in place with a little icing). Pipe a horseshoe shape, leaving a hollow in the middle. When piping a wavy line, squeeze quite firmly to create a natural wave in the icing. In this instance, the dark icing is on the outer edge of the petals.

4 Pipe another, smaller horseshoe shape on top, then for the third stage, keep the petal nozzle almost on the perpendicular and pipe a little petal in the centre.

5 To create various stages of the bud opening, pipe 1, 2 or 3 narrow petals.

 *Tip* If you wish to make a large amount flowers for different purposes, you may prefer to keep them all plain and dust them accordingly when required.

# Rose

In addition to the basic items you will need a small piece of sugarpaste, SK Cyclamen Professional Liquid Food Colour (or other liquid colour of your choice) and a large petal nozzle.

1 Prepare a bag of dark and light coloured icing with a large petal nozzle in same way as for the sweet pea.

2 Make the appropriate size of flower centre from a small cone of sugarpaste. The size will depend on the size of flower you wish to create. Stick the cone onto a piece of cellophane or waxed paper on an icing nail.

3 Keep the nozzle perpendicular to the nail with the thick part at the bottom and the narrow edge at the top. The point of the sugarpaste cone should reach halfway up the nozzle. Turning the nail anticlockwise if you are right-handed or clockwise if you are left-handed, pipe round approximately 1½ times to make the bud.

4 Hold the nail straight and pipe in 3 petals around the bud so that they are slightly interlocked at the edges.

5 Hold the nozzle at an angle of approximately 45° and pipe in 5 petals around the first set. This will give a full, open rose.

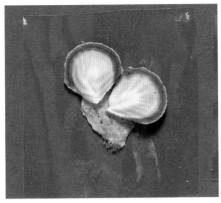 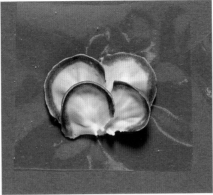 

# *Pansy*

In addition to the basic items you will need SK Daffodil and Violet Professional Liquid Food Colours and a petal nozzle.

1   To make a 3-tone flower such as a pansy, make a narrow bag of deep mauve coloured icing, a regular bag of pale mauve icing, and a bag of yellow (all with no nozzle).

2   Place a petal nozzle in another bag. Snip off the tip of the yellow bag and pipe a line of yellow icing on the same side as the thick part of the nozzle. Snip off the tips of the other 2 piping bags and pipe a line of dark mauve up the side of the narrow edge and a line of light mauve icing up the centre.

3   Prepare a piece of greased cellophane on an icing nail, as before. Using the prepared bag with the petal nozzle, pipe 2 large petals, keeping the nozzle quite flat. Pipe another 2 petals on top, slightly smaller this time, altering the angle of the nozzle slightly. Starting at the bottom of the petals, pipe a full petal in almost a whole circle by rotating the nail.

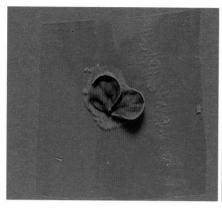

# Violet

This flower is piped in more or less the same way as the pansy, except there are 2 narrow petals at the sides. You will need SK Cyclamen (optional) and Violet Professional Liquid Food Colours, a small petal nozzle (no. 56) and a no. 1 plain piping nozzle.

1 Fit a piping bag with a small petal nozzle and fill with deep purple coloured icing. To make a warm violet colour, add a little Cyclamen Liquid Food Colour to the icing. Hold the nozzle fairly flat with the thick edge in the middle of the nail and pipe 2 petals.

2 Holding the nozzle perpendicular to the icing nail, pipe another pair of petals to the left and right of the first 2. In the same way as for the pansy, pipe a large, rounded petal at the bottom.

3 Put a little yellow royal icing into a bag with a no. 1 nozzle and pipe a tiny stamen in the centre of the flower.

# Apple blossom

This is one of the simplest flowers to pipe. It consists of 5 petals and a few piped stamens in the centre. In addition to the basic items you will need a small petal nozzle (no. 56) and a no. 0 plain piping nozzle.

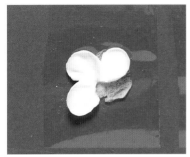

1 Prepare a square of cellophane on an icing nail, as before. The easiest way to pipe a 5-petal flower is to pipe the first petal on the diagonal towards the corner of the square. Pipe the second one next to it towards the top and the third one going across the diagonal, then you should have enough room for the last 2 petals. Alternatively, draw a circle onto card and divide into 5 equal sections. Attach this to the icing nail and use as a template for the 5 petals in the blossom.

2 Place some royal icing into a piping bag with a no. 0 nozzle and pipe a few small pull-ups in the centre for the stamens.

# Cherry blossom

In addition to the basic items you will need SK Cyclamen Professional Liquid Food Colour, a small petal nozzle (no. 56) and a no. 0 plain piping nozzle.

1 Prepare a narrow bag of deep pink royal icing and snip off the tip. Make another bag with a small petal nozzle. Pipe a line of the deep pink up the inside of the piping bag where the narrow edge of the petal nozzle is, then fill the bag with pale pink (as shown here) or white royal icing.

2 Prepare a piece of cellophane on an icing nail. Pipe the petals in a similar way to the apple blossom but move your hand back and forth slightly as you pipe to achieve a wavy edge. Pipe 5 small petals in the same way as before and add small pull-ups for the stamens.

# *Carnation*

In addition to the basic items you will need SK Cyclamen Professional Liquid Food Colour, a small petal nozzle (no. 56) and a no. 0 plain piping nozzle.

1 Prepare a slightly bigger square of cellophane on an icing nail. Using the same technique as for the cherry blossom, pipe the flower to about the same size as the icing nail. Move your hand back and forth as you pipe 5 petals to create the effect of a frilled edge.

2 Add a second layer of slightly smaller petals on top, then another 3 and another 2 to finish.

126

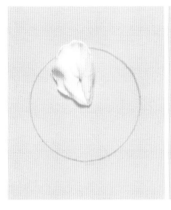   

# Christmas rose and buds

In addition to the basic items you will need SK Daffodil and Holly/Ivy Professional Liquid Food Colours, a large petal nozzle (no. 59 or similar) and a no. 0 plain piping nozzle.

1 Draw a circle template to the size required and stick this to the icing nail with a dot of icing. Place a large petal nozzle into a piping bag and fill with stiff white royal icing. Stick a square of cellophane on top of the template.

2 Pipe the first petal of the flower from the centre to the edge of the circle. Rotate the design and pipe the second petal underneath the first, rather than on the top.

3 Add a yellow centre using royal icing then add the stamens by piping pull-ups with a no. 0 nozzle.

4 To make the buds, you can choose to pipe 1, 2, 3 or 4 petals. Pipe the first petal starting at the top then bring the nozzle down to finish at the base. Add a second petal to one side. (If you are right-handed, it is easier to pipe this petal on the right and vice versa.) Add a third petal on the other side of the first. For the fourth petal, place the thick side of the nozzle at the base of the bud, pipe over the top and stop level with the other petals. Add a green calyx at the base.

5 To pipe the side view of a flower, pipe 1 vertical petal and 1 horizontal petal starting from the same point. Add another petal between the first 2, then pipe 2 petals on top. Add a green calyx at the point where the petals meet.

127

# GREETINGS

Best Wishes

Noel

Anne

Mother

Congratulations
on your
Silver Wedding

# Lettering & Numerals

Whether you decide to royal ice your cakes in the traditional way or opt for a sugarpaste covering, piped greetings will add a professional touch to any celebration cake. When piping lettering onto cakes, it is important to make sure that it is legible, balanced, and in keeping with the style of the cake. By following a few simple guidelines, you can ensure that your lettering is a success.

Lettering and numerals can also be created using run-out techniques, as shown in the examples in the second half of this tutorial.

Cake tops showing how freestyle lettering can be used in different compositions can be seen on pages 194 and 196. Cake tops featuring run-out lettering and numerals are on pages 200 and 211.

# *Tips* for successful lettering and numerals

- Lettering must always be legible. Always start with the simple form of the letters, making sure they are large enough. When embellishing letters, make sure that you don't overpower the basic form of the letter.

- The style of lettering and numerals you use will depend on the occasion (and recipient, see below). Ornate lettering – such as Old English and gothic styles – is usually limited to Christmas cakes, wedding cakes and anniversaries. Make sure that when using Old English letters, you use upper and lower case letters (i.e. start with a capital letter and continue with lower case) as using capital letters only in these styles will not be legible on the cake.

- Make the lettering appropriate to the person receiving the cake. If you are making a cake for a young child, use block lettering; for an older child or adult, use upper case and lower case (except when making run-out letters, as shown on the Noel plaque, page 211).

- It is important to achieve a good balance in lettering. When piping upper and lower case inscriptions, the lower case letters should be no less than half the height of the capitals. The only

exception to this rule is with illuminated letters, but there should still be a balance of parts to the design (such as fitting the letter into a coat of arms).

- When printing on cakes (i.e. in capitals), keep the letters slightly narrower than normal as this makes it easier to fit onto the plaque or cake top. Use your chosen style of block letters, then add embellishments on top, as required.

- The basic lettering should be piped in the same colour as the cake in most cases before the embellishment is added in your chosen colour. If you make a mistake, this can be removed easily. (There are exceptions to this rule: for example, if you are confident at piping, it is feasible to pipe script lettering directly onto the cake in colour. This does, however, take a great deal of practice.)

- The lettering or numerals should be the focal point of the cake and other decoration should not detract from this. Once you have chosen an appropriate style of lettering for the cake, make sure the colouring stands out, e.g. by using a stronger or brighter version of any colour used in other decorations, or by gilding the bottom of the letters

with edible metallic paint to draw the eye towards them. Always make any extra decoration, such as piped flowers, to suit the lettering. When feasible, pipe the lettering first then add other decoration to the cake afterwards.

- Use freshly beaten royal icing without added glycerine (this will cause the icing to run, like putting wet paint on top of wet paint). The icing should be beaten to off-peak consistency, not full-peak; do not over-beat the icing as this will create large air bubbles, making it difficult to pipe. To test the consistency of the icing, dip a palette knife in then lift it out: it should make a peak that bends slightly (see page 32).

- Food colours containing glucose, glycerine or glycerides cannot be used in royal icing when piping lettering onto cakes as they absorb moisture. Always used water-based colourings.

- If space is lacking, keep the letters narrow. There are various forms of letters that can be used in limited space, but the main structure is normally based either on the square or oblong. If the lettering you choose is based on the square form, ensure that letters such as 'o's and 'a's fit into a square shape.

# Freestyle lettering

All of the examples of freestyle lettering shown here require the same basic materials and equipment. You can, of course, change the size and colour of the letters to suit the cake. When you are confident at piping you can pipe straight onto the cake with coloured icing; if the cake is covered with sugarpaste you can use a scriber to mark out the lettering on the surface (this cannot be done on royal icing).

## Materials

Royal icing, made to off-peak consistency (see page 33)

SK Professional Liquid Food Colours (in your chosen colours)

## Equipment

Piping bags

Piping nozzles: nos. 2 (for main letters), 1 or 1.5 (for embellishments)

Lettering templates (see pages 287 to 292)

Surface on which to pipe (e.g. spare board, card, plaque or cake top)

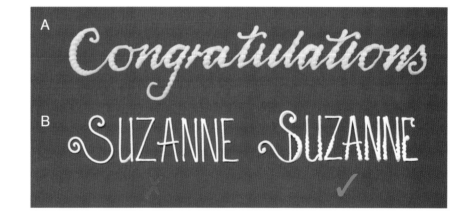

## Styles of lettering

### A: Script

1 This style of lettering is ideal for use on top of chocolate cakes and gateaux as it lends itself to being piped in chocolate as well as in royal icing. To create this style, pressure pipe clean up-strokes and running beads on the down-strokes on a right oblique angle. Use the template on page 287 as a guide.

2 Over pipe the letters with your choice of embellishment (as described overleaf) to suit the colour and style of the cake.

### B: Block lettering

1 Prepare the royal icing for drop line work by rubbing it down on the side of the bowl. Start by piping the basic block form, always piping the lines from top to bottom. It is important to make the letters balanced, even when piping basic block letters. Even a simple letter can make the lettering appear imbalanced, as shown in the first example: the 'U' is too narrow and the 'Z' is too wide compared to the rest of the letters. If you are narrowing the letters, make sure they are the same width at the bottom and top. The correct balance is shown in the second example.

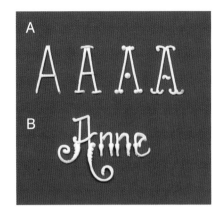

2 Over pipe the letters with your choice of embellishment (as described below) to suit the colour and style of the cake.

## C: Old English lettering

1 Prepare the royal icing for drop line work by rubbing it down on the side of the bowl. Drop line the initial capital letter, using the template on page 287 as a guide.

2 Start the lower case letters just over halfway up the initial letter and continue to pipe your chosen inscription using squared-off lines.

If you find it difficult to keep your lettering straight, place a strip of greaseproof paper just underneath as a guide.

## Basic embellishments

Prepare a bag of white royal icing (or the same colour as the cake covering if different) with a no. 2 nozzle.

### A: Serifs

Start with the basic letter shapes. Pipe serifs onto the ends of the lines: these can take the form of straight lines, dots and scallops.

### B: Scrolls

Full instructions on piping scrolls are given on pages 80 to 93.

1 Pipe the basic letter shapes, as before. Drop line small scrolls around the bottom of the letters, then on the down-stroke, pipe down below the first line.

2 To embellish the letters further, pipe little ropes onto the letters by over piping on the bottom part of

the letter with a no. 1 or 1.5 nozzle. On the lower case letters, pipe small bulbs on the lower half. (This is a useful when piping 2-tone letters, see opposite).

### C: Illuminated lettering

1 Prepare the royal icing for drop line work by rubbing it down on the side of the bowl. Drop line block lettering with small serifs or scrolls at the ends. On the vertical parts, double up each line. For rounded letters such as O, pipe the external circle then make the centre oval, leaving a small space between the two lines at the top and bottom.

2 Fill in the letters with either dots or tiny scrolls for added decoration.

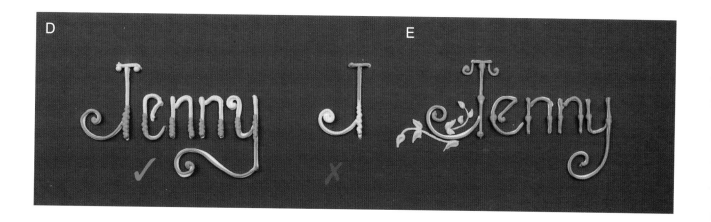

## D: 2-tone lettering

**1** Prepare a bag of white (or self-colour) plus two different tones or colours of royal icing using your chosen SK Professional Liquid Food Colours (I have used Cyclamen in this example).

**2** Pipe the basic shape of the letters in white (or self-colour), taking care not to make bobbles on the end of the lines (unless this is part of the style you wish to create). Aim to create clean lines so that they look neater and can be over piped easily.

*Tip*

When piping dropped line curves, make sure that you lift the nozzle up before dropping the line into position.

**3** Using a no. 1 or 1.5 nozzle, over pipe the letters. Start by piping the top half in the pale colour.

**4** Over pipe the lower half of the letters using the darker colour. Piping back and forth and drop-lining the darker colour will create ornate lettering and give stability to the lower half of the letters. Do not pipe dark colours at the top and light colours at the bottom as this will make the letters imbalanced.

## E: Other embellishments for celebration cakes

Once you have piped the basic form of the letters you can over pipe them with various designs, such as piping dots at given points on the letters or piping small leaves and flowers around the letters. However you choose to embellish your lettering, always ensure that it appears balanced.

### F: Festive embellishments

There are various ways of embellishing or illuminating letters for Christmas cakes. You can achieve this by scratch piping holly leaves, roses and other similar embellishments in the same way.

In addition to the basic materials and equipment required for lettering, you will need SK Poinsettia Professional Dust Food Colour and SK Holly/Ivy and Poinsettia Professional Liquid Food Colours.

1 Place some white (or self-colour) royal icing into a piping bag with a no. 1 or 2 nozzle, depending on the size of the lettering. Pipe your chosen inscription onto the cake or plaque in self-colour using an appropriate style of lettering (in this case, block lettering).

2 Colour some royal icing with Holly/Ivy Liquid Food Colour and place in a piping bag with a no. 0 or 1 nozzle. Colour some more royal icing with Poinsettia Liquid and Dust Food Colours. (Using a combination of both liquid and dust colours will allow you to strengthen the colour without altering the consistency of the icing.) Place in a piping bag with a no. 0 or 1 nozzle.

3 Using the green icing, pipe inward scallops around the initial letter to make holly. Add red berries using the red royal icing.

4 Embellish the initial letter by over piping with the red icing. Over pipe the lower case letters in the same way with the red icing.

### G: Using motifs as embellishments

This musical Christmas design shows how simple motifs can be used with lettering, as long as the writing is clearly legible. More motifs can be seen on pages 94 to 115.

1 Prepare a piping bag of freshly beaten royal icing with a no. 1 piping nozzle.

2 Drop line five ledger lines, keeping them close together.

3 Pipe the treble clef on top of the lines and two sharp (#) symbols to the right of the clef.

4 Write 'Merry Christmas' in block capitals across the stave, again using the drop line technique. If required, the letters can be over piped in a different colour.

5 For further embellishment, add Christmas roses around the design using the brush embroidery technique (see pages 168 to 175). To create quick holly, simply pipe inward scallops to form the outline and leave as a skeleton. Alternatively, brush embroider the holly outline in the same way as for the roses.

6 To finish, add a few musical notes to the design. These can be piped all over the cake to continue the musical theme.

## Embellishing letters

Any letter can be embellished to suit the style of the cake. These examples show how a basic letter 'A' can be made more elaborate. Practise creating different styles for yourself using different piping techniques, always starting with a basic form.

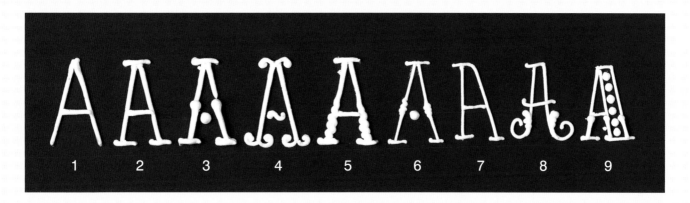

1  Basic form.

2  Basic form with straight serifs at the top and bottom.

3  Basic form with over piped bobbles.

4  A variation on the simple serif, small C and reversed C scrolls are piped on the ends of the lines and a small S scroll added in the centre of the letter.

5  Basic form with over piping. To create this effect, make a back and forth movement with the nozzle as you move down the letter, starting with minimal, light movement, getting heavier towards the bottom.

6  Simple form with serifs and beading on each line.

7  Slanted 'A' with straight serifs.

8  Scrolls and over piped beads are used to create an ornate design.

9  Illuminated letter with a double line, over piping and bobbles. This type of decoration is normally used for single letters, monograms or the first letter of an inscription.

An example of simple block lettering.

If space allows the first letters of each line can be linked together for added interest.

*Cake tops using different styles of lettering can be seen on pages 194 to 293.*

135

# Numerals

There are several different approaches to making decorative numerals in royal icing. From simple, piped numerals to double-sided run-outs with piped decoration, choose a style to suit the project you are working on. The same principles of lettering apply: the style must be suitable for the occasion, the numerals should be well balanced and any embellishments should not be overpowering.

## Materials

Royal icing, made to off-peak consistency (see page 33)

SK Professional Liquid Food Colours (in your chosen colours)

## Equipment

Palette knife

Piping bags

Piping nozzles: nos. 2 (for main numerals), 1 or 1.5 (for embellishments)

Numeral templates (see pages 293 to 294)

## Single-line numerals

Single-line piping is a basic style widely used for speed and commercial purposes. These numerals are piped freestyle, usually in self-colour (i.e. the same colour as the cake covering) and then over piped in the appropriate colour. You can pipe directly onto the cake in colour if you are confident, although piping in self-colour then over piping has the added advantage that it can be removed easily (if the age of the recipient is wrong, for example!).

Rub down (paddle) the icing slightly on the side of the bowl to remove some of the air and to help the icing settle on the cake surface. If the icing is too stiff it is harder to achieve sharpness around the edges of the numbers. If you are having this problem, use an artists' brush to neaten the edges of the lettering.

Single-line piping can be either serif or sans serif (serifs are the little 'tails' on the letters). Choose the style that best suits the cake.

**A:** Plain numerals (sans serif)

1 Prepare the royal icing for drop line work by rubbing it down on the side of the bowl. Place in a piping bag with a no. 2 nozzle.

136

B

C

2 Pipe the basic numerals, making sure they are well-balanced: for example, when piping the number 8, make sure that the top is smaller than the bottom to give the numeral stability. When piping the 0, start on the side of the letter, not the top or the bottom, to make the join less noticeable.

3 The joins can be hidden by adding little curves to the numbers. This also makes them more ornate (shown here on the 8 and 0).

*Tip*

These numbers can also be piped on the right oblique to achieve an italic effect.

## B: Serifs

You can also pipe the numbers with serifs at the ends of the lines. If you choose to add serifs, they can be curves, straight lines, inward curves, dots, or reverse 'C' shapes. Different types of serif are shown here using the number '1'.

## C: Over-piped numerals

Once the basic numbers are on the cake or plaque, they can be over piped in many ways, as shown in these examples.

**No. 1** To break up the line, over pipe from the top, make a dot in the middle, then continue down onto the serif (if there is one).

**No. 2** Start by over piping a straight line at the top, move the nozzle back and forth in the middle, then continue straight at the end.

**No. 3** Over pipe using a rope action (see page 83). Rotate the nozzle in the middle of the numeral, increase the pressure to make the icing thicker in the centre, then ease off at the end.

**No. 4** Over pipe with a series of running dots, starting small and increasing in size as you pipe down the vertical line.

*Tip*

There are other alternatives, so you can be as creative as you wish. Whichever design you choose, always keep the over piping the same throughout the numerals – do not alter the style midway through.

# Double-line numerals

To create double-line numerals, pipe the basic numbers, as for the single-line method. Using the same nozzle, double-up the numbers by piping vertical lines onto the numbers (either parallel to another vertical line or inside a curve). These examples show different ways of embellishing double-line numerals.

**A:** Embellishing double-line numerals

**No. 1:** Plain double-line numeral with no embellishment.

**Nos. 2 and 3:** Flood in the empty areas with contrasting colours or monochromatic colours to create a run-out, then over pipe in a contrasting colour. These styles can be piped onto waxed paper or greased cellophane and carefully removed when dry to place on the cake (see page 97). If you choose this method, use a no. 2 nozzle as a finer nozzle will make the lines too fragile to move.

**No. 4:** Add running beads (see page 71) as a decoration in the double-lined areas after over piping in your chosen colour.

**Nos. 5 and 6:** Over pipe the numbers using a rope action (see page 83).

**No. 7:** After piping the basic shape, add a pattern in-between the double lines such as a zigzag.

**No. 8:** Over pipe the numbers with a simple, clean line or add a dot to the double lines.

**No. 9:** Over pipe using a series of small dots, reducing the size towards the top and bottom of the letter. This technique takes a little more time than the others.

**No. 0:** Add scratch piping (see page 69) on the cake around the letter, then over pipe on the top half of the numeral and finish off with wavy lines around the base. You can also add little dots or flowers around the numbers to make them more interesting, but take care not to detract from the basic form.

**B:** Decorating double-line numerals

Numerals can be decorated with patterns, flowers and leaves, and scrolls to transform a simple inscription into an ornate decoration. The extra decoration is piped directly onto the cake and can be piped in colour if required. Make sure, however, that the colour is not too dark as this will take the focus away from the numerals. If the cake or plaque is a dark colour, you can pipe the letters in white so that they stand out. You could also add a contrasting colour to the background (e.g. yellow on blue).

1 Start by piping the numerals in your chosen style on the cake.

2 Drop line some scrolls around the design, then add piped flowers. When piping the daisies and leaves, make sure the icing is not too stiff: rub it down on the side of the bowl before placing it in the piping bag. This will help to give definition to your work.

3 When piping fine, decorative work inside the numbers, keep the lines clean to prevent the design from looking too fussy.

## Run-out numerals

Preparation for run-out work is very important. For full instructions on how to prepare the icing for run-outs, see pages 144 to 146.

## Materials

Royal icing made to off-peak consistency (see page 33)

SK Professional Liquid Food Colours of your choice (optional)

SK Professional Edible Metallic Paint: Gold or Silver (optional)

White vegetable fat

## Equipment

Piping bags

No. 1 piping nozzle (no. 1.5 or 2 optional)

Palette knife

Cellophane or waxed paper

Template

Masking tape

Desk lamp

A

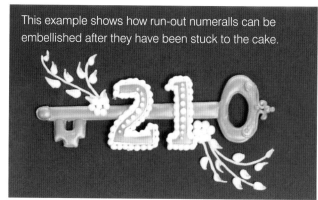

This example shows how run-out numeralls can be embellished after they have been stuck to the cake.

## A: One-piece run-outs

1 Copy your chosen design onto paper (see template for this design on page 294) and secure to a flat surface with masking tape. Cut a piece of cellophane and secure it over the template with tape or a dot of royal icing. If you are using cellophane from a roll, keep the outer side uppermost so that the edges curve downwards, allowing the curve to level out. Lightly grease the cellophane with white vegetable fat.

2 Prepare some freshly beaten royal icing and rub down slightly before use. Place in a piping bag with a no. 1 nozzle and outline the design using the drop line technique (see pages 64 to 65). To avoid bumps in the line work, keep the nozzle at a very shallow angle to the work surface. When piping small radius curves, only lift the nozzle slightly as you work round the curve. (This is why the icing must be rubbed down: if the icing is too stiff it will be hard to create a tight curve and the icing will square off. If the icing is softer, it will follow the curve naturally.)

*Tip*

If you are not confident at drop line piping you can practise by piping straight lines and S and C scrolls. This will help you to establish the correct height-to-angle ratio of the drop for each shape.

When flooding in, make sure that the hole in the piping bag is no larger than the size of a no. 1 nozzle. The finer the aperture, the less chance there is of air bubbles appearing in the icing as they will burst as they pass through the fine hole.

3 Prepare a small bowl of run-out icing (see page 33). Place in a piping bag, snip off the tip and flood the design in stages, starting with the background level. In this case, fill in the key shape first (do not make the run-out too thick) and place underneath a desk lamp. Let it dry for at least 10 minutes underneath the lamp, then flood in the numerals slightly thicker to make the '18' stand out from the key. Place under the lamp again to dry.

4 When the run-out is dry, you may wish to gild it with silver or gold edible paint (see page 47). Allow to dry, then carefully remove from the greased cellophane or waxed paper and secure to the cake or plaque with stiff icing. Add further piped embellishment if required.

## B: Double-sided run-outs

Another method of displaying numerals is to stand them on top of the cake. This is done by using run-outs and reverse run-outs placed back-to-back.

1 Prepare the drawings for your design: you will need a reverse copy of the design as well as the original drawing, so use tracing paper/greaseproof paper, a light box, or hold the design up to the window. Alternatively use the templates provided on page 293. Secure under a piece of greased cellophane or waxed paper, as before.

2 Place some rubbed-down royal icing in a piping bag with a no. 1 nozzle and pipe the outline of both shapes. To achieve sharp definition on the points, always pipe into wet icing then as you 'take off' the nozzle, the point will remain sharp. (Where there are internal lines, you can sometimes cross over the lines to produce a sharp corner, but this is only suitable if the run-out is the same colour as the outline.) Make sure that you stay on the template line so that the two shapes match up exactly when joined together. Rotate the design as you work so that you are always piping towards yourself.

3 Prepare some run-out icing in your chosen colour (see page 33). Flood the numerals, then allow to dry under a desk lamp. If you wish to gild the numerals, allow to dry fully before painting with SK Edible Gold or Silver Paint and allow the paint to dry (see page 47). Carefully release the pieces from the cellophane.

4 To stick the pieces together, use the same rubbed-down icing as before. Make sure that you rub down the icing well; you can even add a drop or two of cooled, boiled water to the icing to make it slacker (this will prevent the run-outs from breaking). Place in a piping bag and snip the tip to the size of a no. 2 nozzle. Pipe a line along the back of each numeral and secure the reverse shape on top, making sure each piece is lined up.

5 In order to display the numerals you will need to make a plaque from sugarpaste for the numerals to stand up in. Instructions for this are given in the cake top example on pages 200 to 201.

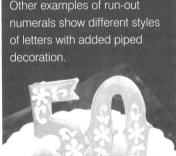

Other examples of run-out numerals show different styles of letters with added piped decoration.

 When making run-outs where the outline of the icing will be defined, the outline must be bold. Use a no. 1.5 or 2 nozzle to pipe the outline, depending on the size of the numerals.

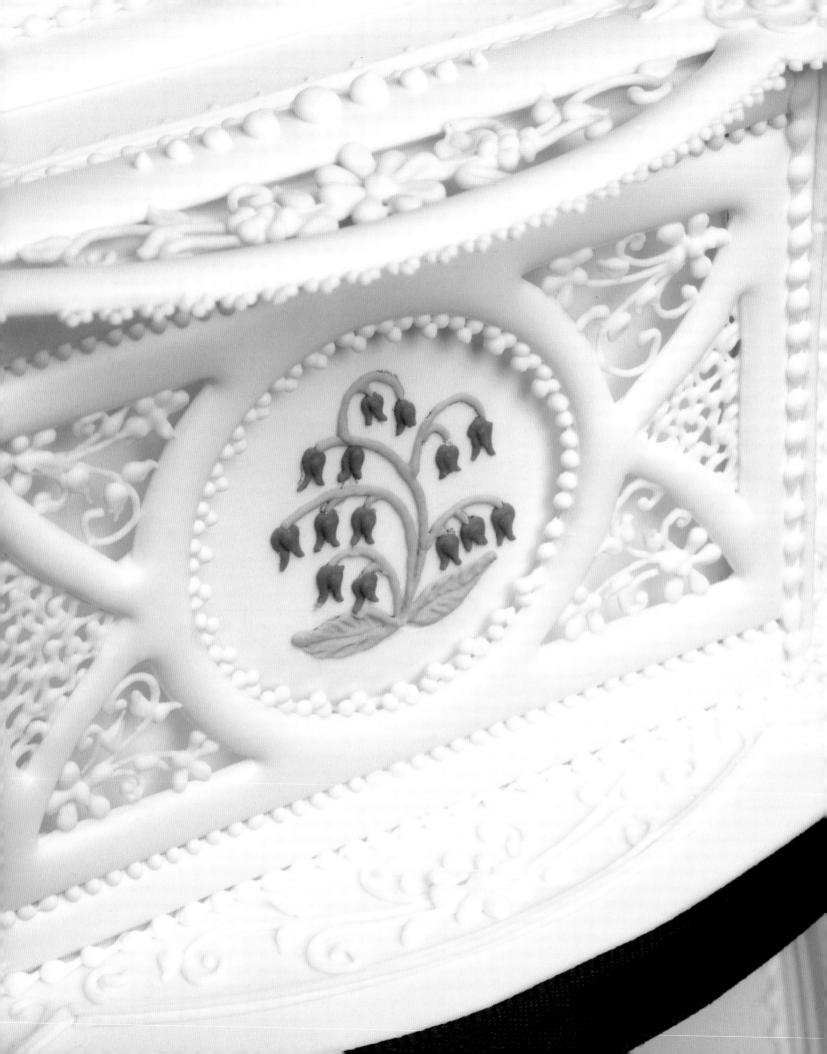

# Run~outs & Collars

Run-outs are made as off-pieces and have many different uses. One of the main reasons for making run-outs is to create flat objects that can either be painted when dry or piped in coloured icing. Plaques can be made as run-outs: these can be prepared well in advance and an inscription or piped decoration added before being transferred to the cake. This technique is also used to make collars for cakes, run-out lettering and numerals (which you can paint or illuminate using pressure piping), and cake top decorations that look extremely impressive when assembled.

I have used the terms 'run-out' and 'flood in' throughout this chapter, but you may also hear this technique described as 'running in' or 'flooding out'.

# *Tips* for making successful run-outs

● Always ensure the icing for flooding is thoroughly rubbed down/paddled on a clean work surface before use to expel all the air bubbles.

● The icing must be at the correct consistency to achieve good results. Use cold water to thin down the icing until the correct consistency is reached: when cut through with a palette knife, it should take approximately 10 seconds to settle (the icing should appear wet and shiny).

● Once you have started a run-out, it must be finished fairly quickly to ensure the icing dries evenly. It is always worth preparing a spare bag of icing in case the first one bursts or runs out.

● Always make sure the cellophane has been greased with white vegetable fat to ensure the figures release easily.

● Allow run-outs to dry under heat (a desk lamp with a 40-watt bulb is ideal). The longer it takes for the icing to dry, the larger the crystalline forms in the sugar will be, which means the icing will appear dull. It also tends to be much softer in consistency, making it hard to work with.

● Use icing sugar made from cane sugar rather than beet sugar: cane sugar has a much harder grain so will produce better results.

● Remember that heat – whether in the atmosphere or from your hands – will cause the air in the icing to expand, which will make the icing 'short' (i.e. it will not flow easily). When piping the outline for run-outs, do not use the same bag of icing for more than 20 minutes as the heat from your hands will cause air bubbles to form and the lines may break.

● Always ensure your equipment is clean and completely free from grease.

● If you are going to store run-outs in airtight, plastic food containers, check that they are completely dry first and place a piece of kitchen towel inside the box to absorb any moisture. If you have decorated a cake with run-outs, do not store it in a plastic container as the moisture from the cake will become trapped, causing the air to become humid and the run-outs to break off. Heavy-duty cardboard boxes are ideal for this purpose and are available from your local cake decorating shop (see page 320 for a list of suppliers).

● When flooding in sections of a run-out, always start at the background and work towards the foreground.

● It is a good idea to make spare run-outs to allow for breakages.

Before making run-outs you will need to ensure you have the correct materials and equipment. You will need:

## Materials

Run-out icing, made to off-peak consistency (see page 33)

SK Professional Liquid Food Colours in your chosen colours

White vegetable fat

## Equipment

Templates (see pages 295 to 297, 302 to 305)

Cellophane

Scissors

Masking tape

Piping bags

No. 1 or 1.5 piping nozzle

Small palette knife

Desk lamp

# Basic run~outs

1 Before you start piping the run-out, draw the template onto paper and secure to a flat surface (such as a non-stick board) with masking tape.

2 Cut a piece of cellophane that is bigger than the template and secure over the top with masking tape. If using cellophane from a roll, keep the outer side uppermost so that the edges do not curve upwards. Lightly grease the cellophane with white vegetable fat.

3 To pipe the outlines of a run-out, prepare some freshly beaten royal icing to off-peak consistency. Using a small palette knife, rub down (paddle) a small amount of icing to expel the air (in the same way as for drop line work).

4 Fit a piping bag with a plain nozzle, usually a no. 1 or 1.5 (depending on the size of the run-out). Half-fill the bag with the rubbed-down icing and fold over the top.

5 Pipe the outline of the run-out using the drop line technique (see page 65). Make sure the ends of the lines join up and try to keep any corners sharp by piping point-to-point. Always hold the bag at least 2.5cm-4cm (1-1½") from the work surface. For the heart design, pipe the outer line first, starting at the top and piping down to the base. Repeat on the opposite side. If the outline is the same colour as the main run-out, cross the internal lines over at the top point.

6 Drop line the inner line, again crossing the internal lines over at the bottom point if the outline is the same colour as the main run-out.

7 When you have finished the outline it is ready to be flooded in with run-out icing. Use a palette knife to place a small amount of royal icing into a bowl. Add a few drops of boiled, cold water or bottled water (preferably from the fridge) and mix. To tell if the consistency is correct for flat run-outs, cut through the icing with the palette knife. Between the counts of 9 and 10 (counting '1 and 2 and 3', etc. or approximately 10 seconds), the line should disappear. If it takes longer, add a little more water and repeat.

8 Place the run-out icing into a piping bag. It will need to have a small aperture so that any air bubbles are expelled before they go through, so either use a no. 1 nozzle or snip off the tip of the bag to the same size.

9 Fill in the run-out. For a narrow area such as this heart design, use a back-and-forth motion. If you are working on a large area, flood small sections at a time and work from 1

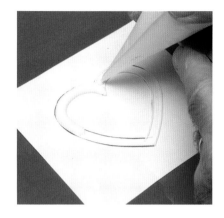

area to another so that you are always piping onto wet icing. (Do not allow 1 area to skin over otherwise the join will show.) Lightly tap the work board on the table to level out the icing then place under a desk lamp to dry.

10 When dry, carefully peel away the cellophane (this should be easy if it was greased properly). To secure a run-out to a cake, pipe bulbs of stiff icing onto the back and press into place very gently, taking care not to break the run-out.

Mark the piping bags with an 'R' for 'rubbed' and 'S' for 'stiff' so as not to confuse the bags when you are working.

# Run~outs as plaques

## (solid run-outs)

When dry, these plaques can be decorated with inscriptions, piped flowers or pressure piped designs. They can be used on used on the top or sides of a cake. Templates for these shapes are given on page 295.

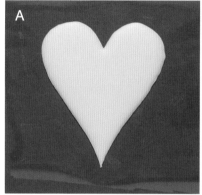

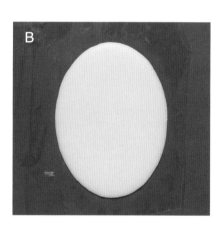

**A:** Heart

1 Drop line half of the heart outline, starting at the top and coming to a point at the end. Start the line just inside the shape so that, when you pipe the second half, the internal lines are crossed.

2 Prepare a bag of run-out icing and snip a small hole in the tip. Pipe just inside the outline then fill in, working quickly so that the icing doesn't dry.

For a quick way to level off the icing, slide a palette knife underneath the cellophane and move it back and forth, keeping it flat under the icing.

**B:** Oval

1 For an oval or circle, start the outline at the bottom and pipe round, working directly over the top of the design.

2 Using run-out icing, pipe just inside the perimeter of the plaque and continue round, bringing the icing in a little each time. It is normal for the surface to appear wavy and you may hear the air bubbles bursting. Continue until you reach the centre. Place under a desk lamp to dry.

*To see how run-out plaques can be used on a cake, see the cake designs on pages 219 and 241.*

# Run~outs as figures and motifs

Some figures and motifs are more suited to run-outs than pressure piping. The run-out technique is suitable for any motif where you require a smooth, shiny surface.

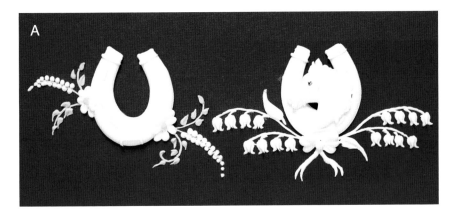

**A:** Horseshoe motif (see template on page 295)

1 Prepare the template underneath a sheet of greased cellophane. Using a no. 1.5 nozzle, outline the horseshoe shape.

2 Rub down some royal icing to run-out consistency. Flood in the horseshoe shape and allow to dry under a desk lamp.

3 Secure the horseshoe to the cake with royal icing. At this stage, you can choose to add a pressure piped horse's head (for instructions, see page 98), or simply add pressure piped flowers. The 2 examples shown here (with and without the horse's head) feature different piped flowers to balance the design.

**B:** Heart and dove design (see template on page 295)

For this design you will also need SK Black QFC Liquid and a no. 2 piping nozzle.

1 Prepare the heart template under greased cellophane. Pipe the outline of the heart with a no. 1 nozzle and then flood the heart with run-out icing. Allow to dry under a desk lamp.

2 Prepare the 2 dove templates under greased cellophane. Outline and flood the doves, excluding the wings, and allow to dry. When dry, pressure pipe the wings using off-peak royal icing and a no. 1 or 1.5 nozzle. Allow to dry.

3 Attach the heart to the cake then attach the doves to the heart with a small amount of royal icing. Pipe in the claws then add rope-effect scallops around the edge of the heart (see scratch piped designs, page 69). Using a fine artists' brush and SK Black QFC Liquid, paint an eye on each dove.

4 If required, pressure pipe initials onto the heart using a no. 2 nozzle (see pages 131 to 132 for styles of freestyle lettering).

Allowing the parts of a run-out to partially dry will prevent the icing running together and therefore give each section definition.

**C:** 2-dimensional bell design (see template on page 296)

1 Prepare the template under greased cellophane. Outline both bells using rubbed-down icing in a piping bag with a no. 1 nozzle.

2 Flood the bottom (internal) part of the bells first then place under a desk lamp for a few moments to skin over. Fill in the remaining part of the bells to complete the run-out and allow to dry again.

3 Secure the bells in place with stiff royal icing, then pressure pipe a ball at the top of each bell and a ball for each clapper. Decorate the bells with dots or small scrolls as required.

4 Add some simple pressure piped flowers and leaves to balance the design (see pages 51 to 57).

*To make a 3-dimensional bell motif, see page 107.*

*This design can be used on mini cakes to give to guests at a wedding or anniversary celebration. Instructions for guilding with edible gold or silver paint are given on page 47.*

## D: Car motif using colour

This example shows how to use colour in run-outs.

For this design you will need to prepare royal icing in your chosen colours, in this case red, black and white (SK Poinsettia and Black Liquid Food Colours).

1 Prepare the template under greased cellophane. To achieve a distinct outline, pipe it in dark grey or black icing using a no. 1 nozzle. Work from left to right and top to bottom to avoid smudging your work.

2 Using run-out icing, flood in the design 1 section at a time. Start by piping the lights, windows and bumpers in white. Allow this icing to skin over.

3 Use red run-out icing to pipe alternate sections of the car: start with the bonnet then add the alternate panels down the side of the car. Place under a lamp to skin over. This will ensure each section remains defined and does not run into the next.

4 Flood the remaining sections to complete the run-out and allow to dry fully under a lamp.

5 Paint on the final detail using a fine paintbrush and liquid food colours.

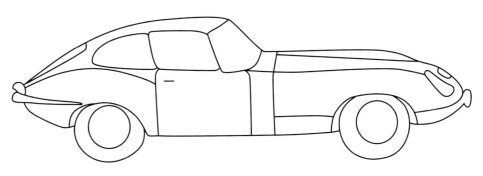

*Tip* Use a photograph of the recipient's favourite car as a template. You could also use any image to suit the recipient's hobby, such as a motorbike, boat, plane or train.

 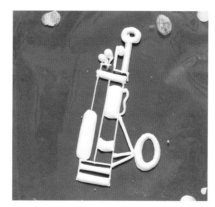 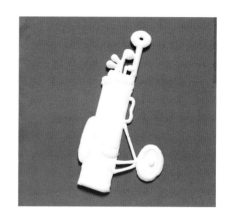

**E:** Golfer and trolley motif using colour (see template on page 295)

This example also shows how to use colour in run-outs. As well as the basic materials and equipment required for run-out work, you will also need SK Professional Liquid Colours of your choice and a no. 2 plain piping nozzle.

### Trolley

1 Prepare the template under a piece of greased cellophane. Place some white off-peak royal icing into a piping bag with a no. 2 nozzle. Drop line the outline of the handle of the trolley, then add the 3 golf clubs on the left-hand side. Pressure pipe the head of the driver (large club).

2 Outline the rest of the trolley bag with a no. 1 nozzle. To pipe the back of the trolley, first pipe the struts with a no. 2 nozzle. Outline the wheel with the no. 1 nozzle.

3 Rub down no more than 2 tablespoonfuls of royal icing on a clean surface to remove the air. Place into a small container and thin down with a few drops of cold water until it is at run-out consistency (see page 33). Place in a piping bag, snip off the tip and flood in alternate areas in the design. Allow to dry under a lamp until the icing has skinned over.

4 Using the same run-out icing, flood in the remaining sections of the trolley and bag.

### Golfer

1 Prepare the template under greased cellophane. Start by outlining the face using a no. 0 nozzle and flesh-coloured rubbed-down icing (add a touch of SK Chestnut Liquid Food Colour or Bulrush for a darker tone). Create a dimple at the top of the nose for the eye then fill out the cheek and vibrate the tip of the bag to smooth out the icing.

2 Pipe in the hair with stiff icing in the colour of your choice. Pipe down over the forehead, down the sideburns and round the back, leaving a gap for the ear. For curly hair, pipe in a round, swirling motion, leaving the indentations in the icing. You can also use an artists' brush to emphasise the texture.

*Tip* It is essential that you pipe clean, even lines with no bulbs, particularly at the joins in the line work (this occurs if you squeeze too hard at the beginning and end of the line). You can tidy up any lines that are not flush with a fine artists' brush dampened with cooled, boiled water.

3 For the trousers, make a small bowl of royal icing in the colour of your choice, rub down with a palette knife and place in a piping bag. Pipe the outline of the trousers, starting with the leg in the background first.

4 Use stiff icing in the colour of your choice to pipe the shoes.

5 Pipe the back arm using rubbed-down icing in your chosen colour.

*Tip*

When rubbing down icing always remember to clean it off the work surface each time. Any dried icing that gets into the piping bag will cause blockages in the nozzle. A good technique is to rub the icing onto a slightly damp surface so that it does not dry so quickly.

6 Use stiff brown royal icing to pipe the handle of the golf club. Using the stiff flesh coloured icing, pipe in the fingers round the back of the handle followed by the other hand on top.

7 Using stiff white icing, pipe the collar. By this time, the face and hair should have dried slightly so will not run into the collar. At this stage leave the run-out to dry under a lamp.

8 There are 2 ways to pipe the trousers: either outline and flood in the area, or pressure pipe them, working from side to side rather than up and down. Vibrate the nozzle in the icing to create natural-looking creases.

9 Prepare a bag of rubbed-down icing and snip off the end. Pipe the jumper, leaving a space for the waistband (this will be piped in separately). Start at the back, go round the shoulder and down to the waist again. Place under a lamp for around 5 minutes to allow the icing to skin over.

10 Using the same rubbed-down icing, pipe in the sleeve at the front, using a back-and-forth motion to give shape and form to the sleeve.

11 Place some stiff green royal icing into a piping bag and snip off the end. Pipe in an up-and-down motion along the waist at the end of the sleeve to create a ribbed effect.

12 Leave the figure to dry under a desk lamp and transfer to the cake or plaque when dry. The shaft and head of the golf club can be piped directly onto the cake when the figure is stuck down, otherwise it may break when being transferred to the cake.

*A single-tier birthday cake for a golf fanatic featuring this design can be seen on pages 260 to 262.*

# Run~out lettering and numerals

The basic principles for creating run-outs can be used to make virtually any shape: simply make a template and pipe onto greased cellophane. Lettering and numerals are no exception: it is feasible to create inscriptions or monograms which can be used on the top and sides of cakes. See pages 139 to 141 to see how single and double run-outs can be used to create lettering and numerals. An example of run-out lettering can also be seen on page 211, Noel plaque.

# Run~outs as cake top decorations: gazebo

This impressive cake top decoration can be used on wedding cakes, christening cakes, and any other special occasion cake. Although it looks complicated, once you know how to make run-outs and pressure pipe, it is a great project for all skill levels. The gazebo can be made in advance and the colour can be altered to suit the cake using liquid colourings.

In addition to the basic run-out requirements you will need royal icing made with strengthened egg white (see method below), fine netting (tulle), a no. 2 plain piping nozzle, templates (see page 296), paper, stiff card, a polystyrene block (a separator is ideal) and a cocktail stick.

## Preparation

1   Beat the egg white (preferably fresh, but dried if preferred) a day before needed and leave in the refrigerator overnight. This will help to strengthen the albumen.

2   Make up the royal icing, including the strengthened egg white, to off-peak consistency (see page 33). If using fresh egg white, you may need to add a few drops of acetic acid (white vinegar) or citric acid (lemon juice) to achieve the correct consistency. This icing will be used to pipe the outlines of the run-out pieces.

3   To prepare the icing to flood the run-outs, use a palette knife to rub down a small amount of the freshly beaten icing on a clean work surface. Place the rubbed-down icing into a small bowl and stir in a teaspoon of very cold water to thin down the icing to run-out consistency (see page 33).

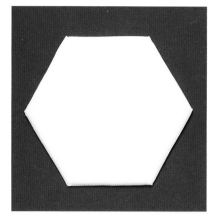

### Solid run-outs

**4** Prepare the templates for the hexagonal solid run-out pieces on paper. Cut around the shape, leaving a 'tongue' at the side so that you can remove the template easily. Secure a piece of cellophane over the template using masking tape and grease the cellophane with a little white vegetable fat.

**5** Place a no. 1.5 nozzle into a piping bag and half-fill the bag with stiff royal icing. Pipe the outline of the solid hexagons. When possible, pipe the lines from point to point to achieve sharp corners. If the corners are not sharp, they can be neatened using a damp artists' brush.

**6** Use the run-out icing prepared earlier to flood in the run-outs. When flooding in, you may use a no. 1 piping nozzle, though I prefer to make a tight piping bag and cut a small aperture in the tip. The smaller the aperture, the better the run-out will be.

*Tip* When flooding a large area, pipe towards the outline, no more than 5cm (2") along to start, then flood in the area. Vibrate the tip of the bag/nozzle on the surface and give the work board a gentle knock on the table periodically to level out the icing and create an even run-out. The idea behind piping into the line is to always pipe onto wet icing to keep the finished result smooth.

**7** Flood in 1 large and 1 small hexagon for the base and the plinth of the gazebo respectively. (The plinth will hold the side panels and doors in position.) Place the completed run-outs under a desk lamp or in an airing cupboard to dry.

### Roof pieces and fillets

**8** Prepare 6 triangular templates and 6 curved fillet pieces (to go around the roof edge) under lightly greased cellophane. Make a bag of stiff royal icing and start by piping the internal lines. At the corners, the lines can be crossed over, which will not only give sharp corners but will form a dam for the icing when you flood

the run-outs. Once the internal lines are complete, pipe all external lines point-to-point. When feasible, pipe towards yourself and finish on the point to retain sharp corners. The last line can be cleaned up using a damp, fine artists' brush.

**9** When all the outlines are complete, use run-out icing to flood the pieces. When flooding into corners, fill in towards the point. When flooding in-between narrow lines, squeeze the piping bag gently and use a back-and-forth motion, keeping a steady pressure on the piping bag. The weight of the icing will pull itself along and level itself out.

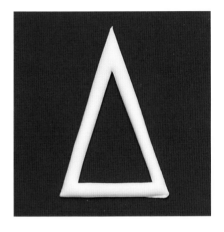
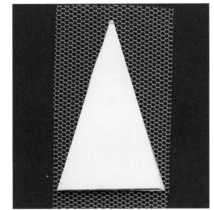
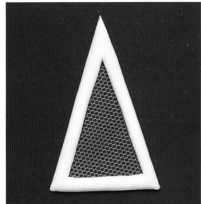

10    Continue to flood all the run-out pieces. Place under a desk lamp or in an airing cupboard to dry.

## Tulle backing

This looks delicate and has the added advantage of holding the scroll work in place. Remember, however, that tulle is not edible so the gazebo must be removed before the cake is eaten.

11    Make a new set of templates from stiff card, this time slightly smaller than the templates for the framework (see secondary line on template). Make 2 templates for each piece, i.e. 4 doors, 10 side panels, and 12 roof sections.

12    Prepare the tulle netting by ironing it underneath a damp cloth to ensure it is completely flat. For each piece of the gazebo, fold the netting over and place between a pair of cardboard templates. Cut out the shape from the netting, creating 2 at a time.

13    To stick the netting onto the run-out framework, prepare a small bag of well rubbed-down royal icing. Half-fill a piping bag fitted with either a no. 1 or 1.5 nozzle or cut a small hole in the tip to this size (no larger). It is imperative that you use rubbed-down icing: if the icing is too stiff there is a greater risk of breaking the run-outs. Pipe a line along the edge of the net piece. Place the run-out on top and gently place it into position. Gently stroke your finger along the run-out to adhere the net to the back of the run-out; do not push the run-out as it might break.

14    Place the template for the scroll work onto a flat board and tape a piece of greased cellophane over the top. Place some rubbed-down royal icing into a piping bag with a no. 1 or 1.5 nozzle. If the icing is too stiff, it will not settle onto the netting and is more likely to break. The rubbed-down icing will also give strength to the scrolls.

155

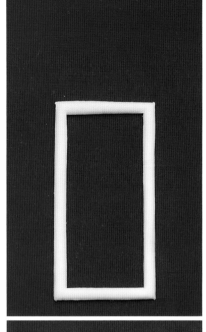

 *Tip* When piping onto netting, you do not have to touch the sides of the framework. However, for competition pieces where you would not use net, the scrolls must touch the frame to hold them in place.

15 Pipe the large S scroll first, followed by the reverse S. Add the small scroll inside the S and reverse S. When 2 lines meet, raise the icing on top of the first scroll so that the line disappears as the icing settles. Add the flowers, leaves and other decoration and use a damp artists' brush to neaten any sharp points. (For more instructions on piping scrolls, see pages 66 to 67.)

16 Repeat the same method to make pieces for the doors and arches on top of the side pieces. You can add your own piped decoration on top: examples of simple and more complex designs are shown here.

17 Allow all of the run-out pieces to dry thoroughly before assembly.

## Assembly

18 Draw the small hexagon template onto paper and draw lines from each corner to locate the central point. Place on top of a piece of polystyrene (such as a separator or cake dummy), then place a piece of cellophane on top of the drawing and tape in position. Grease the cellophane with white vegetable fat.

19 Dip the end of a cocktail stick into white vegetable fat and push this end through the centre of the hexagon and into the polystyrene to hold it upright.

20 Half-fill a piping bag fitted with a no. 2 nozzle with freshly beaten royal icing. Using the hexagonal template prepared earlier, pipe a line of icing slightly to the outside edge of the hexagon. Place 1 of the triangular roof pieces into the icing and lean the point on the cocktail stick. This part can be rather fiddly but it is worth persevering! Pipe a line down the right hand side of the triangle, then continue the line along the next side of the hexagon. Work anticlockwise if you are right-handed and vice versa. Place the second piece in place, joining it to the side of the first piece. As you attach each piece, clean up the edges using a damp artists' brush. Proceed in the same way all round the hexagon to create the roof. When attaching the last piece, pipe down the sides of both adjoining pieces (and along the base) before positioning the last piece.

21 Pipe running beads along the joins using a no. 1 or 1.5 nozzle (see page 71) to disguise any

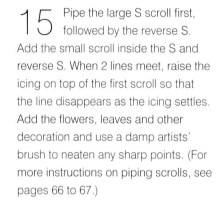

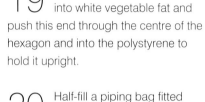

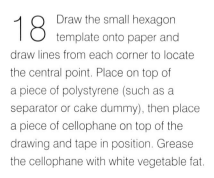

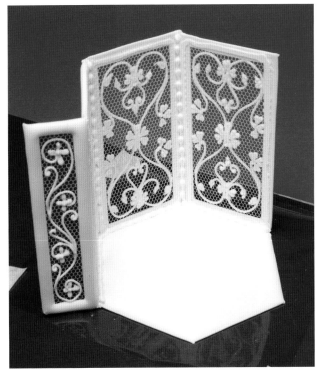

slightly rough edges (you can use a slightly larger nozzle if needed). Place the roof under a desk lamp for at least 1 hour then leave in a warm, dry place to dry overnight. This should make it easy to remove from the cellophane and cocktail stick.

**22** Use a small, cranked palette knife to lift the curved fillets off the cellophane. Pipe a line of stiff royal icing 7mm (¼") in from each corner using a no. 2 nozzle, then place the fillet in place so that it sits vertically. Use an artists' brush to neaten the edge. When all 6 pieces are in place and in the right position, pipe running beads along the bottom edge. This neatens up the edge and also gives it extra strength.

**23** Use the same bag of icing to pipe a line along 2 adjacent sides of the hexagonal base (smaller hexagon). Pipe a line of icing along the right-hand side of 1 side panel, pick up a second panel and press the 2 side pieces against the base. Lift the 2 sides into position and stick them together. If you are worried about this stage, place a support behind each panel to hold them in situ. If the icing is stiff enough, however, this should not be necessary. Take a damp artists' brush and clean up the edges along the base and up the join between the panels. Repeat along 5 sides of the hexagon, piping down the side of each panel individually. When dry, pipe running beads down the sides of the panel.

*Tip*

For added decoration you can pipe running beads on the inside of the joins, but only on the back panels before the others are attached. You will not be able to reach the joins between the other panels so these are left plain.

**24** Once you have attached the 5 side panels you can attach the doors. Ease each door off the cellophane. Pipe a line down the side panel then position the doors so that they are open. When dry, stick the doors onto the larger hexagonal plinth made earlier.

**25** To attach the roof, pipe a line of stiff royal icing using a no. 2 nozzle around the top edge of the side panels. Place the roof on top straight away: do not allow the line of icing to dry first, otherwise the roof will not stick.

*Instructions for making a celebration cake featuring a cake top gazebo with a domed roof can be seen on pages 219 to 225. Directions for making the pedestal of flowers are also given here. An alternative gazebo design is given on page 243.*

# Curved run~outs

In addition to the basic materials required for making run-outs you will need a curved former (such as a piece of guttering).

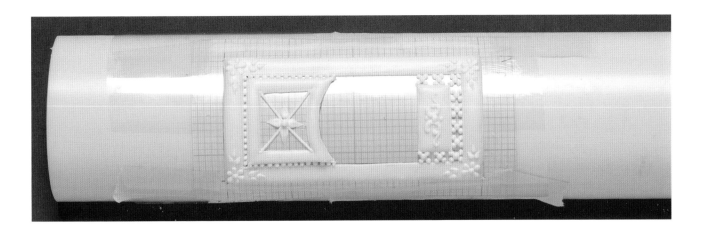

1 Make a template and stick this to a curved former, such as a piece of guttering. Secure a piece of cellophane on top and grease. The curve of the cellophane should follow the curve of the former.

2 Tilt the former so that you can pipe lines perpendicular to the curve (i.e. along the length of the guttering) onto the template in a straight line as you work. Start by piping the outline in the usual way, tilting the former as required so you are always piping on top of it.

3 It is very important to rub all of the air out of the royal icing by paddling well with a palette knife. Once all the air has been expelled it will appear wet and shiny. It is worth making sure this has been done before the next stage, otherwise the icing will be difficult to work with. Transfer to a small bowl.

4 Make the icing for the curved run-out slightly less fluid than normal. Using very cold water, add a few drops at a time to the small bowl of rubbed-down icing. Cut through the icing with a palette knife: it should settle on the count of 16 (see page 33). Add more water a little at a time until the desired consistency is achieved. If the icing is too runny, the icing will run off the curve.

5 Flood in the run-out in the same way as normal and leave to dry in the former under a lamp.

6 When dry, pipe a line of stiff icing along the edges of the run-out and secure in place.

# Corner run~outs for wedding and celebration cakes

The beauty of using corner pieces as opposed to full collars is that, if 1 gets broken, you only have to make 1 small corner piece to replace it. When you are making corner pieces, it is always advisable to make at least 2 spares: these do not necessarily have to be fully decorated unless the finished designs are in colour, in which case it is better to complete them at the same time to ensure all the colours match.

In addition to the basic run-out requirements you will need templates (see page 297) and a no. 0 plain piping nozzle.

## Preparing the template

1. Draw the template for the size of cake you are going to use (you will only need to make 1 corner template rather than 4). The templates here are suitable for a 20cm (8") square cake, which will measure approximately 22cm (8½") when it has been covered with marzipan and iced. If you are making a larger cake, enlarge the templates accordingly.

## Tip

Whatever the size of your cake, make sure that the corner pieces will fit inside the square (i.e. each piece must be no longer than half the length of 1 side). If there is a gap between them, you can pipe in a small design to fit in the gap.

2 Prepare the template and secure under a sheet of greased cellophane (for full instructions, see page 145). Only secure the cellophane along 3 sides so that the template can be removed and used again.

## Piped framework

3 To make the framework for the design, place a no. 1 nozzle into a piping bag and half-fill with rubbed-down royal icing. Pipe the outline of the design using the drop line technique (see page 65). Cross the internal lines over by approximately 5mm (1/8") where they meet so that the corners are sharp. When you are piping the scallop shapes, always pipe towards the point (where feasible) and cross the lines over to create a sharp point.

4 Carefully remove the template from underneath the cellophane and repeat the same method to make 4 corner pieces plus at least 2 spares.

## Flooding in

5 Scoop out some of the royal icing from the bowl and rub it down (paddle) on a clean work surface with a palette knife. Continue to paddle the icing until it looks wet and shiny, then transfer it into a clean bowl. Repeat the process to make as much icing as required. Add a little cold water and stir; do not beat as this will create air bubbles. Check that it is the correct consistency for flat run-outs (see page 33).

6 To prepare for the run-outs, make a tight piping bag, adding at least an extra quarter turn than normal (see page 43). Half-fill the bag with icing and fold over the top. Make a spare bag of icing and leave to 1 side. Snip off the tip of the first bag, ensuring the hole is no bigger than the size of a no. 1 nozzle.

7 Begin to flood in the design, keeping the tip of the piping bag in the icing and using a vibrating movement with your hands to create an even, flat surface. In order to obtain sharp corners, begin by flooding the icing in towards the corners, as shown. When flooding in narrow strips, press the point of the piping bag in the centre of the strip, then flood the central area from side to side. For large areas, start by flooding in from the piped framework, then move the bag up and down with a slight vibrating movement to fill in the area.

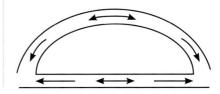

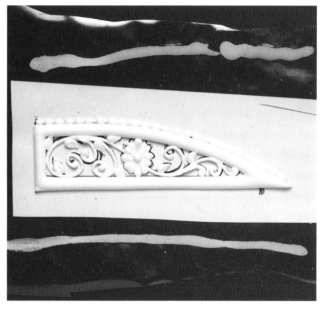

**8** When the run-outs have been flooded in, place them under a desk lamp or into an airing cupboard to dry out.

### Adding the decoration

**9** To pipe the scroll decoration onto the run-out, place some off-peak royal icing into a piping bag with a no. 1 nozzle. Pipe the scrolls into the design using the drop line technique (see pages 66 to 67). Make sure the scrolls touch the edges of the run-outs so that they will hold in position when dry.

**10** To pipe the picot dots, rub down some stiff royal icing to ensure that all the air is expelled. When the icing appears wet, place 1 teaspoonful at a time into a piping bag fitted with a no. 0 nozzle. (For even smaller dots, use a no. 00 or

000 nozzle.) To see if the icing has the correct consistency, pipe a dot and check that the point disappears. If so, it is ready to use; if not, rub down the icing again.

**11** Starting in 1 corner, begin to pipe dots along the edge. The gap between the dots should be no more than half the width of a dot. Pipe a complete line of single dots and allow to dry. If you wish to add a second line, pipe in every alternate dot to give groups of 3 dots. For groups of 6 dots, pipe 3 and miss 1, then add 2 above and 1 to finish. This creates a lace effect.

If you are making a run-out piece with small radius curves, it is advisable to pipe single dots rather than groups of 3 or 6, otherwise the curved edges will appear to be squared off.

### Upright corner pieces

The upright pieces add height to a cake and frame the cake top design. However, they are optional so if you are short of time you can leave them off. More freestanding designs using pressure piping and drop line techniques can be seen on pages 75 to 77.

**12** To make the freestanding corner pieces, prepare the template and drop line the outline in the same way as before. Flood in the narrow lines with run-out icing, making the hole in the piping bag as small as possible to ensure the air is expelled. Make 4 pieces plus at least 2 spares and allow to dry under a desk lamp.

13 For the decoration, rub down some off-peak royal icing for drop line work. Place a no. 1.5 nozzle into a piping bag and half-fill with royal icing. Start by piping the largest S scroll first, then continue by reduction, finishing with the smallest scrolls. Add the leaves and the daisy to finish. Ensure the scrolls touch the inner edges of the run-outs so they hold in position when dry.

14 Pipe along the top edge of the piece, either with single dots, picot dots or running beads. (If you are not going to use the top pieces, there is no need to pipe the inner dots on the corner run-out pieces).

Do not stick the corner run-outs or top edge pieces in place until the cake top design is complete.

Once you have made the corner run-outs for a cake, you can add a piped design to the cake top and further embellishments to complement the run-out work. This can be simple or complex, but should reflect the design of the run-outs. Instructions for decorating the cake further and assembling the run-out pieces are given in the example on pages 216 to 218.

# Collars

If you are making a round, hexagonal or octagonal cake a run-out collar frames the cake top beautifully. Try experimenting with different designs and colours but always ensure that the collar is smaller than the cake on the inside circumference and bigger on the outer circumference. A simple scallop design for a round cake is used as an example here.

**A:** Single-colour collars

1 Prepare 2 templates under greased cellophane for the cake: 1 plain collar to go underneath and another one to go on top. The first collar should be slightly smaller than the second.

2 Pipe the outline for the first collar using a no. 1 or 1.5 nozzle. Start at the bottom of the circle and work directly above it to make it even.

3 Flood in the circle, working on small areas at a time to keep the finish smooth. Allow to dry under a desk lamp.

4 Pipe the outline for the top collar. When piping scallops, cross the internal lines over to keep the points sharp. Flood in with run-out icing and allow to dry.

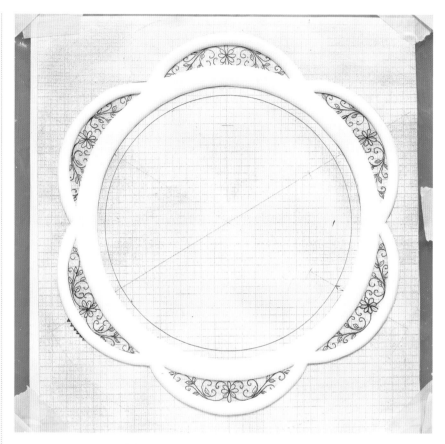

When piping large run-outs such as collars, flood 2.5cm-4cm (1"-1½") wide sections at a time. Continue from 1 side, then do the same on the other side until the run-out joins on the opposite side of the circle. If you work round the circle in 1 direction, the icing will dry as you work and you may see a line at the starting point.

5 Pipe the scroll detail onto the top collar, making sure that the lines touch the edge of the collar so that they are held in place when dry. Allow to dry fully.

6 Pipe a line of stiff icing onto the back of the smaller collar and attach to the top of the cake. The internal line should be smaller than the circumference of the cake. Carefully place into position, taking care not to break the run-out.

7 Pipe a line of icing around the circle of the top collar and attach to the smaller collar. This will raise it up from the top of the cake, making the design look taller and larger.

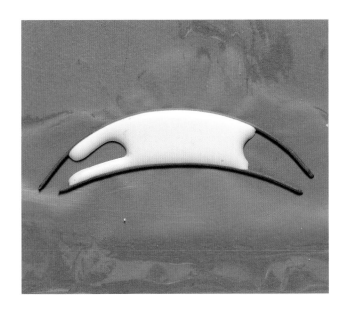

### B: Using colour

This collar is used on the golfer celebration cake featured on pages 260 to 262.

In addition to the basic requirements for run-out work you will need SK Professional Liquid Food Colours of your choice for the outline and run-out icing. Here, I have used Bulrush and Holly/Ivy but you can change the colours to suit the cake.

1. Prepare the collar template (see page 297), again ensuring that the inner circle is smaller than the diameter of the cake and the outer circle larger. Secure under a sheet of greased cellophane.

2. Using a no. 2 nozzle and rubbed-down brown royal icing, outline the design. Start by drop-lining the inner circle of the collar. When piping the outline for a circle, start at the base (nearest to you) and rotate the nozzle as you work round the curve to achieve a perfect circle. Repeat with the ovals: start piping along the long, straighter side rather than at the end as it is easier to create an even shape.

When piping curves or circles, ease off the pressure when you are getting near to the finishing point, touch the end and stop. If you have a point at the join, smooth it off with a damp artists' brush. Practice as much as possible before starting the join-ups: it does take time to master this technique.

3. Drop line the scallops around the outside of the collar. When outlining with a dark colour, drop the lines point-to-point. If you choose to use the same colour as the run-out icing you can cross the ends over to achieve sharp corners.

4. For the run-out, prepare some green run-out icing. (If you are making the whole cake as pictured on page 260, make this a shade lighter than the golfer's jumper.) Flood in the run-out by piping in towards the brown line. Use a back and forth motion then use the tip of the piping bag to vibrate the surface of the icing, making it smooth.

5. Place under a lamp for at least an hour then leave in a warm place overnight to dry completely.

*Instructions on how to assemble this collar on a cake can be seen on pages 260 to 262.*

## C: Using patterns (quick technique)

This is an alternative technique to more complex run-outs and is very quick. In addition to the basic requirements you will need to prepare a small bag of rubbed-down icing (in this case SK Bulrush) and a large bag of rubbed-down icing in a different colour (in this case SK Holly/Ivy).

1 Prepare a circular template underneath a sheet of greased cellophane. The inside edge must be smaller than the diameter of the cake and the outer edge must be larger than the cake but 2.5cm (1") less than the size of the cake board.

2 Prepare a bag of fresh, off-peak white royal icing in a bag with a no. 1.5 nozzle and 2 bags of white run-out icing.

3 Using the off-peak white icing, drop line the inner then outer frame lines, starting at the bottom and working round.

4 Cut a hole in the tip of each bag of white run-out icing around the size of a no. 1 or 1.5 nozzle. This time, pipe round the inner line of the run-out all the way round the circle. If you are using a turntable, use this to turn the template as you work. Pipe another line in towards the outer line in the same way.

5 Start to fill in the area as quickly as possible. Pipe 2 lines inside

the existing lines, then tap the board on the work surface to flatten out the icing.

6 Using the drop line technique pipe a line of brown rubbed-down icing around the centre of the run-out. Pipe a second colour a few millimetres outside the first line and add another line a few millimetres inside the first line. You must work quite quickly when using this technique.

7 Using a cocktail stick, draw a curvy line from side to side through the coloured lines, all the way round the circle. Tap again to flatten off

any raised surfaces then place under a desk lamp to dry.

8 To secure the collar in place, pipe a line of stiff icing onto the back and carefully place it centrally onto the cake.

You can use a third colour in this pattern: simply pipe each coloured line in a different colour.

Examples of how collars can be used on single-tier celebration cakes.

# Embroidery Techniques

There are 3 different types of brush embroidery: shading (a piped outline which is faded into the cake), skeletonized (a piped outline with only the edge broken) and stitch embroidery (using tints and shades of one colour to build up the design). I use rubbed-down royal icing, but if you are new to this technique you can add piping gel to the royal icing to make the icing dry more slowly as you are working. However, do not add too much piping gel as, if there is a high humidity, the icing will start to sweat.

There are other methods for creating embroidery effects but these are the ones I use most frequently.

# *Tips* for successful brush embroidery

- Each method has a slightly different effect, so choose one which suits the cake you are working on.

- Adjust the size of the brush to suit the size of the design: the smaller the design, the finer the brush.

- Using an embosser will make it easier to transfer the design onto a cake or plaque and means that you can use the same design over again. This is only feasible with soft paste such as sugarpaste; if you are working on a royal iced cake, you can scratch the outline of the design onto the surface with a scriber (this technique can also be used on sugarpaste if preferred).

- When you are brushing the icing always use a paintbrush dampened with cooled, boiled water. Blot any excess water onto a piece of kitchen paper beforehand otherwise the coating may start to dissolve.

- If a design is repeated several times on a cake (e.g. on the side panels of a wedding cake or on cupcakes for a display) it is important to keep the colour constant. Weigh the icing and use a pipette to measure the amount of colour used. You can then use the same method to make another batch, keeping the colour the same on each design (see page 45).

# *Reverse* embosser

## Materials

SK Light Confectioners' Glaze
Royal icing, rubbed down (see page 33)

## Equipment

Template of design (see page 298)
25cm (10") square (or larger) piece of acrylic*, washed and sterilised with boiling water
Fine sandpaper
Kitchen paper
Palette knife
Piping bag
No. 1 plain piping nozzle
Desk lamp

*You can buy acrylic from most hardware shops (you may be able to buy an off-cut) or you could even look in charity shops for picture frames made with acrylic. Ensure it is completely clean and sterilised before use to make it safe for food contact.

1 To make a reverse embosser, start by preparing a drawing of the design that you are going to use.

2 Lightly rub 1 side of the acrylic with fine sandpaper to make the surface less slippery (do this away from any edibles to prevent the dust from contaminating them). Draw the design onto this side of the acrylic using a pen or pencil.

3 Turn the acrylic over, smooth side up. Using SK Light Confectioners' Glaze and kitchen paper, lightly cover the acrylic with the glaze and allow to dry slightly until it becomes tacky. This acts as an adhesive for the royal icing.

4 Rub down (paddle) some freshly beaten royal icing using a palette knife until it has a slight flow (see page 33). Place the icing in a piping bag with a no. 1 nozzle.

5 Pipe the outline of the design: remember that it will be in reverse, so any lettering will appear backwards at this stage.

6 Allow to dry overnight in a warm, dry place or under a desk lamp for at least 2 hours.

7 Once you have made the sugarpaste plaque or covered the cake with sugarpaste, lightly dust the surface with a little cornflour and polish with the flat of your hand or a smoother to prevent the embosser from sticking to the paste. Position the embosser centrally over the sugarpaste and press down firmly and evenly: the sugarpaste should be fresh rather than firm. You can then proceed to brush embroider the design using your chosen technique.

*Embossers are not only useful for brush embroidery techniques: they can also be used for pressure piped designs and cake tops decorated with piping gel. Cake tops using the reverse embosser technique can be seen on pages 202 to 205.*

# Shaded brush embroidery

This method is suitable for piping onto solid panels and onto netting, as well as on the top and sides of any celebration cake. I used this technique on Prince Charles and Lady Diana's wedding cake (see page 17).

This style of brush embroidery is effective on both monochrome and coloured designs. Choose a style and design to suit the cake you are working on then follow the same method to create the embroidery effect.

## Materials

Royal icing, rubbed-down (see page 33)

SK Piping Gel (optional, see note on page 169)

Cooled, boiled water

## Equipment

Template (see page 298)

Nos. 0, 1 and 1.5 plain nozzles

No. 3 or 2 paintbrush

**A:** Monochrome design

Prepare a bag of rubbed-down royal icing in a piping bag with a no. 1.5 nozzle.

1 Pipe one petal at a time: the petals on the rose diagram (see below) have been numbered to show the order in which they should be piped. Dampen the paintbrush with cooled, boiled water. Starting on the first outer petal, brush in towards the central point at the base of the petal so that the lines look like they all go towards the centre. When brushing through the icing, aim to keep the outer line unbroken: brush in from the middle of the piped line to create the effect of a clean outline with softened inner lines.

2 Work round each set of petals, starting with the outer petals and working in towards the centre. Brush each petal as soon as you have piped the outline to prevent the icing from drying out before it has been brushed.

3 To create the leaves pipe a serrated edge in a zig-zag motion using a no. 1 plain nozzle. Use a damp paintbrush to brush in the lines, making sure the veining comes down diagonally towards the base of the leaf. When piping leaves, pipe only one side at a time so the icing does not have time to dry out.

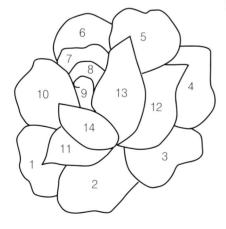

For most designs you will need to work from the background to the foreground. To avoid smudging your work, work round the design clockwise if you are right-handed, anticlockwise if you are left-handed.

4 Using a no. 0 nozzle, pipe in a few veins on the leaves then pipe in the stems.

5 For the main stem, pipe a rope stitch back and forth to fill in the stem from one side to the other using the no. 0 nozzle.

*To see how this design can be used on a cake top, see pages 263 to 265.*

**B:** 2-tone design

To recreate this design you will need SK Cyclamen and Holly/Ivy Professional Liquid Food Colours. Prepare rubbed-down dark pink and light pink royal icing (or a colour of your choice in 2 tones) and rubbed-down dark green royal icing, all in piping bags with no. 1 nozzles.

1 Pipe the outline of the first petal with the dark pink icing, then pipe a line inside this with the light pink.

2 Dampen a paintbrush with cooled, boiled water and brush from the outer line inwards, bringing both colours together. Work in the same way as before, pulling the icing towards the central base of the petal. Work round the flower one petal at a time (clockwise if you are right-handed, anticlockwise if you are left-handed).

3 Outline the leaves with dark green icing using no. 1 nozzle, giving them a serrated edge. Pipe a line of lighter green icing inside and brush them together towards the centre of the leaf.

4 When dry, paint SK Holly/Ivy Liquid Food Colour on top of the brush embroidery to add depth.

Leaves and petals made this way can be piped as off-pieces onto greased cellophane and stuck onto the cake when dry. They can also be dried on curved formers such as guttering to give them shape and movement.

# Skeletonized brush embroidery

This technique is similar to shaded embroidery but is not blended as much, thus giving more of a skeleton outline effect. This is the simplest technique of the 3, is a good way to achieve results quickly and is useful where a lighter effect is required.

You will need the same materials and equipment as for shaded brush embroidery (see page 172) except you will need to use a finer nozzle (such as a no. 0 or 1) to pipe the outline of the design.

1 Emboss or scratch the design onto the cake top or plaque in the usual way.

2 Prepare a piping bag filled with rubbed-down icing and fitted with a no. 1 nozzle (or no. 0 if the design is small). Pipe a fine outline of 1 petal then lightly brush the icing in towards the centre of the petal by only a few millimetres. You are essentially following the same method as for the shaded brush embroidery but you will need to make much shorter brush strokes.

3 Continue to work around the design in the same way as described for shaded brush embroidery. Complete the other parts of the design using the same technique. Other elements of the design, such as flowers and leaves, should all be piped using the same technique.

# Stitch embroidery

This technique is made up of a series of lines piped side-by-side. You can either pipe your chosen design directly onto the cake top using an embosser or scriber to mark the outline, or pipe off-pieces onto greased cellophane (see page 97).

Emboss or scribe the design onto the cake top or prepare a template of the design under greased cellophane. You will also need to prepare a bag of fresh, off-peak royal icing in each colour: in this case pale and dark pink (SK Cyclamen). The size of the nozzle will depend on the size of the design, but is usually between a no. 00 and 1.

1 Pipe the background of the design first and work forward. For the fuchsia design, pipe the stamens in dark pink royal icing, then pipe the two side petals then the central petal with pale pink icing.

2 Using the bag of dark pink royal icing, pipe the three large sepals, starting from the outside and working in. Pipe 3 lines tapering to a point, then pipe 5 lines, then 5 again as the petal gets wider, then 4, then 3 coming to a point.

3 Using a rope technique (see page 83), pipe in the seed pod of the fuchsia.

If the icing starts to run together, add a little sieved icing sugar to make the consistency stiffer.

175

# Oriental String Work

Oriental string work is made up of a series of loops that overlap to create a border around a cake. With a little practice it is an easy technique to master and you can create your own designs using the basic principles described in this chapter. Although simple, this technique is time consuming: the cake covering must be firm enough to handle and each set of loops must be completely dry before the cake is inverted. Make sure that you allow enough time to complete your cake and take extra care when you are handling it as the fine piping work will be very fragile.

You can pipe oriental string work onto a royal iced or sugarpasted cake: I have used a pale blue cake here so that the string work can be seen easily, but you can choose any colour for the coating and piping; white piping on a white cake can look particularly elegant.

# Tips
## for successful string work

- Make sure you leave enough time to prepare: the iced cake should be left at least overnight, preferably two days before the string work is added, so as not to damage the icing.

- The cake will be turned upside down so it is essential that there is no decoration on the top of the cake. If you wish to add decoration to the cake top, this can be done once the string work is complete. Remember, however, that the loops will come above the top of the cake so it may be difficult to pipe directly onto the cake.

- Stick the cake firmly to the board with boiled apricot jam before coating with marzipan so that it does not become dislodged when the cake is inverted.

- When piping the drop lines, always use freshly beaten royal icing to ensure the lines don't break (more tips for successful drop line work are given on page 64).

- Once the string work is complete, the lines are crossed over so the icing supports itself and becomes stronger, even though it still looks delicate. The more lines in the design that are crossed over, the stronger the work will be, making it easier to transport.

## Materials

Round cake and cake board, coated with royal icing or sugarpaste (see pages 34 to 41)

Freshly beaten royal icing, made to off-peak consistency (see page 33)

SK Sugar Florist Paste (SFP): Pale Yellow

Cornflour duster

## Equipment

Template for cake top (see example on page 299)

Compass and pencil

Turntable

Side scraper or straight edge

Piping bags

Nos. 0, 1 or 1.5 and 2 plain piping nozzles

Thin cake board, smaller than the diameter of the cake

Sticky tape

Separator (e.g. polystyrene dummy or cake tin), smaller than the diameter of the cake

Small, non-stick board and rolling pin

Miniature blossom plunger cutter

Piece of food-grade foam sponge

# Basic scallop design

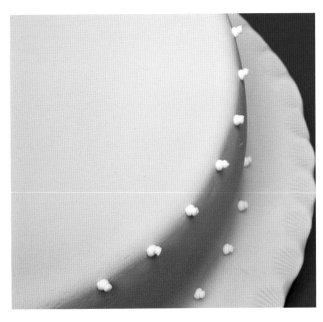

## Stage 1: dividing the cake

1 Make a template for the top of the cake. For a round cake, use a compass to draw a circle slightly smaller than the cake top itself.

2 Use the compass to divide the template into equal sectors: the number of sectors will depend on the size of the cake but you should aim for each one to be no more than 1.3cm-1.6cm (½"-⅝") wide at the edge of the cake. If the sectors are any wider the string work will be too long and may touch the side of the cake. Place the template centrally on top of the cake and place the cake on a turntable.

3 Using freshly beaten royal icing and a no. 2 nozzle, pipe dots all the way round the top edge of the cake. The dots should be around double the width of the nozzle. If you are using a sugarpasted cake, make sure the dots are on the flat edge, not on the rounded corner, otherwise the string work will touch the sides of the cake.

4 Repeat around the base of the cake, ensuring the dots are directly in line with the top set. When working round the cake, hold a side scraper or straight edge against the side of the cake, resting on the board to help keep the dots in line with the top set. Work clockwise if you are right-handed, anticlockwise if you are left-handed.

5 Allow the dots to firm slightly then pipe a set of smaller dots on top of both the top and bottom sets with either a no. 1 or 1.5 nozzle. These dots will keep the string work away from the side of the cake.

6 Using the same nozzle (no. 1 or 1.5) pipe a small dot halfway up the cake, between the two rows of dots. Pipe another dot above and below this one, approximately 4mm (⅛") away. These must all be in line with the top and bottom rows.

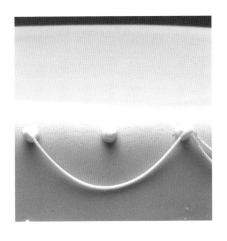
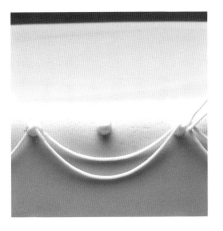
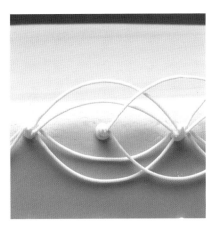

## Stage 2: piping the dropped lines

7 Place some of the icing into a small bowl and 'knock back' (beat slightly) with a palette knife to bring it back to off-peak consistency (do not over-beat the icing).

### Tip

If the icing has been left overnight, beat it again before use to make sure it is fresh. If you do not re-beat the icing, the lines will tend to break.

8 When piping dropped lines, work from left to right if you are right-handed (vice versa if you are left-handed), holding the nozzle on the horizontal. Work to alternate dots (dot 1 to 3, 3 to 5, etc.), then pipe a

second line on each curve, making it slightly shorter so that it drops slightly less. Repeat around the cake. As you pipe from dot-to-dot, keep holding the nozzle in line with the dots (rather than moving in an up and down motion) and let the icing fall naturally into a curve. As with all drop line work, keep the pressure constant and stop when you reach the finishing point.

9 Pipe another set of double dropped lines from the other alternate dots (2 to 4, and so on) so that they cross over.

10 Using a no. 0 nozzle, pipe a small set of curves around the middle of the cake, working from the top point of the set of three and letting the line drop so that the curve reaches the bottom point at the centre. Again, work on alternate dots to create the sequence.

## Stage 3: piping the inverted dropped lines

11 Place a smaller board in the centre of the cake and use a piece of tape to make a loop on the board so you can remove it easily later. Place a polystyrene separator that is smaller still on top. (If you do not have a separator you could use a jar, container or large tumbler; something that is wide but not too heavy.) Slide the cake to the edge of the turntable, place your fingers halfway across the separator/container (so you can remove your hand easily later), upturn the cake and separator/container and place back onto the turntable. Take extra care not to knock the cake as it is very likely to tip over!

12 You can now pipe the inverted lines at the top and base of the cake. Prepare a new bag of freshly beaten icing with a no. 1 nozzle. Always make up a new bag because, when handling the icing, the heat from your hands will cause the air bubbles in the icing to expand, causing the line work to break.

13 Drop double curved lines around the top of the cake in the same way as before, this time in reverse so that they will curve upwards when the cake is the right way round. Repeat around the base of the cake.

When piping the lines around the base of the cake, ensure you keep them in the same sequence as the top set. In other words, start on the same drop as on the first sequence on the top of the cake and continue round the cake. You can mark this dot with a piece of tape stuck to the bottom of the cake drum. You will find it easier pipe on this pattern at eye level.

14 Pipe the second set of lines on alternate dots over the top and allow to dry in the inverted position.

15 Pipe a set of inverted dropped lines around the side of the cake with a no. 0 nozzle to make a symmetrical pattern. You may find it easier if you elevate the cake and turntable by placing them onto a cake tin or box.

16 Allow all of the inverted scallops to dry: this should take approximately 10 minutes (depending on the amount of moisture in the air). When the icing is dry, carefully turn the cake back the right way round and place it back on the turntable.

## Stage 4: final decoration

17 Pressure pipe a simple dot and daisy design inside the lozenge and diamond shapes around the sides of the cake using a no. 1 nozzle (see page 52 for instructions on pressure piping daisies).

18 To hide the dots where the lines are joined you can make

tiny blossoms to place over the top. Thinly roll out some SFP (in this case, Pale Yellow) on a non-stick board dusted with cornflour and cut out as many blossoms as required using a miniature plunger cutter. Push each blossom shape out onto food-grade foam sponge to cup them, then attach to alternate points on the string work using a dot of royal icing on the back. When sticking them on dots around the base of the cake, tilt them up at 45° to balance the design.

The tiny blossoms are difficult to handle so use the icing on the tip of the nozzle to pick up each one and place it into position.

19 Using white royal icing and a no. 0 nozzle, pipe a tiny white dot in the centre of each blossom.

# Other string work designs

There are many different patterns that can be created using this technique but the basic principles of piping string work apply to all designs:

● Make sure the coating (royal icing or sugarpaste) is firm enough for when you invert the cake and always ensure the cake has been stuck to the board before covering.

● When preparing the template, make sure each sector is no wider than 1.3cm-1.6cm ($^1/_2$"-$^5/_8$").

● Repeat the first set of lines around the whole cake (on dots 1, 3, 5, and so on) before overlapping them with a second set (on dots 2, 4, 6, etc.).

● Always ensure that the patterns on the top, sides and base of the cake are lined up with each other.

*A celebration cake featuring oriental string work (pictured right) can be seen on pages 256 to 259.*

*Other design templates for string work are given on page 299.*

# Extension Work

Extension work is an advanced technique that looks exquisite on cakes. Sometimes known as bridge work, it consists of a series of parallel piped lines which start on the cake side and finish on a piped bridge so that they extend away from the cake. It takes a great deal of time and patience to achieve so is usually seen in competition work; however, this chapter covers the different methods that can be used to create extension work, some of which are slightly easier to master. It is advisable to practise on dummy cakes before attempting this technique on a real cake, then you can decide which of the methods you wish to use.

# *Tips* for creating successful extension work

● The icing sugar you use should be passed through a very fine sieve at least twice before use. Pre-mixed (and pre-sieved) extension icing made specifically for this purpose is available from cake decorating suppliers.

● Always ensure that the nozzles you are using are completely clean, i.e. that there is no hard icing inside them. Place used nozzles into warm water after use to dissolve any remaining sugar crystals.

● Always make sure you have a fine, damp artists' brush to hand to clean up any edges on the extension lines or to take off a line if it collapses.

● Most extension work designs require the lines to be straight and at an angle to the cake. To do this, tilt the cake towards yourself on a turntable and pipe the lines straight down, on the perpendicular.

● An easy way to finish off extension work and tidy up the ends of the lines is to pipe running beads along the top (see page 71). Pipe in towards the lines rather than on top of them to avoid breakages.

● Extension work is very fragile so is not easy to transport. Make sure the cake is stable and clamped into the box so there is no movement; do not bump the box otherwise the extension work is likely to break.

● The piping is extremely fine and needs to be consistent so the nozzles you use must be flawless. Look after your nozzles and avoid knocking or dropping them. If there is a dent in the tip of a nozzle this will cause the icing to curl as it is piped, so use a fine needle from the inside to straighten out the edge.

● When piping onto a cake with straight sides (such as a square or hexagon) use a ruler or graph paper to measure equal divisions on the cake. For cakes with curved sides (round and oval) fold a long strip of paper (such as a till roll) into equal sections.

## Materials

Coated cake, iced with royal icing or sugarpaste (see pages 34 to 41)

Royal icing, made to off-peak consistency (see page 33)

Extension icing

## Equipment

Strip of paper for template (a till roll is ideal)

Ruler

Small, round cutter or compass

Low-tack masking tape

Scriber

Tilting turntable

Nos. 0 and 2 plain piping nozzles

Piping bags

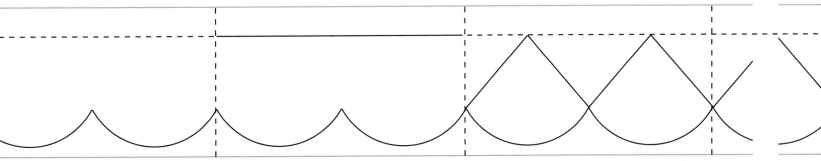

# *Preparation*

Before you can start piping extension work you must carefully measure and mark the cake into equal sections. An example of a design for a template is given on page 300.

1 Take a strip of paper such as a till roll, place it around the cake, mark the circumference then remove from the cake and cut the paper to size.

2 Fold the paper in half, into quarters, then, depending on the size of the cake, fold again as many times as necessary, keeping the proportions equal. Each section should measure between 2.5cm and 5cm (1" and 2") as a rough guide. If the cake has straight sides, fold the paper into sections to match the cake sides (i.e. quarters for a square cake, sixths for a hexagon, etc.) before folding into smaller proportions. This will ensure you have an equal pattern on each side.

3 Measure up approximately 1.3cm (½") from the base of the paper then mark this all the way along the strip on each fold with a pencil and ruler. Use a small, round cutter in the required size or a compass to make a scallop pattern along the paper, making sure the ends of the scallops meet the marks on the paper. These are the guides for the bridge work.

4 Mark a straight line near the top edge of the paper. The height of this line will be the guide for the top of the extension lines and should measure approximately 3cm (1¼") from the base of the scallops. Alternatively, you can create a triangular design by marking the centre point above each scallop and drawing from this point to the ends of each scallop.

5 Cut the template along the line and then place it round the cake and tape into position (make sure the tape does not touch the icing). Use a scriber to scratch along the top edge of the template and prick between each scallop.

*Tip* If you are using a sugarpasted cake, you may choose to cut the scallops out of the template, tape it round the cake then use a scriber to scratch the scallops into the icing as a guide for the drop line work. For royal iced cakes, it is better to drop the lines onto the cake freehand (this may take a little practice) because scratching the surface of the royal icing will create a powder and the drop line work will not stick to the side of the cake.

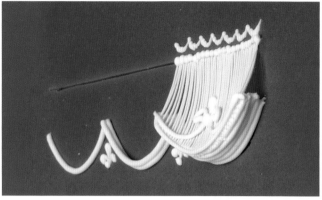

# Bridge work

## Method 1: built-up drop line bridges

1 Prepare a bag of freshly beaten off-peak royal icing with a no. 2 plain piping nozzle. Using the drop line technique (see pages 62 to 79), pipe the scallops all the way round the cake following the guidelines you have marked in the coating.

2 Using the same nozzle, drop another scalloped line directly on top of the first so that it stands proud of the cake side. Continue round the cake and allow to dry for at least 10 to 15 minutes.

 It is important to let the piped work dry at this stage. Never drop any more than 2 lines at a time before it dries out, otherwise the bridge work will tend to sag.

3 Repeat the same method as before with a further 3 lines to create a bridge, allowing the icing to dry after the 3rd and 4th lines. You will need to pipe no less than 5 lines in order for the bridge work to stand out enough from the side of the cake.

## Method 2: curved drop line bridges

This method is similar to the first but gives a slightly different effect. You will need to scratch the scallop pattern around the side of the cake using the template before starting to pipe.

1 Prepare a bag of freshly beaten off-peak royal icing with a no. 2 plain piping nozzle. Using the drop line technique, start at the bottom of the scallop and pipe a line no longer than 6mm (¼"). Continue round the cake.

2 Pipe another line on top of the first on the same radius, making it slightly longer, and repeat around the cake.

3 Follow the guide to make a third line: by this time the lines should start to form a curve that stands proud of the cake. At this point allow the piping to dry, otherwise the bridge work will collapse.

4 Pipe at least another 3 or 4 lines in sequences and leave to dry between every 2 sets. Eventually the ends of the scallops should meet up.

5 Let the bridges dry for at least half an hour in a warm, dry atmosphere before attempting to pipe the extension work.

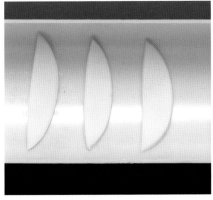  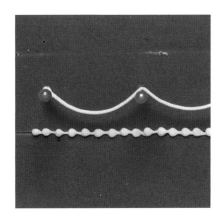

## Method 3: solid paste bridges

This is the easiest method if you are not confident at piping. In addition to the basic materials and equipment you will also need equal amounts of white sugarpaste and white flower paste mixed together, a small non-stick rolling pin and board, a round cutter, a small, sharp knife and a curved former or kitchen roll inner tube.

1 Blend equal amounts of sugarpaste and flower paste, knead together well then roll out to a thickness of approximately 2mm ($\frac{1}{16}$"). Using a round cutter with the same radius curve as the sections on the template, cut out the circles from the paste. Using a sharp knife, cut across the circle approximately 0.7cm to 1.3cm ($\frac{1}{4}$" to $\frac{1}{2}$") from the top: this top section will be used to form the bridge. Make as many as required for the cake plus at least 4 spares.

2 Place the pieces into curved formers and allow to dry for several hours.

3 In order for the bridges to be held firmly in position, stiffen approximately 60g (2oz) of royal icing by adding a level teaspoon of sieved icing sugar. Place this into a piping bag with a no. 1.5 or 2 nozzle.

4 Pipe a line onto the straight edge of 1 of the bridge pieces and stick it onto the side of the cake, following the marked guidelines made earlier. Repeat all the way round the cake, cleaning up any excess icing with a damp brush as you go. Allow to dry for approximately 30 minutes before piping the extension work, as described overleaf.

*Tip* You can use straight or curved bridges, as required for the design. For straight bridges, allow to dry flat on a sheet of food-grade foam sponge.

## Method 4: floating bridges

In addition to the basic materials and equipment you will also need sterilised glass-headed, stainless steel pins and white vegetable fat.

1 Divide the cake into equal sections using a paper template as described previously. Pinprick the sections all round the cake using a scriber.

2 Sterilise some glass-headed, stainless steel pins then lightly coat each one with white vegetable fat. Push them into the cake where the pinpricks are.

3 Place some freshly-beaten, off-peak royal icing into a piping bag with a no. 2 nozzle. Using the drop line technique, pipe scalloped lines from pin to pin. When piping this type of bridge, look down from the top of the cake as you pipe to keep the lines equidistant from the cake (approximately 1.3cm/$\frac{1}{2}$"). Leave the bridge work to dry for at least an hour before piping the extension lines (see overleaf).

4   When all the extensions have been piped (see below), leave in a warm place for at least an hour. When the icing is dry you can start to remove the pins carefully.

5   You may wish to pipe a double bridge above the first line: if this is the case, use the pins again to create bridges above and between the first set. Pipe the second bridges, leave to dry again for approximately 1 hour and then finish piping in the extension lines.

## Tip

To gain confidence with this technique it is better to extend the line slightly over the bridge; after every third line take an artists' brush and clean up the edges. Once you have mastered this art you will rarely need to use the artists' brush as you will be able to create clean edges as you go along with the piping nozzle.

# Extension lines

1   Prepare the extension icing for the fine lines. To make sure the icing is suitable, I recommend using specialised extension icing which has been sieved at least twice through a very fine sieve. Alternatively, you can refine royal icing in 1 of 2 ways:

- Place the icing into a square piece of (new) nylon stocking 1 heaped teaspoon at a time. Gather the corners of the nylon square and place it into a piping bag with a no. 0 nozzle: this will trap any large particles and will prevent the nozzle from becoming blocked.

- Cut a large square of nylon and force the icing through it into a bowl: this should then be fine enough to use with any fine nozzle.

2   Place the cake onto a tilting turntable so that the back of the cake is lifted slightly. The front of the cake should be at the lowest point so that, when piping the extension work, the lines will drop straight down on the perpendicular. If the cake is not tilted you may find that the lines start to sag.

3   Place a no. 0 nozzle into a piping bag and half-fill with extension icing. Starting just above or below the scratched line at the top of the design, pipe straight lines

down to the bridge. In order to achieve a professional result the spacing of the lines should be no greater than the width of the nozzle. However, when you are practising you can pipe them slightly wider.

# Tip

You may wish to start with a bigger piping nozzle for practising the extension work, such as a no. 1 or 1.5. Whichever size you choose, always aim to keep the spacing between the lines equal to the size of the nozzle.

4 Continue around the whole cake, turning the cake between each stage of the design to ensure that you are always piping on the perpendicular. If you are right-handed you will find it easier to work from left to right and

vice versa. If you make any mistakes, carefully remove the line with a damp artists' brush while the icing is still wet.

# Finishing touches

Once the extension work is complete you can add a few finishing touches to neaten up any uneven edges and complement the design. There are a few suggestions below; the main thing to remember is to keep the balance of the designs and not to overpower them.

- Add some pressure piped detail such as little daisies, chrysanthemums, fleurs-de-lys, or other flowers to suit the recipient or match a cake top design.

- Over pipe with scallops to balance the bridge work.

- To neaten the top edge of the extension work, pipe either running beads or drop a single line with a no. 1 nozzle.

# Cake Tops

A sugarpaste plaque is a quick and easy way to decorate a cake top and is also useful for practising your piping skills. The beauty of making a decorated plaque is that it can be made in advance and simply placed on top of the cake when it is needed. Instructions for making sugarpaste plaques are given on page 42.

This design shows how you can pipe lettering freehand onto a plaque or cake top and achieve good balance and composition. The lettering here is piped in the centre and to one side. If you are not confident at piping, it is feasible on sugarpasted cakes/plaques to pinprick the letters onto the surface with a scriber (you cannot do this on royal icing).

# 'Happy Birthday' Cake Top

## with freestyle lettering and piped flowers

## Techniques used:

Making a cake top plaque (see page 42)

Freestyle lettering (see pages 131 to 134)

Piped flowers (see pages 116 to 127)

Scrolls (see pages 80 to 93)

## Materials

Round sugarpaste plaque

Royal icing, made to off-peak consistency (see page 33)

SK Professional Liquid Food Colours: Holly/Ivy, Nasturtium (or your chosen colour)

Piped blossoms and buds in your chosen colour

## Equipment

Basic equipment (see pages 22 to 23)

No. 2 plain and no. 43 rope piping nozzles

1   Starting approximately a third of the way down from the top of the plaque and 5cm (2") from the left side, use a no. 2 nozzle and self-coloured (in this case white) royal icing to drop-line the 'A' in your chosen style.

2   Leaving a gap of 7mm (¼"), pipe the down stroke of the H beneath it, then pipe in the rest of the letter.

3   Pipe the down stroke of the B, ensuring you have even spacing, then pipe the rest of the letter, ensuring the bottom part is wider than the top to give stability.

4   Add the rest of the words 'Happy' and 'Birthday', keeping the letters even and straight.

5   Colour a bowl of royal icing orange (or your chosen colour) and fill a piping bag with a no. 1.5 nozzle. Over pipe the lettering, starting with the down strokes of the capital letters. The colour you choose for the over piping should complement the flowers, either in a monochromatic colour scheme or a harmonious colour scheme (see page 318).

6   Decorate the plaque as required to suit the recipient and the style of cake. To make the flowers shown here, pipe blossoms with sugar centres on a curved stem with buds and leaves. To ensure that the design is balanced, pipe the stem 4cm (1½") in from the edge of the cake and make sure the flowers are equidistant from the edge and the writing.

7   If you are piping onto a plaque, place it in position on top of the cake. Using a no. 43 rope nozzle, pipe shells around the edge at an angle of 45° to hide the join. Piping at this angle will also make the cake appear larger. Pipe a C scroll and reverse C scroll at the side of the plaque using a rope action, then add smaller C scrolls on top and a teardrop in the centre.

This cake top design shows how to create a composition with the lettering at the bottom.

# 'Best Wishes' Cake Top

## with freestyle lettering and piped flowers

### Techniques used:

Making a cake top plaque (see page 42)

Freestyle lettering (see pages 131 to 134)

Piped flowers (see pages 116 to 127)

Scrolls (see pages 80 to 93)

### Materials

Round sugarpaste plaque

Royal icing, made to off-peak consistency (see page 33)

SK Professional Liquid Food Colours: Bulrush, Cyclamen, Holly/Ivy

Piped roses in your chosen colour

### Equipment

Basic equipment (see pages 22 to 23)

No. 1 plain and no. 43 rope piping nozzles

1 Prepare a piping bag with white (or self-colour) royal icing and a no. 1 nozzle. Starting halfway down the plaque, approximately 2.5cm (1") in from the side, begin by piping the B for Best, followed by the lower case letters.

2 Pipe the W approximately 2.5cm (1") further in and below the B. (There are various ways of piping a W, but here it is shown with an X in the middle: this should not be any higher than the lower case letters to achieve good balance.) Add the rest of the word Wishes.

3 Over pipe all the letters in a deep colour, such as SK Cyclamen. Always remember that the bottom part of the letters should be larger to give them stability.

4 Decorate the plaque with your chosen decoration to suit the recipient. To create the rose design shown here, pipe a trellis in brown royal icing to balance the inscription. Pressure pipe wavy stems and two-tone green and brown leaves (see page 79), then add the piped roses and buds, using bulbs of royal icing to hold them in position.

5 If you are using a plaque, place it on top of the cake. Place some white royal icing in a large piping bag with a no. 43 rope nozzle and pipe a shell design around the outer edge of the cake or plaque. Pipe an S scroll and reverse S scroll at the bottom of the plaque, then add a C and a teardrop in the centre. Over pipe the shells and scrolls with dark pink icing using a no. 1 plain nozzle.

This design combines the techniques of simple stencilling and pressure piping to create a cake top scene. It is worth practising the stencilling technique on a spare plaque first so that you can experiment with the different effects that can be created.

# *Easter Cake Top*

## with pressure piped figure and stencilling

## Techniques used:

Making a cake top plaque (see page 42)

Pressure piped motifs (see pages 94 to 115)

Freestyle lettering (see pages 131 to 134)

Scrolls (see pages 80 to 93)

## Materials

Round sugarpaste plaque

Royal icing, made to off-peak consistency (see page 33)

SK Professional Dust Food Colours: Bluebell, Edelweiss (or cornflour)

SK Professional Liquid Food Colours: Bulrush, Holly/Ivy, Rose

Pressure piped Easter figure (see pages 101 to 102)

## Equipment

Basic equipment (see pages 22 to 23)

No. 10 SK paintbrush (for dusting)

No. 2 plain and no. 43 rope piping nozzles

1 To make the sky effect on the plaque, cut a cloud template from paper. Mix some Bluebell Dust Food Colour with either Edelweiss Dust Food Colour or cornflour to make a pale blue. Position the template a third of the way up the plaque and, using a no. 10 dusting brush, dust outwards from the centre of the template. Build up the colour gradually, taking care not to use too much at once.

2 Tear a piece of paper roughly in a straight line and place the torn edge along the horizon line. Use downward brushstrokes and Holly/Ivy Dust Food Colour to create the hill effect.

3 Carefully remove the prepared pressure piped figure (in this case the chick) from the cellophane, pipe a large bulb of icing onto the back and gently position it in the centre of the plaque, ensuring it stands proud of the sugarpaste surface.

4 Colour a small bowl of royal icing brown, place it in a piping bag and snip off the tip. Pressure pipe a tree and a fence directly onto the plaque. Do the same with a bag of green icing and pipe the leaves and the grass.

5 Make a piping bag narrower than normal and half-fill with pink royal icing. Snip off the tip to the size of a no. 4 nozzle. Pipe two lines of pink up opposite sides of another piping bag, fill this second bag with white icing, then cut a small 'V' at the tip and pipe little blossoms in a circular motion onto the tree. Hold the bag to one side and pipe in some buds.

6 If you are piping onto a plaque, place it in position on top of the cake. Place a no. 43 rope nozzle into a large piping bag and half-fill with white icing. Pipe a rope C scroll around the edge of the plaque at an angle of 45° to hide the join. Piping at this angle will also make the cake appear larger. Over pipe with a no. 2 nozzle using pink royal icing.

7 Using the drop line technique, pipe an inscription onto the cake top with the same bag of pink royal icing.

Upright numerals always look impressive on a cake. You could complement this cake top design by adding more run-out numerals to the sides of the cake and the cake board.

# 'Happy Anniversary' Cake Top

## with double-sided run-outs

## Techniques used:

Making a cake top plaque (see page 42)

Double-sided run-outs, see page 141

Freestyle lettering (see pages 131 to 134)

Pressure piping (see pages 48 to 61)

## Materials

Round sugarpaste plaque, plus extra sugarpaste for small plaque

Royal icing, made to off-peak consistency (see page 33)

SK Professional Liquid Food Colours: Berberis, Cyclamen, Holly/Ivy (or the same colours as the plaque and numerals)

Extra icing sugar

Run-out and reverse run-out for each numeral (see page 141)

Sugar roses

## Equipment

Basic equipment (see pages 22 to 23)

Oval cutter

No. 1 piping nozzles

Food-grade foam sponge

1 To make a plaque for the numerals, roll a piece of sugarpaste to approximately 7mm (¼") thick and cut out an oval (or the shape of your choice). Using an icing ruler, indent a line across the middle of the plaque to hold the numerals in position.

2 To hold the numerals in suspension, mix up a small bowl of royal icing coloured the same as the plaque (in this example, ivory using a hint of SK Berberis). Add a teaspoon of icing sugar to make it a stiffer consistency and place into a piping bag with no nozzle. Make up bag of rubbed-down royal icing, again to the same colour as the plaque, with a no. 1 nozzle. Colour some icing with liquid food colour to match the numerals (in this example, SK Cyclamen), rub down (paddle) with a palette knife and place into another piping bag with no nozzle.

3 Place the dried run-out numerals on a piece of food-grade foam, upturn the cellophane and carefully peel it away from the back. Stick the back and front pieces together with the same colour rubbed-down icing.

4 Snip off the tip of the bag of stiffened icing and pipe a line along the indentation in the plaque.

Carefully position the numerals into the icing, holding them in position for a few moments if necessary. Fill in the gutter with ivory-coloured royal icing and use a palette knife or artists' brush to smooth over the surface.

5 Using the bag of rubbed-down icing the same colour as the plaque, pipe filigree decoration over the top of the plaque to disguise the gutter across the centre (see page 237). For competition or fine work, you could use a no. 0 nozzle to make the filigree. Emboss a simple pattern around the edge using a shell tool then add scallops around the edge of the plaque using the same bag of icing.

6 Place the finished oval plaque on top of the cake top plaque, then add the inscription of your choice in a co-ordinating colour using freshly beaten icing. Add extra decoration, such as sugar roses, piped leaves and stems to complement your design. Finally, transfer the plaque to the cake top.

 *Tip*

For anniversary cakes, colour the numerals to co-ordinate with the anniversary, e.g. gold for 50 years.

If you are making a celebration cake in a hurry or do not feel confident enough to pipe directly onto a cake, this is a great way to add a special cake top decoration. Here, I have described how to create an embossed royal iced design on a sugarpaste plaque, but you could, of course, work straight on a cake (coated with sugarpaste) if required. One of the main advantages of using this technique is that it is much quicker and easier than modelling or piping sugar flowers.

 When you are piping in a design, always work from left to right if you are right-handed, vice versa if you are left-handed, and always top to bottom. This allows you to see where you have piped and prevents smudging.

# 'Happy Birthday' Embossed Cake Top

## with coloured gel design

## Techniques used:

Making a cake top plaque (see page 42)

Freestyle lettering (see pages 131 to 134)

Making a reverse embosser (see pages 170 to 171)

## Materials

Round sugarpaste plaque

Royal icing, made to off-peak consistency (see page 33)

SK Professional Liquid Food Colours: Cyclamen, Holly/Ivy

SK Scintillo Piping Sparkles: Gold

SK Piping Gel

## Equipment

Basic equipment (see pages 22 to 23)

Acrylic embosser prepared with your chosen design (see template on page 301)

Nos. 1 and 1.5 piping nozzles

1 Make a reverse embosser with the 'Happy Birthday' inscription (or other message of your choice) and the floral design. Remember that the lettering will appear backwards at this stage. Allow the embosser to dry fully.

2 Make the sugarpaste plaque (or cover a round cake with sugarpaste, see pages 40 to 41), then lightly dust the surface with a little cornflour and polish with the flat of your hand or a smoother. This will prevent the embosser from sticking to the paste. Position the embosser centrally over the sugarpaste and press down firmly and evenly (the sugarpaste should be fresh rather than firm).

3 Make up the required royal icing and piping gel for your chosen colour scheme; here, I have used SK Holly/Ivy and Cyclamen coloured royal icing and piping gel and SK Gold Scintillo Piping Sparkles.

4 Start by piping in the framework of the leaves using Holly/Ivy coloured royal icing in a piping bag with a no. 1 nozzle. Add the stalks using a no. 1.5 nozzle.

5 Place some Cyclamen coloured royal icing in a piping bag with a no. 1 nozzle. Pipe the outline of the lettering and the flowers.

6 Place some Gold Scintillo Piping Sparkles into a piping bag with no nozzle. Snip a tiny hole in the tip and fill in the lettering. Pipe in the centres of the flowers using the same bag.

7 Place the Cyclamen and Holly/Ivy coloured piping gel into piping bags, snip off the tip and fill in the flowers and leaves.

8 To finish, use a shell tool to emboss around the edge of the plaque. Using Cyclamen coloured royal icing and a no. 1 nozzle, pipe a rope action around the shell pattern to decorate. Place the plaque in position on top of the cake.

## Tip

For a slightly different effect, pipe the outline of the design as before, then paint with liquid colours of your choice to fill in the design. Pipe over the colour with neutral (uncoloured) SK Piping Gel.

# 'To Mother' Cake Top

## with piped flowers and freestyle lettering

## Techniques used:

Making a cake top plaque (see page 42)

Making a reverse embosser (see pages 170 to 171)

Combining drop line work with pressure piping (see pages 62 to 79)

Freestyle lettering (see pages 131 to 134)

Scrolls (see pages 80 to 93)

## Materials

Round sugarpaste plaque

Royal icing, made to off-peak consistency (see page 33)

SK Professional Liquid Food Colours: Cyclamen, Holly/Ivy

Extra icing sugar

Cornflour

## Equipment

Basic equipment (see pages 22 to 23)

Acrylic embosser prepared with your chosen design (see template on page 301)

Nos. 1, 1.5 and 2 plain, 43 rope, 56-58 petal (left- or right-handed) piping nozzles

This design also uses the embosser technique (as on the previous cake top) but the single-line lettering is piped freehand. If you are not confident at piping lettering, you can include this on the embosser so that you have a guideline on which to pipe. The fuchsias in this design are piped directly onto the cake, but you can use prepared piped flowers if you are short of time.

1 Prepare an acrylic embosser with a fuchsia design using the template. Allow to dry.

2 Emboss the fuchsia design into a sugarpaste plaque (or the top of a sugarpasted cake) while the paste is still soft. Make sure the outside edge of the flowers is equidistant from the edge of the circle around one side, press down evenly then remove the embosser.

3 Prepare a dark shade of SK Cyclamen coloured royal icing and place into a piping bag with a no. 1 nozzle. Pipe in the stamens of the flowers (each one should have a slight curve) and add a dot at the end.

4 Prepare a lighter shade of Cyclamen coloured royal icing and place in a piping bag with a no. 57 petal nozzle. Pipe in the skirt of each flower.

5 Rub down (paddle) some dark Cyclamen coloured, fresh royal icing with a palette knife and place into a piping bag with a no. 2 piping nozzle. Add the seed box of each flower by piping a teardrop, ease off the pressure and finish with a dot.

6 Take a piping bag and make a tight cone. Using fresh, stiff Cyclamen coloured royal icing (with a teaspoon of icing sugar added), half-fill the piping bag. Cut a small 'V' in the tip of the bag, checking the size of the hole against the size of the flowers to ensure they are in proportion to one another. Pipe the back two petals first, then the last two on top. Give the top petals a curve and lift the nozzle up as you pipe to add dimension to the flower.

7 Place some SK Holly/Ivy coloured royal icing into a piping bag with a no. 1.5 nozzle. Pipe in the stems using the drop line technique. When joining a short stem to a main stem, make sure it curves gracefully. Using the same nozzle, pipe in two of the smaller leaves.

8 To pipe the buds, place some pale Cyclamen royal icing in a piping bag with a no. 1.5 nozzle. Keep the nozzle upright, squeeze and pull through in the same way as for a teardrop.

9 Place some Holly/Ivy coloured royal icing into a piping bag with a petal nozzle (the size will depend on the size of your design). Hold the bag so that the nozzle is at an angle of around 40° (no more than 45°). Pipe down one side of the leaf using a back-and-forth motion, ensuring that the wider part of the nozzle (i.e. the thicker line) is in the centre. Pipe down the second side, again with the thicker piping in the centre. Using an artists' brush or a cocktail stick, draw down the centre of the leaf to create a central vein.

10 Add an inscription to the plaque/cake in your chosen style. Here, I have piped 'To Mother' freehand using the scratch piping technique with a rope effect.

11 If you are using a plaque, place it centrally on top of a cake. To disguise the join, pipe shells around the edge of the plaque using a no. 43 rope nozzle. Holding the piping bag at 45°, start at one side of the design, rather than at the top. Pipe 'S' scrolls over the shells with a dark shade of Cyclamen coloured royal icing.

12 If extra decoration is required, scratch pipe a few S and C scrolls in white around the writing.

# 'Merry Christmas' Cake Top

## with lettering motif

## Techniques used:

Making a cake top plaque (see page 42)

Lettering: using motifs as embellishments (see page 134)

Scrolls (see pages 80 to 93)

## Materials

Round sugarpaste plaque

Royal icing, made to off-peak consistency (see page 33)

SK QFC Liquid: Black

SK Professional Designer Dust Food Colour: Jet Black (optional)

SK Professional Liquid Food Colours: Daffodil, Holly/Ivy, Poinsettia

50:50 mixture of Squires Kitchen White Sugar Florist Paste (SFP) and white sugarpaste

SK Professional Dust Food Colour: Mint

Sugar flower centres (optional) (see page 119)

SK Sugar Florist Paste (SFP): Holly/Ivy

SK Confectioners' Glaze

## Equipment

Basic equipment (see pages 22 to 23)

No. 1 or 1.5 plain, 43 rope piping nozzles

Nos. 5 or 6, 10 SK Paintbrushes

Dimpled foam

SK Great Impressions Holly Leaf Veiner

This design shows how you can create a festive theme around central lettering. By changing the inscription and flowers to suit the recipient, this design can also be used for other celebrations such as birthdays and weddings.

1 Colour some royal icing with SK Black QFC Liquid. Add some SK Jet Black Dust Food Colour if required to strengthen the colour. Place in a piping bag with a no. 1 or 1.5 nozzle.

2 Using the drop line technique, pipe a long S scroll for the musical stave. Add four more lines then pipe a vertical line at each end. Pipe a treble clef and two sharp symbols.

3 Colour some royal icing with SK Poinsettia Liquid Food Colour and place into a piping bag with a no. 1 nozzle. Pipe the lettering over the top of the stave to spell 'Merry Christmas'. The capital letters should be just below and above the stave, with the smaller letters in-between the middle lines.

4 Using SK Holly/Ivy coloured royal icing in a piping bag with the tip cut off, pipe an S scroll flowing to the right above the stave and another flowing to the left below the stave to create the rose stems.

5 Make several Christmas roses from a mixture of sugarpaste and SFP (see page 213) and dust in the centre with SK Mint Dust Food Colour. Either pipe a series of yellow dots in the centre or use yellow centres made from granulated sugar (see page 119) and secure in place with a dot of royal icing.

6 Secure flowers and buds down the stem using the green royal icing. Using a piping bag with the tip cut off, pipe calyces on the back of the buds and add some mistletoe.

7 Thinly roll out some Holly/Ivy SFP and cut out several leaves using a small holly cutter. Vein in an SK Great Impressions Holly Leaf Veiner and allow to dry in a curved shape. When dry, brush with SK Confectioners'

Glaze and allow to dry for 24 hours. Secure in place with a little green royal icing.

8 Pipe in a few white berries on the mistletoe. To finish the design, add a few musical notes using the black royal icing.

9 Place the plaque in position on the cake. To pipe the decorative edge, place some royal icing in a piping bag with a no. 43 rope nozzle and pipe a continuous S scroll around the edge. When piping each S scroll, start off fine, get thicker in the middle, then taper off again to form a natural shape, emulating the acanthus leaf. When piping scrolls and shells around the edge of a cake, always finish on the side, not the top, so that any slight discrepancies won't be noticed.

*Tip* Make the flowers and leaves in advance so that they are ready to be placed on the plaque; this way you can complete all of the piped work in one go. Alternatively, you could use piped flowers and leaves for a slightly different effect.

This festive design shows how lettering can be piped on the lower half of the plaque with the decoration at the top. This is a particularly quick design to make, particularly if you make the motif in advance.

# 'Christmas Greetings' Cake Top

## with pressure piped motif and freestyle lettering

## Techniques used:

Making a cake top plaque (see page 42)

Pressure piped motifs (see pages 94 to 115)

Freestyle lettering (see pages 131 to 134)

Brush embroidery (see pages 168 to 174)

Scrolls (see pages 80 to 93)

## Materials

Round sugarpaste plaque

Royal icing, made to off-peak consistency (see page 33)

SK Professional Liquid Food Colours: Holly/Ivy, Poinsettia

Pressure piped Father Christmas motif (use head only from template, see page 114)

## Equipment

Basic equipment (see pages 22 to 23)

Nos. 1.5 plain, 44 rope piping nozzles

SK Paintbrush: no. 2

1 Using your chosen style of lettering, pipe the 'Christmas Greetings' inscription in self-colour (in this case, white) on the cake top or plaque using a no. 1.5 nozzle. Start the lettering halfway down the plaque, ensuring any decoration you wish to use will fit neatly above the inscription. Allow to dry.

2 Colour some royal icing with SK Poinsettia Liquid Food Colour and place in a piping bag with a no. 1.5 nozzle. Over pipe the lettering.

3 Make up some green royal icing using SK Holly/Ivy Liquid Food Colour, place in a piping bag and snip off the end to approximately the size of a no. 1 nozzle. Pipe stems above the

inscription. Add holly leaves on the end of the stems, then use a slightly damp no. 2 paintbrush with a fine point to brush-embroider the leaves. Add red berries down the stems of holly using the red royal icing.

4 Peel the Father Christmas motif away from the cellophane, pipe bulbs on the back at the top and bottom and carefully press into position on the plaque.

5 Place the plaque in position on top of the cake. Pipe a simple shell edging using a no. 44 rope nozzle. Using green royal icing in a piping bag with a no. 2 nozzle, pipe an S scroll over the top of the shells, starting in the centre.

# 'Noel' Christmas Cake Top

## with run-out lettering and lantern design

This festive design can be applied to a royal iced or sugarpasted cake. The beauty of this kind of design is that it can be applied directly to the cake top, or to a plaque that can be made in advance and placed on top of the cake at a later stage. If you are not yet confident using the skills required here, it is advisable to use a plaque so that you do not risk spoiling the cake. A plaque is also ideal to use on top of a gateau or torte where the surface is too soft to decorate.

### Techniques used:

Making a cake top plaque (see page 42)

Run-outs and collars (see pages 142 to 167)

Lettering as run-outs (see page 152)

Pressure piping (see pages 48 to 61)

Using an airbrush, see right

## Materials

Round sugarpaste plaque, at least 18cm (7") in diameter

Royal icing, made to off-peak consistency (see page 33)

SK Professional Metallic Lustre Dusts: Classic Gold, Copper

SK Professional Edible Metallic Paint: Gold

SK Confectioners' Glaze

SK Professional Liquid Food Colours: Bulrush, Daffodil, Holly/Ivy, Poinsettia

SK Professional Dust Food Colours: Holly/Ivy, Marigold or Nasturtium, Poinsettia, Sunflower

SK Professional Paste Food Colour: Holly/Ivy

50:50 mixture of Squires Kitchen White Sugar Florist Paste (SFP) and white sugarpaste

White vegetable fat

Clear alcohol (e.g. gin or vodka)

## Equipment

Basic equipment (see pages 22 to 23)

Template (see page 302)

Nos. 1 and 2 plain, 43 rope piping nozzles

SK Paintbrushes: nos. 1, 5, 6, 10

Kitchen paper

Holly leaf cutters: 2 sizes

Dimpled foam

## Using an airbrush

● When spraying run-outs, be extremely careful not to over-wet the sugar as fragile pieces may break. It is better to apply two or three coats of paint, allowing each stage to dry before applying the next.

● If you are using an airbrush which has not been used for some time, put a little vegetable oil into the needle and blow this through before use. This will protect against rust. After use, if you do not intend to use the airbrush for some time, put some vegetable oil into the needle and blow through. Wash with warm, soapy water before use to remove the grease.

● To clean the airbrush between colours, blow some clean, warm water through it until the spray is clear.

● To clean the airbrush after use, use lukewarm water and a little washing up liquid then rinse thoroughly.

1 Trace the lantern design onto a piece of paper and prepare a template underneath a piece of greased cellophane. Pipe the outline of the candle and the internal line work with freshly beaten royal icing and a no. 1 nozzle. Outline the basic structure of the lantern with a no. 2 nozzle.

2 Prepare a bowl of icing for run-out work (see page 33) and half-fill a piping bag with no nozzle. Snip off the end and flood the areas within the piped outlines. Always pipe alternate areas first (as shown) and allow to firm under a desk lamp before completing the design. When the first stage of the run-outs has dried (after approximately 10 minutes), flood the remaining areas of the design and leave to dry under the lamp for an hour.

3 Pipe in the scrolls and finishing touches on the lantern. If the sharpness of the outlines has been lost, over pipe the main structure using a no. 1 piping nozzle.

4 Make a thick, gold paint in a palette by adding some SK Classic Gold Metallic Lustre Dust to SK Edible Gold Paint. Using a soft no. 6 paintbrush, paint over the entire lantern with the gold paint. Add another coat if necessary to intensify the colour. Gild the candle in the same way with a mixture of SK Copper Metallic Lustre Dust and clear alcohol.

5 Paint over the flame with SK Daffodil Liquid Food Colour.

Dip a fine (no. 1) paintbrush into SK Poinsettia Liquid Food Colour and, starting at the base of the flame, paint an S scroll in an upwards direction. Next, paint a shallow C shape at the base of the flame but do not join the lines together.

6 Prepare the template for the run-out lettering under greased cellophane. Pipe the outline of the lettering using a no. 1 nozzle, then flood the letters with run-out icing. Place under a desk lamp to dry. Ideally, the run-outs should be left under the lamp to dry for 1 hour, then transferred to a warm, dry place overnight (such as an airing cupboard). However, if you are short of time, leave to dry under a lamp for 3 hours: the icing should then be firm enough to spray or dust.

7 Place a strip of greaseproof paper over the lower half of the lettering. Make sure you have opened up the knarled end of the airbrush for a wide spray. Place some SK Holly/Ivy Liquid Food Colour into the well of the airbrush and spray some colour onto a piece of scrap paper. When you are happy with the colour, carefully spray the top half of the letters.

8 Spray cooled, boiled water through the airbrush until it runs clear. Next, place some SK Poinsettia Liquid Food Colour into the well, cover the top half of the lettering and colour the lower half of the letters.

9 Place the traced design on top of the cake/plaque and pierce a dot in the middle of the flame with a scriber. Remove the template. Dip a dry, flat paintbrush (no. 10) into SK Sunflower Dust Food Colour, dab away the excess on a piece of kitchen paper and dust lightly from the centre of the dot. Brush the colour outwards, keeping the colour light. Add a pale orange tinge in the centre by brushing on a little SK Marigold or Nasturtium Dust Food Colour.

10 Place a no. 1 or 2 nozzle into a piping bag and half-fill with royal icing. Carefully remove the lantern run-out from the cellophane and pipe several bulbs of royal icing onto the back. Position the lantern on the cake so that the flame is over the dot and push down gently so that the design is slightly raised.

11 Take the tracing of the 'NOEL' letters and pierce a dot at the top and bottom of each letter to mark their position on the plaque. Remove the letters from the cellophane, pipe a line of royal icing on the back of each letter and secure in place. To illuminate the letters, pipe little flowers in the centre of each one (this also softens the line where the colours meet).

12 Secure the plaque on top of the cake and cover the sides if required. Use a no. 43 rope nozzle and freshly beaten royal icing to pipe shells around the edge of the cake at a 45° angle. This will hide the join and will also make the cake appear larger.

13 To lighten the design, pipe S scrolls over the shells using freshly beaten royal icing and a no. 2 nozzle. Start at the centre of the shell and pipe clockwise, working to the outside edge of each shell. Remember to keep the edge piping fairly simple so as not to detract from the central design. Pipe in extra detail such as scrolls, snow and icicles on the letters.

14 To make the flowers and leaves, use a 50:50 mixture

*Tip* Here, I have used an airbrush to create a two-tone effect. If you do not have an airbrush, you can dust or paint the letters as required. For monochrome lettering, you can colour the outline and run-out icing itself using SK Liquid Food Colours.

When colouring 2-tone letters, always use the darkest or strongest colour at the bottom to give the illusion of stability. Alternatively, use tints and shades of one colour: fading out the colour (without masking off) can create a soft, subtle effect.

of sugarpaste and SFP. Colour some paste with SK Holly/Ivy Paste Food Colour and cut out several holly leaves in two sizes. Twist each leaf and leave to dry overnight on dimpled foam. Mix together some SK Holly/Ivy Liquid Food Colour and SK Confectioners' Glaze and paint over each leaf. Add an extra layer of glaze if required.

**15** To make the Christmas roses, roll out some of the white sugarpaste/SFP mix and cut out several blossom shapes. Using a ball tool, thin the edges of the petals then cup each petal by pulling the tool from the centre of each petal to the edge. Cup each flower by pressing the tool into the centre of each flower and allow to dry.

**16** Using a dry, medium paintbrush (no. 5 or 6), dust the centres with a touch of Holly/Ivy Dust Food Colour. Take a small bag of Daffodil coloured royal icing and pipe a few dots in the middle of each flower to represent stamens.

**17** To make the rose buds, form a carrot shape of white paste and flatten out one side with your finger to thin the paste and create a fine edge. Roll up the length of the paste to create a bud shape, then roll the bud in your fingers and pinch off the excess paste at the base. You can create buds of different sizes using this method.

**18** Colour some royal icing with SK Bulrush Liquid Food Colour, place in a piping bag and snip off the tip. Pipe in the stems of the holly sprays. Add some leaves using light Holly/Ivy coloured royal icing.

**19** Secure the roses and buds in place using royal icing and add a green calyx on the buds. To achieve a strong red colour for the berries, colour some royal icing with SK Poinsettia Liquid and Dust Food Colours and leave (covered) for an hour for the colour to develop. Pipe berries onto the design to add a final touch of colour.

If you would prefer to use piped flowers and leaves in your design, instructions for the Christmas rose and buds are given on page 127. The holly leaves can be piped as off-pieces or piped directly onto the cake.

# Cake Projects

These cake designs show how you can put your royal icing skills into practice. They are given as a guide so you can change the colour scheme, piped detail and number of tiers to suit the celebration. Once you gain confidence you can create your own original cakes for weddings, anniversaries, christenings and other special occasions.

# Single~tier Celebration Cake

## with corner run-outs, scrolls and pressure piping

### Techniques used:

Run-outs (see pages 142 to 167)

Scrolls (see pages 80 to 93)

Pressure piping (see pages 48 to 61)

### Cake

20.5cm (8") square

### Cake covering

1.14kg (2lb 8oz) SK Marzipan

1.14kg (2lb 8oz) royal icing

*Full instructions for covering a cake are given on pages 34 to 41.*

### Materials

Royal icing, made to off-peak consistency (see page 33)

Corner run-out pieces (see pages 160 to 163)

### Equipment

Basic equipment (see pages 22 to 23)

30.5cm (12") square cake drum (board)

No. 1.5 or 2 plain piping nozzle

Greaseproof paper

Scriber

Templates (see page 297)

1.25m (49") x 15mm width satin ribbon for board edge

1 Cover a 20.5cm (8") square fruitcake with marzipan (see pages 34 to 37), then place centrally on a 30.5cm (12") square cake drum. Allow to firm.

2 Coat the top and sides of the cake with 2 coats of royal icing; for a finer finish, apply 3 or 4 coats (see pages 38 to 39).

3 Coat the board on which the cake is placed with royal icing using your chosen method (see page 39). Leave to dry overnight. When dry, the cake is ready to decorate.

4 Make a 10cm (4") square template from greaseproof paper, thus allowing 5cm (2") on each side for the run-outs. Fold the template in half twice to locate the centre and place in the centre of the cake. Using a scriber, mark the centre and the 4 corners of the square in the icing.

5 Beat some royal icing well to expel any air and place in a piping bag with a no. 1.5 or 2 piping nozzle. Using the drop line technique, pipe a cross in the centre of the cake, extending each line out to the corners of the square marked earlier.

6 Pipe a little dot approximately 1.3cm (½") from the centre in-between each line of the cross. Using these dots as a starting point, pipe an inward curve and finish as an S scroll. Repeat on either side of each line of the cross. Add C scrolls and reverse C scrolls in towards the centre and at the base curve of each S scroll. Curve the centre of each of these scrolls to meet the base of the S scrolls.

7 Pipe petals in the centre of each quarter of the design, similar to the shape of a fleur-de-lys, by making a dot and pulling through with the piping nozzle. Add a dot in the centre and then pipe in a few leaves with a slight inward curve. Add a few more curved leaves to the design, then add 1 at the end with a dot. The main leaf at the end of the scroll is straight.

*Tip* This design can be adapted for a larger square or an oblong: simply adjust the template as required to fit the cake.

8 Make up some royal icing to a stiff consistency (see page 33) and pipe a large dot in the centre of the cake. Pipe a series of pull-ups around the dot to create the spiky dahlia for the centre of the design (see page 73).

### Tip

Depending on the design of the cake, you could also pipe a wild rose or large blossom instead of a dahlia; the flower can be in colour if required. If you are piping a dahlia, a graduated, monochrome colour scheme works well: simply pipe the first, lower petals in the darkest tint, then add a little more white royal icing with each layer.

9 Mark the centre of each cake side using a ruler and a scriber. Pressure pipe a simple daisy design on all 4 sides of the cake. Add straight lines down the sides from the corners and finish with a dot to balance the design.

10 You will need 4 horizontal corner pieces and 4 upright pieces for this design, plus spares to allow for breakages. Prepare the run-out templates under greased cellophane and pipe all of the run-out pieces (see pages 160 to 163). Allow to dry fully under a lamp.

### Tip

If you wish to make the run-out pieces before covering the cake, they can be kept in a safe place until the cake is required. Alternatively, you may choose to make and cover the cake first but remember to allow enough time for the run-outs to be made.

11 To stick the corner pieces onto the cake, pipe dots of royal icing underneath where each piece will be placed and gently press the run-outs into position. Make sure the icing is well rubbed down so that the edge pieces settle into the icing; if the icing is too stiff, you will have to press the piece down onto it, thus increasing the risk of breaking it. Allow to dry.

12 Secure the upright pieces in place along the inner edges of the corner pieces using fresh, stiff royal icing to hold them securely in place. These pieces are optional so can be omitted from the cake if required.

13 To finish the cake, pipe a running bead around the base of the cake to hide the join between the cake and the board. Secure a length of ribbon around the board edge with the join at the back.

# Three~tier Hexagonal Wedding Cake

with gazebo, run-out panels and collars

## Techniques used:

Dowelling a cake (see pages 46 to 47)

Run-outs and collars (see pages 142 to 167)

Scrolls (see pages 80 to 93)

## Cakes

15cm (6") hexagon

20.5cm (8") hexagon

25.5cm (10") hexagon

*NB: All cakes are measured point-to-point.*

## Cake covering

2.78kg (6lb 2oz) SK Marzipan

2.78kg (6lb 2oz) royal icing

*Full instructions for covering a cake are given on pages 34 to 41.*

## Materials

Royal icing, made to off-peak consistency (see page 33)

SK Professional Liquid Food Colours: Bluebell, Holly/Ivy, Violet (or colours of your choice)

SK Edible Silver Paint

Gazebo with pedestal of flowers (see pages 153 to 158)

50:50 mixture of Squires Kitchen White Sugar Florist Paste (SFP) and white sugarpaste (optional, to make a domed top for gazebo)

## Equipment

Basic equipment (see pages 22 to 23)

28cm, 33cm, 38cm (11", 13", 15") round cake drums (boards)*

8 cake dowels

Collar and panel templates (see pages 302 to 304)

Spare boards, at least 23cm, 30.5cm and 40.5cm (9", 12" and 16") square

Nos. 0, 1 and 1.5 (optional) plain piping nozzles

SK Paintbrushes: fine and large

8cm (3¼") round cutter

Rounded former (e.g. a teacup)

SK Barley Twist pillars: 4 x 10cm (4"), 4 x 12cm (4¾")

3.35m (11ft) x 15mm width satin ribbon for board edge

*You can use hexagonal boards if preferred – either will work with this design. Be aware that some boards are measured flat-edge to flat-edge. Always ensure the board is 13cm (5") larger than the cake, i.e. 6.5cm (2½") on either side when the cake is positioned centrally.

1. Marzipan all three cakes, starting with the top then covering each side one at a time (see page 37). When trimming the corners, remember that the marzipan must be cut towards the opposite point so that the corners can be chamfered. Allow to firm.

2. Coat the top of the cake with royal icing and allow to dry (see page 38). Follow on with the first set of alternate sides (sides 1, 3 and 5), allow to dry, then complete the remaining alternate sides (2, 4 and 6). When applying the second coat, start with the top again, followed by the second set of alternate sides (2, 4, 6), then the first three (1, 3, 5) to keep the sides even. Repeat if a third coating is required.

3. Once the cakes are coated, cover the boards in the usual way (see page 39). Dowel the middle and base tiers with 4 dowels each, cutting the dowelling rods to size according to the type of pillars you are using (see page 47). Position the dowels so that they are lined up with 4 corners of the cake (rather than 4 sides).

4. Draw the templates for the no. 1 (plain) collar on each cake: check that the internal framework is approximately 1.3cm (¼") inside the cake sides and the external framework 1.3cm (¼") outside the cake sides and adjust to fit if necessary. Repeat for the three large collars (no. 2), this time making sure that the internal framework is the same size as the cake and the external framework is approximately 1.3cm (¼") wider than

the first collar on each side. Secure each template to a spare board and cover with a sheet of greased cellophane.

5 Make the templates for the panels, again checking that they are the correct size for the coated cakes: each panel should be the same height as the cake sides and the same width as the outside edge of the first collar (this is what they will be attached to).

These panels are made for 3 different sizes of cakes which are all 7.5cm (3") high. They can easily be enlarged or made smaller as required. If you need to increase the height of a panel but not the width you can add extra strips at the top and bottom, as shown in the template (see page 304).

6 Outline collars 1 and 2 for each tier using a no. 1 or 1.5 piping nozzle (see pages 164 to 166 for further instructions on making collars). Cross over the internal lines on the larger collar to achieve sharp corners.

7 Make up a bowl of run-out icing (see page 33), place in a piping bag and cut a small hole in the end no bigger than a no. 1 nozzle. Flood in all 6 collars and leave under a desk lamp to dry.

8 Pipe in the scroll work on the no. 2 collars, ensuring that the scrolls touch the internal lines of the collar. Add some extra detail on the run-outs and scalloped pieces if required, making sure you do not overpower the design. For the picot dots around the edge of the collar, rub down some off-peak icing well: you may have to add a few drops of water so that, when piping, the take-off comes away cleanly without a point. Place into a piping bag with a no. 1 nozzle and pipe two rows of dots (2 + 1) on the large radius curves and a single line of

dots on the pointed scallops around the outside edge. Allow to dry.

9 Prepare the template for the side panels under greased cellophane. Pipe in the filigree sections on the left and right with a no. 0 nozzle (see page 237), making sure it goes just over the lines of the template to strengthen the panel (this will prevent it from dropping out when the panel is dry).

10 When the filigree is dry, outline the whole panel with a no. 1 nozzle. When complete, flood in with run-out icing and allow to dry under a desk lamp.

If the filigree doesn't look strong enough to hold in place, add in a few leaves touching the sides of the run-out to strengthen it.

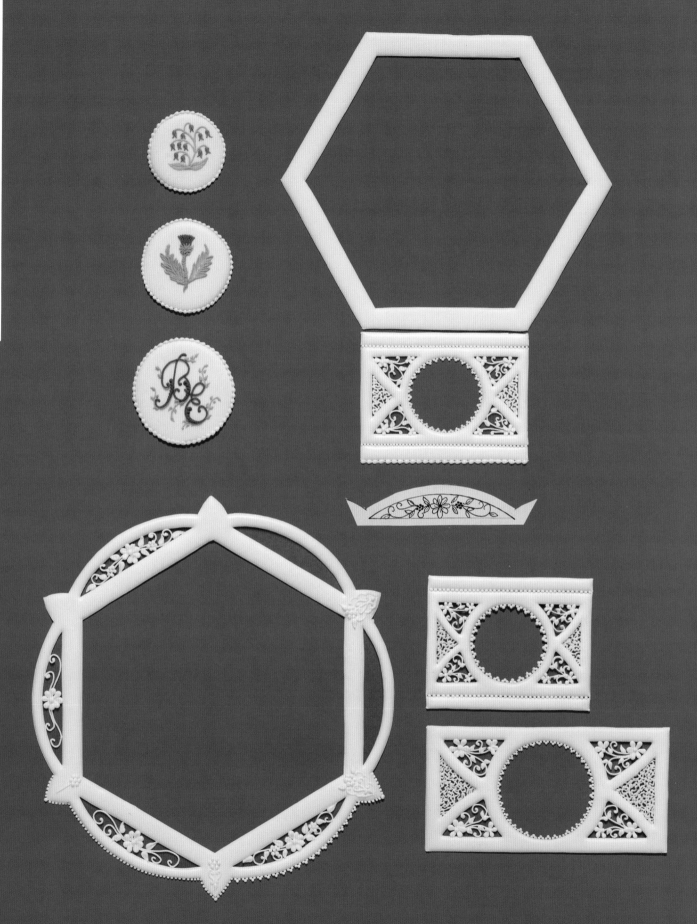

**11** Pipe in the scrolls and flowers, making sure that the scrolls touch the edges of the panels so they stay firmly in place. If there are any slight gaps, pipe in a tiny spot of rubbed-down icing using a fine nozzle to ensure the scrolls adhere to the panel.

**12** Using the centre of the panel templates, draw 6 circle templates for each tier and secure under greased cellophane. Pipe the outlines with a no. 1 nozzle then flood with run-out icing to make solid circular plaques (see page 146). Allow to dry then pressure pipe your chosen details to suit the occasion: this cake features a combination of thistle, bluebell and monogram motifs in blues and greens.

**13** Using the panel templates as a guide, stick the circles to the sides of the cakes with rubbed-down icing, making sure they are central. Finish with a single row of picot dots around the outer edge of each circle.

**14** Stick the no. 1 collars in place on each tier with rubbed-down icing and allow to firm. Make up a bag of off-peak royal icing with a no. 1 or 1.5 nozzle and pipe a line along the top and bottom edges of one of the panels. Stick it in place so that the top edge touches the collar. Pipe down one side of this panel, then repeat with the second panel, ensuring it adheres to the first panel and the collar. Repeat all the way around the cake and then pipe running beads along the base and sides of the panels to neaten the joins.

**15** Once the panels are in position, you can pipe the decoration on the board to match the design on the no. 2 collar. To make a template for the board, copy the template of the top collar design for each tier and cut along the outside edge and 1 scallop. Make a tab on the top from tape so that you can lift it off without damaging the piping. Place on the board and pipe the outside edge with a no. 2 nozzle. Pipe the inner line with a no. 1 nozzle, either point-to-point or scalloped. Mark the centre of the daisy through the template with a scriber so that the pressure piped design balances with the top design and then remove the template and pipe in the same detail as on the no. 2 collar. Repeat around all 6 sides of the cake.

**16** Use rubbed-down icing to stick the no. 2 collars in place on top of the first collars. Make sure they are lined up with the first collar on each cake and take extra care not to push down on them as they are very fragile.

When sticking down any collar, make sure the icing is well rubbed-down to expel the air. If the icing is too stiff, the collar is more likely to break when you press it into place. Moreover, if the icing is stiff you will increase the height that the panels need to be in order to reach the collar.

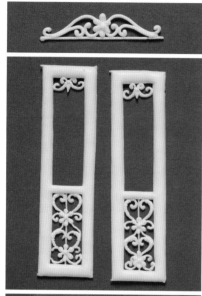

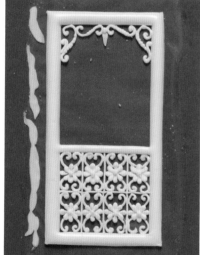

**17** Once all the collars are in place, pipe straight 2-1 dropped lines around the inside of the collars (see page 68) and add scratched scallops to the inside line to give it finer detail (see page 69).

**18** Make the gazebo following the instructions on pages 153 to 158. This one has been made without the tulle backing but you may use it for extra support if you prefer. To make a domed top rather than a pointed one, cut out an 8cm (3¼") circle from a 50:50 mix of SFP and sugarpaste, dust the top and bottom surfaces with icing sugar and place into a rounded former such as a cup. Use a rolling pin to push the paste down into the cup to create a rounded finish. Make 2 in case one doesn't form correctly and allow to dry.

**19** Using a no. 1 or 1.5 plain nozzle, decorate the top of the dome with a scroll pattern (see picture, below left). Repeat the same design on the centre of the middle and bottom tiers to balance the cake, ensuring that each design fits within the pillars. Assemble the gazebo (see pages 156 to 158) and position the flower stand inside.

**20** Paint the 8 pillars with edible silver paint and allow to dry. Trim the 3 boards with ribbon. Place the 4 longest pillars in position on the bottom tier and carefully place the middle tier on top, ensuring that the collars line up. Position the shortest pillars on the middle tier and position on the top tier in place, then place the gazebo on top with the doors at the front.

# Flower stand

To finish off the gazebo, you can place a flower stand inside (or figurines to suit the occasion). This should be done before the roof is attached.

**1** Mix equal quantities of SK White SFP and white sugarpaste or mix up some SK Instant Mix Pastillage. Roll out thickly and cut out 3 hexagons using the templates (see page 296): 1 large for the base and 2 small. Make an indentation in the top of one of the small hexagons to hold the flowers later. Roll a thick sausage of paste and cut to size for the upright piece. Allow all pieces to dry. Secure the pieces for the flower stand together with royal icing.

**2** Colour some SK SFP the colour of your choice for the flowers and use a mini blossom plunger cutter to make several blossoms. Cup the blossoms on a piece of foam by pressing into each one with a ball tool and allow to dry. Make several miniature leaves from SK Holly/Ivy SFP and soften with a ball tool.

**3** Make a cone from the SFP/ sugarpaste mix (or pastillage) and secure this to the top of the flower stand. Attach leaves around the base of the cone, then secure flowers onto the cone itself. Pipe some coloured leaves in-between the flowers, then add a piped yellow centre to each flower.

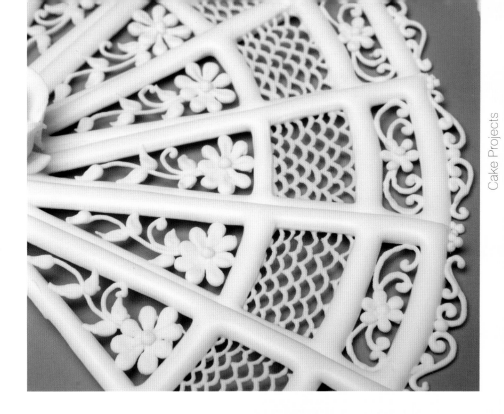

## Techniques used:

Run-outs (see pages 142 to 167)

Pressure piping (see pages 48 to 61)

Scrolls (see pages 80 to 93)

Freestyle lettering (see pages 131 to 134)

## Cake

23cm (9") round

## Cake covering

1.14kg (2lb 8oz) SK Marzipan

1.14kg (2lb 8oz) royal icing (or sugarpaste if preferred)

*Full instructions for covering a cake are given on pages 34 to 41.*

## Materials

Royal icing, made to off-peak consistency (see page 33)

SK Professional Liquid Food Colour: Bluebell

Piped rose (see page 122) or rose moulded from sugarpaste

## Equipment

Basic equipment (see pages 22 to 23)

30.5cm (12") round cake drum

Fan templates (see page 305)

No. 0, 1, 1.5 plain and nos. 43 and 44 rope piping nozzles

66cm (26") x 15mm width satin ribbon for board edge

1 Cover the top and sides of the cake separately with marzipan to achieve squared edges (see pages 34 to 36). Place the cake centrally on the cake drum.

2 Colour enough royal icing to cover the cake and board blue using SK Bluebell Professional Liquid Food Colour (see page 45). Coat the top of the cake then the sides and repeat to create two or three complete coats (see pages 38 to 39). If you would prefer to cover the cake with sugarpaste, cover the top and sides of the cake separately in the same way as for the marzipan.

3 Ice the edge of the board with well rubbed-down blue royal icing or outline and flood in with run-out icing (see page 33). If you are using sugarpaste, cover the edge of the board with a long strip and trim neatly around the edge. Allow to dry.

4 Choose the design you would like to use for the fan and prepare

## *Tip*

While the marzipan and icing is drying you can make the fan pieces to give them plenty of time to dry.

the template of your choice under a sheet of greased cellophane. Make a tab at the end of the template so that you can move it under the cellophane to make each piece separately. Different designs are given on page 305, so you can either use the same one for each piece or alternate them with different patterns.

5 To make the fan design shown on the cake, use a no. 0 nozzle and fresh, stiff icing to pipe in the scallops on the design. Pipe the scallops in lines, making sure there is a slight overlap at the edge and also that they touch each other.

You will find it easier to pipe the scallops if you position the template on its side, with the point on the left if you are right-handed and vice versa.

6 Use a no. 1 nozzle to outline the fan shape, overlapping the internal lines slightly. Once the outline is complete, use run-out icing to flood the design.

7 Make 8 fan pieces to this stage using the template plus 2 extra pieces to allow for breakages. Allow to dry under a desk lamp.

8 When the pieces are dry, pipe in the scroll work with a no. 1 nozzle. Make sure that the lines or the leaves touch the sides of the run-out so that it won't fall out when lifted from the cellophane. Pipe in the daisy (see page 52), again so that it touches the edges. Do this while the scrolls are still soft otherwise the lines might break.

9 While the fan pieces are drying, make a template for the top of the cake and divide into 36 equal sections (or slightly less if preferred, as long as it is divisible by 4): this is done in the same way as for oriental string work preparation (see page 179). Mark the edge of the cake into sections for the scrolls then pipe roped S scrolls

Tip

To ensure that all the pull-ups are the same height you could use a scriber and length of ribbon to mark a guideline all the way around the cake.

around the edge of the cake with a no. 43 rope nozzle (see page 84). Over pipe the scrolls with the same nozzle.

10 Using a no. 44 star nozzle, pipe pull-ups around the base of the cake, piping onto the side of the cake and pulling the nozzle upwards to a point.

11 Use a no. 2 and no. 1 nozzle respectively to pipe dropped line scallops around the side of the cake (see page 67). Use a no. 1 nozzle to pipe vertical lines at each quarter point of the cake then add dots where the scallops join.

12 Using a no. 2 nozzle, over pipe the teardrops at the base with drop line work (see page 92). Over pipe shallower scallops with a no. 1 nozzle then use a no. 1.5 nozzle and rubbed-down icing to pipe dots at the top of the teardrops.

13 Make a paper template of the daisy design if needed and scribe where the daisies will go on the cake. Pipe in the left-to-right

scallop to the centre of where the daisy will be, then the right-to-left scallop. Add the stalks above and on either side, then add the full daisy and then the half daisies. Repeat 4 times around the cake then use stiff icing and a no. 1.5 nozzle to pipe in the leaves.

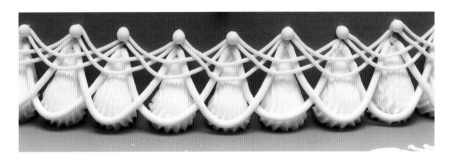

14 Scratch pipe a scallop or reverse S scroll design around the edge of the board (see page 69).

15 Mark the centre of the cake using the template made earlier. Pipe a line of slightly rubbed-down royal icing on the left hand side of the first fan piece with a no. 2 nozzle. Stick the fan piece in place with the point in the centre. Pipe a line on top of the right-hand side of the same piece and place the second one in position so that it overlaps the first. Repeat until the 8th and final piece is in position (you don't need to pipe down the right hand side of the last piece).

16 Pipe the inscription using a no. 2 plain nozzle in your chosen style (see pages 131 to 134). Add leaves or other embellishments to illuminate the letters with a no. 1 nozzle.

17 Pipe in the scroll decoration with a no. 1.5 nozzle then stick 3 piped or modelled roses onto the point of the fan. Cut a V shape from the tip of a piping bag and pipe in the leaves to finish. If the cake looks imbalanced you can add more scrolls or leaves to balance the design.

Different design ideas for the fan pieces

# Barrel Scroll Wedding Cake

## with curved off-pieces and filigree piping

## Techniques used:

Dowelling a cake (see pages 46 to 47)

Drop line work (see pages 62 to 79)

Run-outs (see pages 142 to 167)

Pressure piping (see pages 48 to 61)

## Cakes

15cm (6") round

25.5cm (10") round

## Cake covering

1.9kg (4lb 3oz) SK Marzipan

1.9kg (4lb 3oz) royal icing

*Full instructions for covering a cake are given on pages 34 to 41.*

## Materials

Royal icing, made to off-peak consistency (see page 33)

SK White Sugar Florist Paste (SFP) or equal amounts of White SFP and white sugarpaste

White vegetable fat

SK Professional Liquid Food Colour: Cyclamen (or colour of your choice)

## Equipment

Basic equipment (see pages 22 to 23)

23cm and 33cm (9" and 13") round cake drums

4 dowelling rods

Templates: 2 x cake top, cake sides, large and small barrel (rectangle), large and small petal, large and small scallop piece (see pages 305 to 307)

Thin plastic (side scrapers are ideal) or thick card for stencils

Barrel former (see right)

Curved plastic former or kitchen roll inner tube

Clean kitchen cloths

Nos. 1.5, 2, 3 plain, no. 42 rope piping nozzles

SK Paintbrush: no. 2

10cm (4") SK Barley Twist Pillars

1.3m (51") x 15mm width satin ribbon for board edge

# *Barrel former*

In order to make the barrel decorations on this cake, you will need to make a curved former on which to dry the pieces. I have used a broom handle and shoebox which, once made, can be used again on future projects.

## Materials

Royal icing, made to off-peak consistency (see page 33)

## Equipment

Broom handle (or similar)

Hand saw (for cutting broom handle)

Shoebox (or similar)

2 x nails, at least 6.5cm (2½") long

Hammer

Craft knife

1 Cut the broom handle into lengths approximately 2cm (¾") less than the length of the shoebox; you will need at least 3 pieces of handle or 4 if you are making a three-tier cake. This should give you enough room to dry all the barrel pieces, plus a few spares to allow for breakages.

2 Hammer 6.5cm (2½") nails into the ends of the broom handle lengths, keeping them central.

3 Cut grooves into the ends of the box with a craft knife and place the formers (broom handle lengths) into position so that the nails rest in the grooves.

 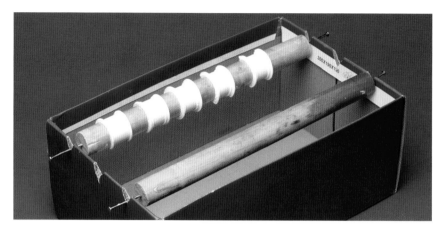

1 Cover the top and sides of the cakes separately with marzipan to give a clean, sharp edge (see pages 34 to 36). Place the cakes centrally on their respective cake drums and allow to firm.

2 Cover the cakes with two or three coats of royal icing as required then cover the boards (see pages 38 to 39). Once the icing is dry, dowel the bottom tier with 4 dowelling rods, ensuring you cut them to the required length for the pillars you are using (see pages 46 to 47). Dowelling the cake is essential if you are using a fruit cake for the top cake, otherwise it will collapse. While the template is on the cake, mark the central point with a scriber; this will be a marker for the lily.

3 Using the template, cut the barrel (rectangle) and petal shapes out of thin plastic side scrapers or thick card to make the stencils needed for the cake.

4 Cut lengths of cellophane at least 2.5cm (1") bigger than the

stencils. Stick to a flat surface with masking tape and grease with white vegetable fat.

When taking the cellophane off the roll, keep the curved side uppermost, the same as the curve of the barrels.

5 Prepare a bag of fresh, off-peak royal icing with a no. 2 nozzle and put to one side with a damp cloth covering the tip to prevent the icing from drying out.

6 Using a small, cranked palette knife, rub down (paddle) the icing to expel the air. Hold one of the rectangular stencils on a piece of greased cellophane and spread the icing onto the stencil, leaving the shape on the greased cellophane.

7 Use the piping bag prepared earlier to pipe a line of icing on the broom handle former. Stick the end of the cellophane onto the icing, roll the cellophane around the former by turning the nail and stick the other end to the former with icing to hold it in place.

8 Clean the stencil using a damp cloth and wipe with a dry cloth. This will give you a clean edge each time you use it. Make sure the stencil is at right angles to the former so that it dries straight.

9 Repeat this process to make 8 curved pieces plus 4 spare in the larger size for the top edge of the cakes and 8 plus 4 spare in the smaller size for the base of the cakes. If you work quickly enough you may be able to make two or three stencils at a time; start with one or two at a time until you develop confidence with this technique.

10 Using no. 3 and no. 2 nozzles, outline the barrel

design with freshly beaten icing. You will find it easier to work on the former in the cradle that is closest to the edge of the box: hold the nail with your left hand and turn the former anticlockwise. Rest your piping hand on the edge of the box to keep it steady and pipe a dropped line with the no. 3 nozzle on the outer edges of the rectangles. Repeat the process using a no. 2 nozzle, this time piping a dropped line just inside the no. 3 lines. Over pipe on top of the no. 3 line with the no. 2 nozzle. Allow to dry.

11 Prepare a length of greased cellophane, this time the other way up so the edges curl upwards. Stick to the work surface with masking tape. Use the template prepared earlier, rubbed-down icing and the cranked palette knife to make the petals in the same way as before. Make no more than 4 at a time and place into a curved former so that they dry on the inside of the curve. Stick the edges of the cellophane to the former with a line of royal icing to hold them in position.

12 Repeat this method to make 8 large petals plus 4 spares for the bottom tier and 8 large and 8 small plus 4 spares of each size for the cake top decoration. Allow to dry.

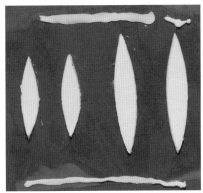

13 To make the cake top decoration, prepare a piping bag of fresh, off-peak icing with a no. 1.5 nozzle. Place a small amount of icing into a bowl and add a little cold water to make it the correct consistency for run-outs (see page 33).

14 Prepare the larger scallop template underneath a piece of greased cellophane (see page 145). Pipe the outline using the no. 1.5 nozzle, overlapping the internal lines to achieve sharp corners. Snip off the tip from the bag of run-out icing so that the hole is no more than the size of a no. 1 nozzle. Fill in each segment of the shape until they join in the middle.

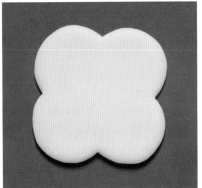

15 Make two smaller scalloped pieces in the same way and allow all the pieces to dry under a desk lamp. When dry, the cake top decoration can be assembled.

16 To make the flower centre for the cake top decoration, grease a small square of cellophane and use a no. 1.5 nozzle to pipe a dot the size of a large pea. Pipe pull-ups around the base of this dot, then continue with subsequent layers to cover it. Repeat to make a second flower centre for the bottom tier and allow to dry.

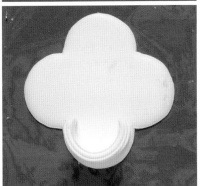

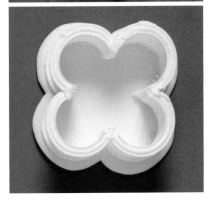

*Tip* The petals for the water lily can be made as run-outs made to guttering consistency (see page 33) if preferred.

**17** Thickly roll out either White SFP or equal amounts of SFP and sugarpaste mixed together to a thickness of approximately 1.3cm (½") and cut to the same size as the larger scalloped base piece. Stick the base run-out on the sugarpaste plaque then stick one of the two smaller scalloped run-outs onto the base pieces with a little rubbed-down royal icing.

**18** Carefully remove 4 small barrel pieces from the former and stick them onto the scalloped shape with royal icing. If there are gaps between the barrels, fill these in using the bag with freshly beaten icing then pipe running beads at the front to neaten the join. Stick the other small scalloped run-out on top of the barrels.

**19** Pipe filigree round the base and running beads around the joins. Pipe a dotted daisy with three leaves on either side on each of the four barrels.

**20** To make the lily on top, pipe a dot of stiff royal icing in the centre and place the stencilled petals on top. Stick the large petals on first, allow to dry, then place the small petals on top and in between the large ones. Carefully stick the flower centre in place. Repeat in the centre of the bottom tier.

**21** Place the top tier onto a tilting turntable. Using the cake top template, mark then pipe 4 dropped line scallops with a no. 2 nozzle down the sides of the cake. Use a no. 1 nozzle to pipe a line directly underneath, then another no. 1 line on top of the no. 2 line to create a 2-1 build-up (see page 68). Repeat on the top of the cake so that the scallops match up. Mark where the daisy will be piped approximately halfway between the centre of the top scallop and the base. Drop line a curve, following the line of the top scallop. Pressure pipe a daisy and leaves (5 or 7 leaves, depending on the size of the cake) on either side of the line.

To make the templates for the 2-1 line work on the cake, copy the whole template then cut out the sections required for each scalloped piece.

**22** Repeat the above step for the lower tier, this time making a triple scallop shape in the 2-1 line work.

**23** Trace the radius curve for the top tier and the curve of the scallop onto paper. Make a template with a small tab on the top made from sticky tape (so you can pick up the template after piping). Place this on the board and pipe 2-1 line work just outside the paper template so as not to damage the piping as you lift the template.

Repeat 4 times around the cake. Make a template in the same way for the lower tier and repeat the same method.

24 Prepare some slightly rubbed-down coloured icing in a piping bag with a no. 0 nozzle. I have used SK Cyclamen but you can change the colour to suit the occasion. Pipe the filigree inside the 2-1 line work on the cakes and boards with the nozzle resting on the surface of the cake. Proceed to pipe wavy, irregular lines to fill in the space. Make sure none of the lines are straight – the effect should look like crazy paving.

25 Using the template as a guide, pipe a dropped line down the sides of each cake from the ends of the scallops and continue in a square shape to outline where the barrel pieces will go on the cake and board.

26 Using a no. 42 rope nozzle, pipe running beads around the base of the cake. In the gaps where the barrels will be positioned, use a no. 2 nozzle to make smaller beads.

27 Carefully remove the barrels from the former. Using fresh, stiff icing and a no. 2 nozzle, pipe a line along both edges of each barrel piece and immediately stick them onto the cake, between the filigree sections. Use the larger (more rounded) pieces for the top and the smaller ones for the base. Allow to dry then use a no. 1 nozzle to pipe running beads along the joins to neaten them.

28 To assemble the 2 tiers, place the pillars in position over the cake dowels and carefully place the top tier on the pillars so that the barrels and scallops line up. Place the top decoration on the top tier and stick in place if necessary with a little royal icing.

*Tip*

When sticking on the barrels, it is useful to have a damp no. 2 artists' brush to hand to clean up any untidy piping.

# Single~tier Wedgwood~inspired Cake

## with pressure piped motifs, run-out panels and collars

## Techniques used:

Pressure piping (see pages 48 to 61)

Run-outs and collars (see pages 142 to 167)

*Tip* If you would like to make this as a 3-tier wedding cake use 10cm, 18cm and 25.5cm (4", 7" and 10") cakes, each on a cake drum 10cm (4") bigger than the cake or 13cm (5") if you prefer (as long as they are all the same).

## Cake

18cm (7") round, no taller than 7.5cm (3") (or you could also use an 18cm (7") hexagon, measured flat-edge to flat-edge)

## Cake covering

650g (1lb 7oz) SK Marzipan

650g (1lb 7oz) royal icing

*Full instructions for covering a cake are given on pages 34 to 41.*

## Materials

Royal icing, made to stiff and off-peak consistency (see page 33)

SK Professional Liquid Food Colour: Bluebell

## Equipment

Basic equipment (see pages 22 to 23)

28cm (11") round cake drum (board)

Nos. 0, 1 and 1.5 (optional) plain piping nozzles

Templates (see pages 308 to 309)

94cm (37") x 15mm width satin ribbon for board edge

1 Cover the cake with marzipan, top and sides separately (see pages 34 to 36). Place centrally on the cake drum and allow to firm overnight.

2 Coat the cake and board with royal icing (see pages 38 to 39) and allow to dry.

3 Using either round cutters or a ruler and compass, prepare a 9cm (3½") diameter circle for the cake top plaque and a 6.5cm (2½") diameter circle for the side plaques. Secure the templates under greased cellophane and prepare some rubbed-down icing coloured with SK Bluebell Professional Liquid Food Colour. Place some of the blue icing into a piping bag with a no. 1 or 1.5 nozzle and pipe the outline of the circles: you will need 2 large ones for the top (including 1 spare) and 8 small circles for the cake sides (including 2 spare).

4 Add cold water to the blue icing to make it the correct consistency for run-outs (see page 33), flood in all the circles and place

under a desk lamp to dry. They should be approximately 23cm to 30cm (9" to 12") away from the bulb to accelerate the drying of the sugar crystals and therefore make the plaques very hard when dry.

5 Prepare the 2 collar templates under greased cellophane. Outline the solid collar (no. 1) then flood in. Outline the secondary collar (no. 2) with the open structure and flood in. Allow to dry under a lamp then leave overnight in a warm place.

6 Prepare the template for the side panels under greased cellophane then outline and flood in the panels. You will need to make 6 plus 2 spare. Allow to dry under a lamp then leave overnight in a warm place.

7 Using a no. 1 nozzle, pipe the detail onto the framework of the secondary collar. Start with the S and reverse S scrolls, then the small C scrolls. Pipe the daisy in the middle, then pipe in the leaves. Repeat around all 6 sections of the collar. Pipe the small S scrolls into the triangles.

*Tip*

When piping in the detail on the collar and panels, make sure the lines touch the edge of the framework so that they will not fall out when dry. All of the scrolls, some of the petals and the primary leaves should touch the edge of the collar.

8 Pipe in the scroll work on the side panels, starting with the large S scrolls then the small C scrolls. Pressure pipe the daisies and leaves then run little beads round the inner circle (see page 71). Repeat on all 8 side panels (6 plus 2 spare).

9 Prepare a bag of well rubbed-down icing with a no. 0 nozzle. On the secondary (top) collar, pipe single dots all the way round the outer edge with no more than half a dot space between each one. If the icing is forming a peak, add a couple of drops of cold water to the icing (be careful not to add too much). When you have worked round the whole collar, pipe a secondary dot between every alternate dot in the first row to make triangles. Pipe a running bead round the inside edge of the collar.

10 Pressure pipe the figures onto the blue plaques to suit the cake (you may choose your own designs here if preferred). To

create the daisy design, use the side panel template, mark the centre of the circle with a scriber then pipe a cross from edge to edge leaving at least 1.3cm (½") from the outside edge of the circle. Pipe a daisy in the centre then add the leaves and a few dots to resemble fern. Allow to dry.

11 Pipe a circle of rubbed-down icing onto the top edge of the cake and place the solid collar onto the cake. Check that the collar is in line with the board by looking at it from overhead. Make a paper template the same size as the side panel, cut out the centre circle, then place it onto the side of the cake in line with the collar. Mark where the plaques need to be positioned on the side of the cake then use stiff icing to stick the plaques in place. Using the same icing, pipe a line along each edge of the solid collar and stick the 6 panels onto the solid collar (they should only be stuck along the top edge).

12 Take a piece of greaseproof paper and make a template

of the outer edge of the top collar. Place this along the edge of each side panel and drop a curved line onto the board to follow the same shape as the collar. Pipe a dot at each point to hide the joins. When this is complete, pipe running beads down the sides and along the base of each panel (not along the top).

13 Pressure pipe the daisies onto the cake board. Use the radius of the inner circle as a guide for the length of the daisy design.

14 Stick the cake top plaque onto the centre of the cake. Pipe running beads round the inner edge of the solid collar. Pipe 6 daisies round the top of the cake in line with the corners of the plaques.

15 Using the drop line technique, pipe a line of rubbed-down icing on the outer edge of the solid collar then place the top collar in position, making sure the points match up with the edges of the panels. Trim the board with ribbon to finish.

A similar design can be created using a hexagonal cake and slightly different collars based on a hexagon rather than a circle. You can also replace the panel on the cake top with a gazebo for a more ornate finish (see instructions on pages 153 to 158).

# Victoriana Cake

## with scroll work, piped flowers and baskets

### Techniques used:

Scrolls (see pages 80 to 93)

Piped baskets (see pages 78 to 79)

Piped flowers (see pages 116 to 127)

### Cake

2 x 18cm (7") round

### Cake covering

1.3kg (2lb 14oz) SK Marzipan

1.3kg (2lb 14oz) royal icing

*Full instructions for covering a cake are given on pages 34 to 41.*

### Materials

Royal icing, made to stiff and off-peak consistencies (see page 33)

Small amount of SK White SFP or MMP

Approximately 24 piped violets (see page 124) or violets modelled from 50:50 mixture of SK Sugar Florist Paste and sugarpaste

SK Professional Liquid Food Colour: Holly/Ivy

Small amount of sugarpaste

### Equipment

Basic equipment (see pages 22 to 23)

28cm, 30.5cm and 33cm (11", 12" and 13") round cake drums (boards)

Double-sided tape (optional)

Templates (see page 309)

Nos. 1.5, 2 and 3 plain, nos. 43 and 44 rope piping nozzles

6.5cm (2½") circle cutter

Shallow curved former (e.g. grapefruit dish)

18cm (7") square cake board or drum

1.1m (43") x 15mm width satin ribbon for board edge

1 Stick the 3 boards together with stiff royal icing or double-sided tape.

2 Roll out the marzipan to a thickness of 7mm (¼") and cover the top of each cake (see page 35). Brush the top of 1 cake with apricot glaze and stack the other cake on top. The overall height of the cakes when stacked should be approximately 18cm-19cm (7"-7½").

3 Roll out the marzipan to a thickness of 4mm (⅛"), making sure it is wide enough for both cakes together, and coat the sides (see page 36). Place the cake centrally on the boards and allow to dry.

4 Coat the top and sides of the cake with royal icing (see pages 38 to 39); when coating the sides use a straight edge (or something similar such as a sheet of rigid food-grade plastic: whatever you use must be food-grade, lightweight and tall enough to smooth the cake). Repeat this method to apply 2 or 3 coats of icing.

 *Tip* You can coat the board and make the off-piece decorations between coating the cake top and sides.

5 Start coating the 3 boards together. Fill in the gaps with stiff icing; you will probably need 3 coats to achieve a smooth, sloped finish. The board on which the cake is placed should be iced last: outline the edge of this then flood in with run-out icing up to the edge of the cake. Allow to dry.

6 Prepare the scroll templates under greased cellophane and pipe the S and C scroll off-pieces for the sides and top of the cake using a no. 43 nozzle. Keep the nozzle quite high so that the icing drops into the shape of the scroll; in each case, drop line the small inner C scroll first, then the outer scroll. As you are coming down on the outer scroll on the base design, make sure it tapers away into the first C scroll so that it blends in. Do not get mixed up with the various scrolls for the design: the smallest scroll is for the top edge of the cake, the large scroll is for the bottom of the cake and the middle size is for holding the basket on the top. Make 4 of each shape for the top edge, bottom edge and cake top and at least 1 extra of each to allow for breakages. Allow to dry under a

desk lamp. When dry, take the scrolls off the cellophane, turn them over and pipe the scrolls in reverse on the back.

7 Using a no. 2 nozzle, pipe 4 baskets plus 1 spare onto a greased patty tin (see pages 78 to 79). For the basket on top of the cake, cut out a 6.5cm (2½") circle from flower paste or modelling paste. Allow to dry on a slightly curved former such as a grapefruit dish.

8 To divide the cake into 4, place an 18cm (7") square board on top of the cake and mark the 4 points with a dot of icing before removing the board. Take the top edge scrolls and place into position using stiff royal icing. Mark the centre point between the each pair of scrolls then use a no. 44 nozzle to pipe an S and C scroll pattern around the top of the cake.

9 Stick the 4 large scrolls around the base of the cake in line with the top scrolls (you may wish to use a straight edge to make sure they are in line). Using the no. 44 nozzle again, pipe S scrolls all the way round

*Tip* Always remember that the scroll is based on a natural form (see Scrolls tutorial, pages 80 to 93). There should be no 'dog legs' or sharp corners, only nicely rounded shapes. The S and C scroll derive from the acanthus leaf, so remember that, when piping the scroll, the stalks should run into one another alongside the main stem. This is achieved by easing off the pressure.

then pipe a scallop with a no. 2 nozzle above them. Over pipe the S scroll all the way around the cake with a no. 43 nozzle. Pipe the trellis from the scallop to the S scroll at an angle of 45° (see pages 85 to 86).

10 After piping the trellises all round the cake, over pipe the base of this piece with a no. 2 nozzle to hide the join. Over pipe the top of the trellis with a no. 3 nozzle.

11 Using slightly rubbed-down icing and a no. 2 nozzle, pipe running beads down the scroll pieces to hide the join down the centre.

12 Pipe 2-1 drop line work down the sides of the cake with no. 3 and 2 nozzles (see page 68) then pipe scallops around the base scrolls with a no. 1.5 nozzle.

13 Use stiff icing to stick the baskets in situ, making sure each one is central.

14 Pipe a running bead round the top edge of the sloped boards with a no. 43 rope nozzle.

15 Using a no. 3 nozzle, pipe the double C scrolls round the middle of the board using a rope action then use a no. 43 nozzle to pipe scallops underneath the C scrolls around the edge, again using a rope action and following the shape of the C scroll.

16 By this time the baskets should be held firmly in position. Take some green icing and either pipe the leaves as off-pieces or pipe them directly onto the top edge of the basket. When you have

finished the leaves, stick the violets in place.

17 For the cake top decoration, stick the 4 medium scrolls on top of the cake using stiff royal icing so that they don't tip over. Stick the dish on top of the 4 scrolls then add piped prepared leaves. Make a small pyramid of green sugarpaste and then stick the violets onto this with royal icing (this gives it height).

18 Stick a violet in the centre of each trellis at the bottom of the cake and position 8 violets on the cake top to balance the design. Pipe in a few simple leaves to finish.

19 Trim the edge of the cake board with co-ordinating ribbon, ensuring the join is at the back of the cake.

# Christening Cake

## with run-out crib and extension work

## Techniques used:

Extension work (see pages 184 to 191)

Run-outs (see pages 142 to 167)

Lettering (see pages 128 to 135)

Scrolls (see pages 80 to 93)

Pressure piped motifs (see pages 94 to 115)

## Cake

18cm (7") square

## Cake covering

850g (1lb 14oz) SK Marzipan

850g (1lb 14oz) royal icing

*Full instructions for covering a cake are given on pages 34 to 41.*

## Materials

Royal icing, made to off-peak consistency (see page 33)

Extension icing

White vegetable fat

SK Professional Liquid Food Colours: Bluebell (for a boy), Bulrush, Cyclamen (for a girl), Nasturtium

SK Professional Paste Food Colour: Chestnut

50:50 mixture of Squires Kitchen White Sugar Florist Paste (SFP) and white sugarpaste

## Equipment

Basic equipment (see pages 22 to 23)

25cm (10") square cake drum (board)

Spare round cake board

Templates (see page 309)

Nos. 1 and 2 plain piping nozzles

SK Paintbrushes: fine and flat

Small, round cutter

Oval fluted cutter set

Plain oval cutter

Small head mould

Piece of dried spaghetti

1.02m (40") x 15mm width satin ribbon for board edge

1 Marzipan an 18cm (7") square fruit cake, coating the top and sides separately (see pages 34 to 37). Stick the cake to the centre of a 25cm (10") square cake drum with boiled apricot jam. Allow to firm.

2 Coat the top and sides of the cake with royal icing: you will need to apply 2 coats, or 3 for a fine, professional finish (see pages 38 to 39).

## Tip

In between applying coats of icing prepare the cradle, lettering and scrolls for the top of the cake, as described below.

3 Prepare the templates for the cradle pieces under greased cellophane. You will need 1 back piece, 1 front, 1 base, 2 sides and 4 rockers. (The rockers can be quite fiddly to assemble so these can be left off if preferred.) Outline the cradle pieces with a no. 1 nozzle and off-peak royal icing. When piping to a point (such as on the back piece), always pipe towards yourself and always into wet icing to achieve a sharp point.

4 Add cold water to a bowl of icing to bring it to run-out consistency (see page 33) and flood in all of the cradle pieces. Place the run-outs underneath a lamp for at least 1½-2 hours: the icing will dry to a fine crystalline form giving a slight gloss to the icing and making it very hard. After this, leave in a warm, dry place such as an airing cupboard so they can dry out completely.

5 For the lettering, prepare your chosen inscription as a template in the size and font required. Choose a style of lettering that is suitable for a baby (see page 130) and thick enough for run-out work. Secure under a sheet of greased cellophane.

6 Weigh out 60g (2oz) of royal icing into a bowl and add 2 to 3 drops of SK Cyclamen, Bluebell or your chosen liquid food colour. Make a note of how much colour you use then if you run out of icing or it dries out, you can make the same colour again using the same quantity of icing and colouring.

7 Place a no. 1 nozzle into a piping bag and half-fill with the coloured icing. Outline the lettering and tidy up any discrepancies with a damp artists' brush.

8 To achieve a very pale tone of the same colour, weigh out 60g (2oz) of white royal icing and mix in a level teaspoon of the coloured royal icing. When flooding in fine work such as lettering, rub down (paddle) the icing first to eliminate any air bubbles then thin with cold water to a run-out consistency.

9 Make a tight piping bag, half-fill with the pale icing and cut a small hole in the tip, no greater than the size of a no. 1 nozzle. Keeping the hole small will force the icing through it, causing any air bubbles in the icing to burst, thus giving a smoother finish. When you have flooded in all of the lettering, place under a lamp for approximately 2 hours then leave in a warm place overnight to dry fully.

10 Prepare the templates for the scrolls under a sheet of greased cellophane. Place some freshly beaten off-peak icing into a piping bag with a no. 2 nozzle and pipe the straight line along the base. Add the S and C scrolls: start with the large S scroll first, then pipe the small C scroll in towards the centre of where the flower will be, followed by the smaller S scroll to the edges. Make sure all of the lines touch the straight edge at the base. While the icing is still soft, pipe in the daisy (see page 52).

11 Repeat to make 4 scroll pieces, plus 1 or 2 spares in case of breakages.

*Tip*

If you would like to incorporate the baby's initials or birth date into the cake, use the alternative scroll design template on page 309. Start with the base line then outline the oval in the centre. Proceed to pipe the scrolls as above, making sure that the lines touch each other. Use a tiny amount of run-out icing in white, the pale colour or another colour of your choice then fill in the oval. When dry, you can pipe the baby's initials or birth date onto this.

12 Before piping the bridge work on the cake sides, use a ruler to measure 1.3cm (½") up from the base of the cake, then divide each cake side into quarters and pipe a dot at this level. Pipe the scalloped bridges to the dots with a no. 2 nozzle, allowing the icing to dry between every 2 lines to prevent the bridges from collapsing. (See pages 188 to 190 for full instructions on piping bridge work.)

13 Measure up 1.5cm ($^5/_8$") from the central scallop and mark with a dot of icing. Measure 4cm (1½") up from the 2 adjacent scallops and mark two more dots. To achieve the curve, use a round cake board as a guide and scratch a line from point-to-point with a scriber. Clean up any dust from the icing with a dry, flat brush before proceeding.

14 At this point, finish off the bridge work at the side of the cake: you will need to pipe a total of 5 lines on top of each other, allowing them to dry after the 4th set.

15 Measure in just under 2.5cm (1") from all 4 corners on the top edges of the cake and mark with a dot of icing. Take a small, round cutter and scribe a curve onto each corner. Use a no. 0 or 1 nozzle to pipe filigree into this area, then use a no. 2 nozzle to pipe a curve around the edge of the filigree.

16 Drop a straight line using a no. 2 nozzle approximately 3mm ($^1/_8$") in from the top edge of the cake on all four sides and allow to dry. This will help support the scrolls and keep them upright when they are in place.

17 Tilt the cake slightly towards yourself so the drop line work falls away from the cake. Place some extension icing in a piping bag with a no. 0 nozzle and pipe the extension work around the sides of the cake. Follow the curved line scribed earlier and pipe down to the edge of the bridge work on all 4 sides of the cake.

18 Pipe running beads around the base of the cake and around the edge of the extensions. Make sure

that you pipe downwards onto the line to avoid accidentally touching and breaking the extension lines. Instead of the beads you may prefer to make small lace off-pieces and stick them in position around the scallops when dry.

19 Pipe the stork straight onto the cake (see page 109) and add the scroll. Pipe the fleurs-de-lys then the daisies to finish.

20 To assemble the cradle, use slightly stiffened icing in a piping bag with a no. 2 nozzle to hold the pieces in place (add a level teaspoon of sieved icing sugar to approximately 60g (2oz) of royal icing). Stick the base onto a piece of greased cellophane with a dot of icing. Take the back of the cradle, pipe a line of stiff icing along the top edge of the base then hold the back piece in position (shiny side outermost) until dry. Stick the two sides then the end piece in position and leave to dry. You should find that you can handle it quite easily after an hour. If you wish to use the rockers, stick them together in pairs

*Tip*

You may prefer to make the cradle from pieces of pastillage instead of run-outs. Pastillage does dry very hard so is usually only used for ornamental decoration rather than to be eaten. You may also wish to add initials or flowers on the back of the cradle: if so, allow to dry fully before assembly.

using rubbed-down icing, leave to dry then stick onto the base of the cradle with the stiff icing.

21 For the frill on the back of the cot and the blanket, thinly roll out a 50:50 mix of sugarpaste and SFP. Cut out a fluted oval shape then cut out a plain oval from the centre to make a ring approximately 1.3cm (½") wide. Cut through the paste and straighten it out on the work board. Use a cocktail

stick or paintbrush handle to frill the fluted edge by pushing down and rolling along the edge of the paste. Pipe a line with a no. 2 nozzle from the top of the cradle all the way down to the base and secure the frill in place. Trim if necessary.

**22** Make the baby's head using a small head mould and 50:50 paste coloured with a little SK Chestnut Paste Food Colour. Push onto a piece of dry spaghetti to hold it in place for painting. Using a fine paintbrush paint the eyes, mouth and hair and with SK Bulrush Liquid Food Colour, then paint the lips with Nasturtium (do not use red as it is too dark).

**23** Model a rectangular piece of paste approximately 7mm (¼") thick for the mattress and place it in the cradle. Model a little pillow, make a dimple where the head will be positioned and secure the pillow in position. Make a small oval shape for the baby's body and stick this and the head in place. For the blanket, thinly roll out more of the paste and cut out a 9cm x 6.5cm (3½" x 2½") fluted oval. Cut off the top ⅓ of the oval, frill the fluted edge as before then fold over the straight edge at the top. Place the blanket over the top of the cradle while the paste is still soft.

**24** Using a no. 1 nozzle, pipe a running bead across the top of the covers, then decorate it with a delicate piped design in your chosen colours. Pipe the bootees and rattles

directly onto the cake or make them as off-pieces and stick in position.

**25** Stick the cradle in position above the halfway mark of the cake. Stick the inscription beneath it using rubbed-down icing: position the central letter first, halfway between the end of the crib and the side of the cake. Add the letters to the left then the right, keeping them in line (you may wish to use a ruler or straight edge for this). Finish off the letters with little running beads, flowers, or any other piped decoration.

**26** Using a no. 2 nozzle, pipe a line of icing on the edge of the cake running alongside the other straight line then stick the scrolls onto this on each edge. Carefully place in position and run your finger gently along the base line to position it.

**27** When this is done, pipe a scallop around the outside edge of the cake: this may be done in colour but must be paler than any of the other colours on the cake and must be done very finely, otherwise you will detract from the crib and inscription.

**28** To finish, trim the board edge with co-ordinating ribbon.

 When picking up the scroll pieces, only use 1 hand and lift by the centre part to avoid breaking them. If you use 2 hands you are more likely to snap the icing.

# Mother's Day Cake

## with oriental string work and pressure piping

## Techniques used:

Oriental string work (see pages 176 to 183)

Freestyle lettering (see pages 131 to 134)

Pressure piping (see pages 48 to 61)

## Cake

20.5cm (8") round

## Cake covering

880g (1lb 15oz) SK Marzipan

880g (1lb 15oz) royal icing

*Full instructions for covering a cake are given on pages 34 to 41.*

## Materials

Freshly beaten royal icing, made to off-peak consistency (see page 33)

SK Professional Liquid Food Colours: Holly/Ivy, Rose

Small, pink plunger blossoms (see page 23) or piped flowers

50:50 mixture of Squires Kitchen White Sugar Florist Paste (SFP) and white sugarpaste

## Equipment

Basic equipment (see pages 22 to 23)

28cm (11") cake drum (must be at least 3" bigger than the cake)

Template for cake top (see page 299)

Nos. 1, 1.5 and 2 plain piping nozzles

Thin cake board, smaller than the diameter of the cake

Sticky tape

Separator (e.g. polystyrene dummy or cake tin), smaller than the diameter of the cake

Daisy cutter

Piece of food-grade foam sponge

94cm (37") x 15mm width satin ribbon for board edge

1   Cover the top and sides of the cake with marzipan separately to give a clean, sharp edge (see pages 34 to 36). Stick the cake firmly to the cake drum with boiled apricot jam and allow to firm overnight.

2   Cover the cake and cake drum with royal icing: you will need to apply at least 2 coats of royal icing for a smooth finish. Allow the coated cake to firm for several hours, preferably overnight.

3   Make a template for the cake top and divide into 36 equal portions: each section should be approximately 1.6cm ($^5/_8$") wide at the edge of the cake. Place the template on top of the cake and place the cake onto a turntable.

4   Pipe dots around the top edge of the cake using a no. 1.5 or 2 nozzle. Using a side scraper or straight edge as a guide, pipe dots around the base so that they line up with the dots on top. Leave to dry for approximately 10 minutes then pipe a smaller dot on top with a no. 1 or 1.5 nozzle to make sure that the dropped lines stand proud of the cake.

5 Make a dot in the middle of the cake side level with every second dot to mark the position for the side design.

6 Using a no. 1 or 1.5 nozzle, pipe the first set of scallops around the top edge of the cake. Pipe the lower line first to every other dot all the way round the cake then pipe a slightly shallower scallop from the same dots.

7 Repeat the above step to pipe a second set of double lines all the way round the cake from alternate dots. Make sure the lines fall to the same depth as the first set.

8 Drop a line approximately 7mm (¼") higher than the dots in the centre of the cake side and loop all the way round the side of the cake.

9 Prepare a bag of freshly beaten green royal icing with a no. 1 nozzle. Pipe a small dot on every dot around the top and base of the cake, allow to dry then pipe a shallow

scallop from dot-to-dot all the way round the top of the cake. Leave to dry for approximately 10 minutes.

10 Place a smaller board in the centre of the cake and use a piece of tape to make a loop on the board so you can remove it easily later. Place a separator (or similar) on top of the cake board, carefully upturn the cake and separator and place back onto the turntable.

11 Pipe the inverted string work at the top of the cake, following the same method as for the top edge.

12 Pipe the inverted drop line curves around the cake sides, making a lozenge and diamond pattern.

13 Pipe the inverted string work around the base of the cake, ensuring that the sequence lines up with the top set. Allow to dry then turn the cake the right way up and place back on the turntable.

14 Using fresh icing and a no. 1 nozzle, pipe in the elongated daisies in the lozenge shapes, then a single dot in the diamond shape.

15 Stick small piped flowers or plunger blossoms onto alternate dots around the top and base of the cake.

16 Pipe your chosen inscription on top of the cake and over pipe in pink icing. taking care not to touch the string work. Keep the lettering simple but make sure it is legible.

Tip

To avoid breaking the string work, keep the cake low, around waist height: place it directly onto the table (off the turntable) and stand up so that you can work directly above the cake.

*Tip*

If you have made piped flowers in advance you can use these instead of the paste flowers. This is useful if you are short of time. (See pages 116 to 127 for piped flower designs.)

17 Using fresh, green royal icing in a piping bag with a no. 1 nozzle, pipe the stems approximately halfway between the lettering and the edge of the cake. Keep the leaves simple: pipe a dot with a no. 1 nozzle then pull down to achieve a central vein, giving the leaves a slight curve.

18 The flowers used here are daisies made from 50:50 SFP and sugarpaste coloured with SK Rose Liquid Food Colour to match the piping. Roll out the paste thinly, cut out a daisy shape and place onto a foam pad. Press a ball tool onto each petal from the tip to the centre to lift the petals up. Make a second layer then use edible glue or a dot of royal icing underneath to stick them together. Repeat to make 3 (or as many as required).

19 To make the half-daisy, cut out a daisy shape as before, soften with a ball tool then fold over. To make the buds, cut the daisy shape in half then roll it up to make a tight bud.

20 Using the bag of green icing, stick the flowers in place on the stem. Add the flourishes (embellishments) to the lettering to balance out the design. Keep a gap around the edge of the cake to prevent it from looking cramped.

21 To finish, scratch pipe a simple scroll pattern around the edge of the cake (see page 69) then pressure pipe dots and teardrops around the edge of the board. Trim the board with ribbon in a colour that complements the flowers.

# Golfer Cake

with run-outs, drop line work and pressure piping

## Techniques used:

Run-outs and collars (see pages 142 to 167)

Drop line work (see pages 62 to 79)

Pressure piping (see pages 48 to 61)

Freestyle lettering (see pages 131 to 134)

## Cake

20.5cm (8") round

## Cake covering

880g (1lb 15oz) SK Marzipan

880g (1lb 15oz) royal icing (or white sugarpaste if preferred)

*Full instructions for covering a cake are given on pages 34 to 41.*

## Materials

Royal icing, made to off-peak consistency (see page 33)

SK Professional Liquid Food Colours: Bulrush, Daffodil, Fern, Holly/Ivy

SK Professional Edible Silver Paint

White vegetable fat

## Equipment

Basic equipment (see pages 22 to 23)

28cm (11") round cake drum

Collar, golfer and trolley templates (see pages 295 and 297)

Nos. 0, 1, 1.5, 2 plain, no. 43 shell piping nozzles

Ribbon: 90cm (35½") x 15mm width satin for board edge; 80cm (31½") x 25mm width sheer ribbon to tie around cake

Non-toxic glue stick or double-sided sticky tape

In order to create a sense of perspective when painting onto cakes, use paler colours and finer strokes in the background, working towards stronger colours and bolder strokes in the foreground.

1 Cover the top and sides of the cake with marzipan separately to give a clean, sharp edge (see pages 34 to 36). Place the cake centrally on the cake drum and allow to firm.

2 Cover the cake and cake drum with royal icing, or sugarpaste if preferred. If you are using sugarpaste, cover the top and sides separately (as for the marzipan) to give a sharp edge. Smooth the join at the back so that it is less noticeable. Allow the coated cake to firm for several hours, preferably overnight.

3 Make the golfer and trolley as off-piece run-outs on greased cellophane; full instructions for these are given on pages 150 to 151. Allow to dry completely.

4 Prepare the collar template, ensuring that the inner circle is slightly smaller than the cake and

the outer scallops are larger than the cake. Remember that you will need to resize the collar accordingly if you use a different sized cake. Prepare the template under a sheet of greased cellophane (see page 145) and proceed to pipe the collar with brown (SK Bulrush) and green (SK Holly/Ivy) run-out icing following the instructions on page 165. Allow to dry completely under a desk lamp.

5 When the collar is dry, pipe 2 crossed lines for the golf clubs with a no. 1.5 plain nozzle into the holes in the collar, making sure that the ends of the golf clubs touch the edges of the oval. Add a golf ball and the club heads. When the club heads are dry, paint with SK Edible Silver Paint (see page 47). Allow to dry.

6 Next, paint the scene on the cake top. Using a fine artists' brush, paint the background design in pale

green and brown liquid food colours. Use a brighter green (SK Fern) for the putting green.

7 For the foreground, make up some green royal icing using SK Holly/Ivy and a touch of Daffodil Liquid Food Colour. Use a cranked palette knife to spread the icing approximately $^1/_3$ up from the bottom of the cake, using a back-and-forth motion and leaving horizontal lines in the icing to resemble grass. Taper the icing away towards the edges.

8 Carefully remove the golfer and trolley run-outs from the cellophane. Using slightly rubbed-down icing, stick the golfer in place, approximately $^1/_3$ in from the left side of the cake. Ensure that the upper part of the body is slightly raised as this will give shadow and perspective to the cake. Do the same with the golf trolley.

9 Pipe scrolls onto the collar while it is still on the cellophane. If preferred you can use a scriber to scratch the scroll pattern onto the

collar as a guide before piping it in white icing with a no. 1.5 or 2 nozzle. Leave to dry for an hour or so under a lamp.

10 Slide the cellophane onto a surface with a squared edge (such as a tabletop). Position the edge of the cellophane off the edge of the surface, use one hand to support the centre of the cellophane and use your other hand to pull the cellophane down, easing it away from the run-out. Repeat around the collar until it is completely released from the cellophane; do this carefully and do not put too much stress on the collar otherwise it will break.

11 Rub down some white icing and use a no. 2 nozzle to pipe a circle around the very edge of the cake top. Immediately afterwards, place the collar on top of the cake. Do not be afraid to pick the collar up as this design should be very firm and stable. Make sure that the ovals are positioned correctly, i.e. the right and left ovals should be on the horizontal.

12 Prepare a bag of green icing with a no. 0 nozzle. Before adding the scroll work round the edge of the cake, practise the S and reverse S pattern (see page 69), then do this around the inside of the collar. If you find this difficult, make a simple scallop instead.

13 Pipe the inscription of your choice on the cake in your preferred lettering. You could use a pun such as 'Happy Birday' or 'Have a Parfect Day'.

14 Pipe a running shell around the base of the cake in green icing with a no. 43 nozzle then over pipe in brown icing. Finally, pipe a large and small roped scallop pattern around the edge of the board with a few dots using well rubbed-down icing and a no. 1 nozzle.

15 Secure the satin ribbon around the edge of the cake drum with a non-toxic glue stick or double-sided sticky tape, ensuring the join is at the back. Tie the sheer ribbon around the cake and make a neat bow at the front.

## Techniques used:

Embroidery techniques (see pages 168 to 175)

Making a reverse embosser (see pages 170 to 171)

Scrolls (see pages 80 to 93)

## Cake

17.5cm (7") round

## Cake covering

650kg (1lb 7oz) SK Marzipan

650kg (1lb 7oz) Atlantic Blue sugarpaste

*Full instructions for covering a cake are given on pages 34 to 41.*

## Materials

Royal icing, made to off-peak consistency (see page 33)

## Equipment

Basic equipment (see pages 22 to 23)

Template (see page 298)

25.5cm (10") round cake drum

Acrylic embosser prepared with rose design (see pages 170 to 171)

Nos. 0, 1, 1.5 and 3 plain, 43 rope piping nozzles

80cm (31½") x 15mm width satin ribbon for board edge

1 Cover the cake all-in-one with marzipan (see pages 38 to 39), place centrally on the cake drum and allow to firm. When dry, cover the cake and board with blue sugarpaste.

2 While the sugarpaste is still soft, rub a little icing sugar on your hands and gently rub the top of the cake to prevent the embosser from sticking to the cake. Gently press the embosser onto the surface of the cake and rock it back and forth slightly if the cake is not quite level to ensure the design is fully embossed. Once the paste is embossed, immediately lift the embosser off otherwise it will stick to the cake.

 When using sugarpaste with a deep colour, only use a little (or no) icing sugar when rolling out so as not to leave white marks on the paste.

3 Use the tin in which the cake was baked (or a board of the same size) to make a template of the cake top. Divide the circle into 16 equal sectors, lay the template on top of the cake and mark the 16 points with tiny dots of icing. Remove the template.

4 At this point, pipe the brush embroidery rose design onto the cake top (see page 172).

5 Pipe your chosen inscription in a suitable style of lettering so that the cake is balanced.

6 Place some freshly beaten off-peak royal icing into a piping bag with a no. 43 rope nozzle. Leave 3 sectors at the bottom of the cake then pipe 13 barrel scrolls around the edge of the cake top (see pages 83 to 84), making sure you pipe at a 45° angle from the top and sides. Pipe flounces and pull-ups around the base of the cake using the same nozzle.

7 Pipe the S and C scrolls at the bottom of the cake top design, using 1½ sectors as a size guide. Pipe the left to right S scroll first, then the C scroll at the end. Angle the cake 45° away from your body and pipe the right to left scrolls. Pipe the base scrolls in the same way to reflect the top design.

8 The over piping can be done either with a no. 43 rope nozzle for a bold finish or a no. 3 plain nozzle for a more delicate effect; either one will work on this design. Work round the scrolls on the top of the cake then over pipe the flounces and pull-ups around the base. To hide the joins between the flounces and pull-ups, pipe a dot of slightly rubbed-down royal icing so that the point disappears

(neaten with a damp artists' brush if necessary).

9 To lighten the scroll work, pipe a scalloped line with a no. 2 nozzle around the inside of the top edge and the same underneath. Above the S and C scrolls, pipe a simple scroll pattern to decorate the cake top. Pipe a secondary line just beside it with a no. 1 nozzle, then add another no. 1 line on top of the no. 2 line above and below the scrolls to create a 2-1 build-up (see page 68).

10 To finish, pipe 3 straight lines down the sides of the cake where the barrel scrolls join and add a simple embellishment by the S and C scrolls on the cake top.

 If the cake is slightly larger, you may prefer to pipe a 3-2-1 build-up with no. 3, 2, and 1 nozzles (see page 68). This will graduate the scrolls into the cake design.

# Mini Cakes

with pressure piped motifs, scroll work and drop line work

## Techniques used:

Combining drop line work with pressure piping (see pages 62 to 79)

Scrolls (see pages 80 to 93)

Piped flowers (see pages 116 to 127)

Embroidery techniques (see pages 168 to 175)

Lettering (see pages 128 to 135)

## Cake

5cm (2") round and square mini cakes

## Cake covering

60g (2oz) SK Marzipan per mini cake (optional)

60g (2oz) sugarpaste per mini cake

## Materials

Royal icing, made to off-peak consistency (see page 33)

SK Professional Liquid Food Colours (see individual mini cake designs for requirements)

Assortment of piped flowers (see individual mini cake designs for requirements)

## Equipment

Basic equipment (see pages 22 to 23)

Mini plastic cake plates, round and square

Piping nozzles (see individual mini cake designs for requirements)

One of the biggest trends in cake design in recent years is to decorate small, individual cakes. These cakes can be used for weddings, birthdays, christenings, special anniversaries, Valentine's Day, or simply to say 'thank you'. Mini cake pans, liners and cutters are available from Squires Kitchen (see page 320): these are ideal if you are making a large number of cakes.

You can use a sponge cake mixture or a rich fruitcake for mini cakes; the beauty of using a heavy fruitcake mixture is that they can be made up to 6 weeks in advance.

Many of the decorations shown here can be either piped directly onto the cake or made as off-pieces in advance and placed onto the cake when needed. You can also change the colours to suit the occasion: opt for a monochromatic colour scheme for a subtle effect, or choose contrasting colours for a more dramatic result.

1 Brush the cake with apricot glaze. If you are using rich fruitcake, cover the cake all-in-one with marzipan. (You may choose to omit the marzipan if you are using sponge cakes.)

2 Cover the cakes all-in-one with sugarpaste in the colour of your choice, trim neatly at the base and allow to firm.

3 Decorate as required (see design suggestions on the following pages and further templates on pages 310 to 311). Place each finished cake onto a mini cake plate or cake card.

4 Display the cakes as required: for a multi-tiered display place them onto an acrylic stand (ideal for weddings); for a teatime treat arrange on a cake plate or stand; and for individual gift cakes and favours place into little boxes or cellophane bags tied with ribbon.

For added or alternative decoration, tie a ribbon around the mini cakes: this is useful if you are short of time or for colour-co-ordinating a mini cake display.

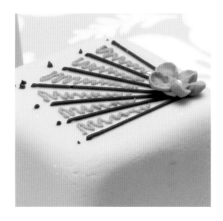

### Design 1: Fan (square)

Piping simple line work on top of the cake in a contrasting colour creates quite a striking design.

1 Place some dark SK Bulrush coloured icing into a piping bag with a no. 1 nozzle. Pipe the fan from corner to corner using the drop line technique (see pages 64 to 67). Start with a diagonal line down the centre and then add 3 lines on either side. Add green (SK Holly/Ivy) wavy lines between them with a no. 0 nozzle.

2 Place a piped or modelled flower on top of the fan then use a no. 43 rope nozzle to pipe running beads around the base.

### Design 2: Rose trellis (round)

1 Place some dark SK Bulrush coloured icing into a piping bag with a no. 1 nozzle. Starting approximately $1/3$ of the way up the cake, drop line 3 horizontal lines followed by 3 vertical lines on the perpendicular.

2 With a no. 1 or 0 piping nozzle, pipe a zig-zagged stem in green (SK Holly/Ivy) royal icing. For a quick rose, make a small piping bag with a sharp point, fill with pink icing and cut a V in the tip at a 45° angle. Using a circular motion, pipe a tiny rose.

3 To finish add a running bead around the base with a no. 43 rope nozzle.

### Design 3: Simple scrolls (square)

1 Place some dark SK Bulrush coloured icing into a piping bag with a no. 1 nozzle. Pipe a straight line from corner to corner, leaving a 7mm (¼") gap around the edge of the cake. Using the same bag of icing, drop line an S and reverse S scroll to the sides of the line.

2 Place a small piped or cut-out flower at the bottom. To make the leaves, make a dot and pull through.

3 Add a running bead around the base with a no. 43 rope nozzle.

*Tip* These little piped roses are useful if you are decorating a large number of cookies, mini cakes or fancies, such as on individual wedding cakes or favours.

### Design 4: Violet (round)

**1** Place some dark SK Bulrush coloured icing into a piping bag with a no. 1 nozzle. Following the template pipe the long dropped line with the loops first. Pipe each line in turn, making them wider each time.

**2** Add a piped violet or other flower on top with a green stalk and a few leaves. Add a running bead around base with a no. 43 nozzle.

### Design 5: Blossom trellis (round)

**1** Place some dark SK Bulrush coloured icing into a piping bag with a no. 1 nozzle. Just in from the outside edge pipe an S scroll, leave a gap of 2cm (¾") at the top then add a C scroll.

**2** Use the same nozzle to pipe the trellis: start with the straight lines going from side to side then pipe the curves from top to bottom on the second layer.

**3** Pipe in a few curved stems and leaves using SK Holly/ Ivy coloured royal icing and a no. 0 nozzle then place a few tiny blossoms on top (see instructions in the oriental string work tutorial, page 182). Add a running bead around the base of the cake with a no. 43 nozzle.

### Design 6: Dahlia (square)

1 Place some dark SK Bulrush coloured icing into a piping bag with a no. 1 nozzle and pipe a cross from corner to corner, leaving a gap around the edge.

2 Working from the centre out, pipe an S and reverse S scroll on either side of the line. Repeat on the other three corners in turn, always piping towards yourself.

3 Pipe a small dahlia in the centre (see page 75) with a few green leaves. Add a running bead around base with a no. 43 nozzle.

### Design 7: Bluebells (square)

1 Prepare a bag of white royal icing with a no. 43 rope nozzle. Pipe a reverse S and C scroll along the top edge of the cake, then do the opposite on the next side and a running shell on the other 2 edges. Pipe a running shell round the base. Using a no. 1 nozzle, drop line a series of scallops round the sides of the cake.

2 Prepare a bag of SK Holly/Ivy coloured royal icing with a no. 1 nozzle. Drop line a C scroll, an S scroll from the top in towards the C then another S and C scroll from the middle towards the corner, keeping 1.3cm (½") in from the edge.

3 Prepare a bag of SK Bluebell coloured royal icing with a no. 1 nozzle and pipe a few blue dots on the cake sides. Add the bluebells to the stems (see page 55).

### Design 8: Daisy motif (square)

1 Pipe a running shell round the top edge of the cake using a no. 43 nozzle. Using the same nozzle, pipe an S and reverse S in a rope action from the centre out around the base of the cake on all 4 sides.

2 Use a no. 2 nozzle to pipe a fleur-de-lys on each corner at the top and one in the centre of the scrolls at the base.

3 Use a no. 1.5 nozzle to drop a straight line from corner to corner, then pipe S scrolls to the left and right. Pipe a daisy then add a few leaves to finish off.

4 Over pipe the top shells around the top edge with scallops using a no. 2 nozzle.

**Design 9:** Valentine heart (square)

1  Cut out a hole in the shape of a heart from thin card. Colour a small amount of royal icing with SK Poinsettia Professional Liquid Food Colour, rub down a little of the icing slightly and use a cranked palette knife to stencil the heart on top of the cake (in the same way as for the curved pieces on the Barrel Scroll Wedding Cake, pages 232 to 237).

2  Place some of the red icing into a piping bag with a no. 1 nozzle. Pipe a running bead around the heart then drop line two curved lines inside the heart to emphasise the shape.

3  Write the 'With Love' inscription with a no. 1 nozzle; if you are not confident at piping, pipe in self colour first then over pipe in red (see page 130). Make sure you do this before adding the embellishments.

4  Drop some simple line work around the edges to balance the design, then add stems, leaves and small daisies on either side of the heart. For the side designs, scratch pipe the stems then pressure pipe the leaves and daisy.

5  Pipe a running bead around the base of the cake with a no. 43 nozzle.

**Design 10:** Vintage lace (square)

1  To make a peach coloured icing, use SK Chestnut and a touch of Fuchsia Professional Liquid Food Colours. Place into a piping bag with a no. 43 rope nozzle then pipe an S scroll from corner to corner, a C scroll on either side then a shell just past the halfway mark to resemble a fleur-de-lys.

2  Using a no. 2 nozzle, drop a line from the edge of the S scroll to the centre of each side. With a no. 1 nozzle, pipe 3 lines from each corner with a dot on the top. Use the same nozzle to pipe in a daisy on the side. Drop a line from midway on the top to the corner and repeat in reverse on the other side in a heart shape. Using the same nozzle, outline slightly round the fleur-de-lys.

3  Pipe a shell round the base with a no. 43 rope nozzle then over pipe with a roped C scroll (see page 90).

## Design 11: Fuchsia (square)

1 Prepare 2 piping bags with SK Cyclamen and Holly/Ivy coloured royal icing, each with a no. 1 nozzle. Pipe a C scroll to the bottom and the reverse on the opposite side in green royal icing. Pipe an oval daisy towards the top of the cake (see page 52). Add yellow dots in the centre for the stamens if required.

2 Take the bag of pink icing and pipe in the stamens of the fuchsia, making sure the angle follows the stalk. In pale pink, pipe a teardrop on either side and one on top. Using a no. 2 nozzle and deep pink icing, pipe an elongated carrot shape and add a dot on the end for the seedpod. Make a dot and pull out on each side of the petals. To make the bud pipe a carrot shape with a dot at the end. Pipe in the leaves and a few dots to balance the design.

3 Use a no. 2 nozzle to pipe running beads around the top edge of the cake then drop lines down the sides of the cake at the corners. Add a few dots in deep pink to balance the design.

4 Pipe running beads round the base of the cake using a no. 43 rope nozzle, then use a no. 1 nozzle and pale pink icing to over pipe the running beads.

## Design 12: Art Nouveau (square)

1 Prepare a bag of white royal icing with a no. 43 nozzle. Mark a spot of icing on the centre point of each side, then pipe an S scroll from the centre to one edge and the reverse on the other side. Repeat on all 4 sides the cake.

2 To pipe the cake top design use freshly beaten dark brown (SK Bulrush) coloured icing in a piping bag with a no. 1 nozzle. Starting from the middle, make a narrow figure of 8 across the centre and repeat on the other 2 opposite corners. Pipe a secondary line, slightly wider and shorter figure of 8 and repeat, then again even wider and shorter.

3 Using a no. 43 nozzle, pipe running shells all the way round the base of the cake. Using a rope action, over pipe round the edges of the shells in the brown icing to emphasise the curve. Using the same bag of icing, drop line scallops round the edge of the top design, pipe 3 dots reducing in size at the join of each scallop, then pipe a fleur-de-lys on each corner.

4 Add a little plunger blossom, edible diamond or other decoration in the centre of the cake to suit the occasion.

## Design 13: Wedding bells (round)

1  Make a template of a small bell design (see page 310) and secure under a piece of greased cellophane. Outline with a no. 1 nozzle, then flood the inside of the bell at the bottom with run-out icing (see page 33). Over pipe the outline of the rim and then flood in the top part of each bell. Leave under a lamp to dry.

2  Use the no. 1 nozzle to pipe a frilly edge around each bell. Decorate the bells as desired with piping, pipe in the clapper, then allow to dry. When dry, gilt with SK Edible Silver or Gold Paint (see page 47). Put under the lamp to dry completely.

3  Attach the bell motif to the centre of the cake. Use a no. 2 nozzle to pipe a butterfly bow on top. Pipe simple line work around the top edge of the cake to frame the design.

4  Using a no. 43 nozzle, pipe a series of pull-ups (see page 92) from left to right around the bottom of the cake. This makes the cake appear larger than it actually is (so is good for commercial cakes). Pipe a running bead round the top of the pull-ups.

## Design 14: Water lily (round)

1  Blend together equal amounts of SK White Sugar Florist Paste (SFP) and white sugarpaste. Roll out the paste thinly and cut out a large and small calyx using cutters for the water lily. Use a ball tool to thin the edges, then use the ball tool again to press from the tip to the centre to lift the petals (sepals). Repeat on all 5 petals on both shapes. Pipe a bulb of icing in the centre of the large one and stick the small one on top. Pipe a few pull-ups in the centre for stamens, either in white or in colour.

2  Divide the cake top into 8 and do the same with the base. At the top, use a rope action to pipe a C scroll round the top edge with a no. 43 nozzle (see page 83). At the base, use a rope action to pipe a barrel scroll with the same nozzle.

3  Use a no. 2 nozzle to pipe scallops point-to-point onto the barrel scrolls, then add a C and reverse C scroll on top (see page 88). Pipe a scallop over the top edge scrolls, again point-to-point.

4  Pipe a fleur-de-lys on the top of the cake using a no. 1.5 nozzle then pipe a drop line under the edge of the scallop. Finish with dots to hide the joins.

## Design 15: Daisies (round)

1 Place some royal icing into a piping bag with a no. 43 nozzle and pipe shells round the top and base of the cake.

2 Pipe the daisies in your chosen colour: start with the 8-petal daisy towards the top left of the cake then pipe a half-daisy to the side at the same level (see page 52). Pipe in an S shaped green (SK Holly/Ivy) stalk from the half-daisy and a C shaped stalk from the open daisy to meet the first one and add 3 or 4 leaves.

3 In the same colour as the daisy, pipe in a roped scallop over the top of the shells with a no. 1 nozzle (see page 69). Pipe little dropped lines on every alternate scallop then over pipe the secondary line in between. Pipe a dot in between each shell when dry to hide the joins.

4 Pipe a running shell around the base of the cake with a no. 43 nozzle then over pipe a rope scallop around the lower edge of the shells.

## Design 16: Cameo (round)

1 Colour some royal icing dark brown or black using SK Bulrush Professional or Black QFC Liquid Food Colour. Prepare the template (see page 310) under a piece of greased cellophane and place some stiff icing in a piping bag with a no. 1 nozzle. Pipe the silhouette as follows: outline the forehead, nose, mouth and chin, then using well rubbed-down icing (so that it flows better), pipe in the head and cheekbone (slightly enlarged). Use an artists' brush to make a dimple for the eye. Pipe in the neck. Use the first bag of stiff icing to pipe in the hair a little at a time and use a brush to make it appear finer.

2 Using a no. 1 or 1.5 nozzle, drop line the 2 C scrolls with a little fleur-de-lys on each side. If the design looks imbalanced it is feasible to pipe in 1 or 2 scrolls.

3 Use the same colour to pipe an S and reverse S scroll pattern round the side of the cake. Add a running shell round the base using a no. 43 rope nozzle and pipe a dot between each shell in the dark icing.

### Design 17: Bootees (round)

1 Pipe 2 bootees in the centre of the cake (see page 108): you can pipe them either directly onto the cake or as off-pieces. Pipe on the bows once the bootees are in place.

2 Divide the cake into 4, pipe 2 C scrolls at the front and at the back, then add a flounce on either side using a no. 43 nozzle (see page 88). Pipe scallops along the top edge and shells round the base.

3 Pipe dots down the cake sides to finish.

### Design 18: Stork (square)

1 Place some white royal icing into a piping bag with a no. 2 nozzle. Starting ¾ of the way up the cake, pipe the stork (see instructions on page 109).

2 Use a no. 1 nozzle to pipe an S and C scroll underneath the stork then add a little flower in the colour of your choice (e.g. blue, pink or yellow).

3 Pipe round the top with a simple scallop design, then add a running bead with a no. 43 nozzle round the base to finish. This can be over piped if desired to complement the colour scheme.

### Design 19: Swan silhouette (round)

1 Start by piping round the side of the cake with a no. 1.5 nozzle and dark brown (SK Bulrush) coloured royal icing. Pipe a repetitive C scroll with an S scroll underneath then the same width pipe a repetitive C scroll underneath, almost to the bottom of the cake (see page 83).

2 Use the same icing to pipe the swan design with a no 1.5 nozzle (see page 108).

**Design 20:** Single daisy in relief (round)

1 Using a no. 56 or 57 petal nozzle, pipe a daisy either directly onto the cake or as an off-piece (see page 97). Stick the daisy to one side of the cake top then add a sugar centre (see page 119).

2 Place some SK Holly/Ivy coloured royal icing into a piping bag with a no. 1 nozzle and pipe a C scroll from the base of the daisy, passing through the centre of the cake towards the outer edge. Pipe the outside edge of one side of the leaf, making the line bold, then brush embroider this side (see page 173). Pipe the opposite side, quite firmly again, then brush into the centre again. Using the same brush, pull down the centre to create the central vein.

3 Add a running bead around the base using a no. 43 rope nozzle.

**Design 21:** Carnation (round)

1 Using a small petal nozzle, pipe a carnation (see page 126), either directly onto the cake or as an off-piece which can then be stuck in place.

2 From the base of the flower, drop a circular line in a silvery/blue green (SK Bluegrass) around the cake for the stem using a no. 2 nozzle. Pipe in the leaves and seedpod.

3 Finish with a running bead around base of the cake using a no. 43 rope nozzle.

**Design 22:** English rose (round)

1 Pipe an English rose from the centre to the outer edge of the cake and add the calyx in SK Holly/Ivy icing between the petals. Use a no. 2 nozzle to pipe the stalk.

2 Brush embroider a leaf on either side by piping the outline and brushing inward (see page 173). Using a fine artists' brush and Holly/Ivy Professional Liquid Food Colour, paint in a few extra veins on the leaf, or use a no. 0 nozzle to pipe in the veins in a darker green.

3 Pipe roped scallops round the edge of the cake using a no. 2 nozzle or use a no. 42 rope nozzle if preferred. Pipe dots between the scallops round the top edge.

4 Using a no. 43 or 44 rope nozzle, pipe a set of pull-ups round the base (see page 92): it is a good idea to mark the height of the pull-ups beforehand using a ribbon tied round the cake and a scriber. Over pipe the pull-ups with a no. 2 nozzle from the top edge of the bulb to the bottom and back up to the top, then use a no. 1 nozzle to pipe the double dropped lines at the top. Finish with a dot at the top.

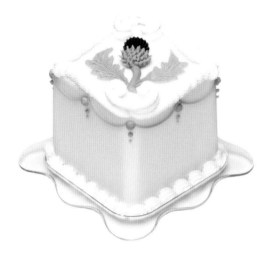

## Design 23: Thistle (square)

1 To make the thistle, colour some off-peak royal icing mauve using SK Violet Professional Liquid Food Colour. Place into a piping bag with a no. 1.5 nozzle and pipe the top in a V shape, coming down to the centre.

2 Colour some icing a pale green using SK Holly/Ivy Professional Liquid Food Colour and place into a piping bag with a no. 1.5 nozzle. Make pointed pull-ups, starting at the base of the flower and working down to the base, creating an oval shape.

3 Pipe the green stalk using a no. 2 nozzle then use the no. 1.5 nozzle to pipe one side of the leaf. Brush embroider the icing towards the centre of the leaf using a damp artists' brush (see pages 172 to 173). Pipe the opposite side and brush embroider again to the centre. Brush down the centre of the leaf from the top to the stalk to create the central vein. Repeat on the other side of the thistle.

4 Using a no. 43 rope nozzle, pipe an S scroll from corner to corner: go left-to-right on one side then right-to-left on the adjacent side. Do the same on the opposite sides then pipe two C scrolls above and below the thistle using the same nozzle. Add a running bead around the base of the cake.

5 Place some rubbed-down icing in the colour of your choice into a piping bag with a no. 1 nozzle. Pipe drop line scallops down the sides of the cake then add dots between them to emphasise the curves.

## Design 24: Ornate fan (square)

1 Place some white royal icing into a piping bag with a no. 43 rope nozzle. Pipe an S scroll along one edge from left to right, turn the cake then do the same from right to left. Pipe 2 S scrolls on the corner make a heart shape. Turn the cake round and pipe the other 2 edges as a reflection of the first set. Use the same nozzle to pipe a running shell round the base.

2 Prepare a bag of white icing with a no. 1 nozzle. Keeping about 1.3cm (½") in from the edges of the cake, drop a line on the diagonal towards the heart. Add three lines on each side then use a back-and-forth movement to pipe in 6 wavy lines, reducing in size towards the point.

3 Add a piped blossom at the base of the fan (see page 125) then pipe under the scrolls to finish.

## Design 25: Dove and heart (square)

1    Prepare a pressure piped dove on greased cellophane (see page 106) and leave under a lamp to dry.

2    Using a no. 3 nozzle, pipe a square around the top edge of the cake, then pipe in a C and reverse C scroll to make the heart. Use a no. 0 nozzle to pipe in little reverse S scrolls around the inside of the square. Using a no. 1.5 or 2 nozzle, pipe in the daisy to the bottom left-hand side of the heart and add a few leaves.

3    By this time, the square will be dry enough to pipe the barrel scrolls round the edge of the cake. Pipe these from corner to corner using a no. 43 nozzle (see page 83). Use a no. 3 nozzle to over pipe reverse C scrolls all the way round the cake. Add a dot to hide the joins on the corners then pipe fleurs-de-lys on the 4 corners.

4    Pipe a flounce towards the bottom of the 4 sides with a no. 43 nozzle and add a pull-up on each corner (see pages 88 and 92). Over pipe with a scallop then a reverse C scroll using a no. 3 nozzle. Over pipe the pull-ups with reverse C scrolls.

5    Rub down some royal icing, place in a bag with a no. 1.5 nozzle and pipe in the dotted daisy and leaves on the cake sides (see page 51).

## Design 26: Piped monogram (square)

This design is useful for personalising a cake e.g. at a christening or birthday. For a wedding or anniversary, you can change the lettering slightly to incorporate 2 intertwined initials.

1    Pipe your chosen letter in the centre of the cake in the colour and style of your choice (see pages 130 to 135). The script lettering used here can be piped directly onto the cake, but if preferred the lettering could be made as a run-out and placed on the cake when dry (see design 28).

2    Divide each side of the cake in half and pipe a repetitive S scroll all the way round the top with a no. 43 nozzle. Over pipe the scrolls with a no. 3 nozzle.

3    Use a fine nozzle such as a no. 1 or 0 to pipe in a few stalks and leaves in green (SK Holly/Ivy) to help balance the letter. Pipe 3 dropped lines down each corner and add dots in the same colour as the lettering.

4    Use the no. 43 nozzle to pipe running shells round the base and then over pipe with an S scroll (see page 89).

**Design 27:** Daisy trellis (round)

1 Place some white royal icing into a piping bag with a no. 2 plain nozzle. Pipe a long S scroll round the top edge of the cake, approximately $1/3$ of the way round. Pipe a C scroll from the middle of the cake to the end of the S scroll. Using the same nozzle and starting at the top, pipe straight lines across from the C scroll to the outer scroll, not too close together. Pipe the secondary lines on top, crossing over at an angle of approximately 45° to make a trellis.

2 Pipe in a few daisies at the top then pipe the stems following the line of the curve to balance the design. Add a few leaves on the stems.

3 Over pipe the S scroll using a no. 43 rope nozzle with a rope action in a clockwise rotation. Over pipe the C scroll with an anticlockwise rope action.

4 Pipe a running shell around the top edge, starting at the end of the scroll. Pipe a shell round the base then add drop line work round the top edge with reducing dots using a no. 2 plain nozzle.

**Design 28:** Run-out monogram (square)

1 Make a template for the letter, ensuring that it is slightly smaller than the cake top. Secure under a sheet of greased cellophane then outline and flood in the letter in your chosen colour. Allow to dry then secure to the top of the cake.

2 Outline the letter in white with a no. 1 nozzle, then over pipe the letter with a daisy and scroll (in white or self-colour if preferred) to take away the solid appearance of the letter. In green, pipe 2 inward C scrolls with a few leaves and pipe in a couple of buds, or use the smallest blossom plunger cutter to add a couple of blossoms if you wish (see page 182).

3 Pipe a running shell round the top edge of the cake and use a no. 1 nozzle to pipe a roped scallop underneath the shells. Pipe in a little fleur-de-lys at the front.

4 To finish, add a shell round the base with a no. 43 rope nozzle.

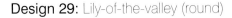

**Design 29:** Lily-of-the-valley (round)

1 Colour some royal icing with SK Holly/Ivy Professional Liquid Food Colour and place in a piping bag with a no. 1.5 nozzle. Leaving a 1.3cm (½") gap around the edge of the cake, drop line a curve approximately ¾ of the way round the cake. Add a smaller one starting in the centre of the cake, down to the base of the stem.

2 Pipe in the little bracts round the inside of both stems, approximately 7mm (¼") apart. Pipe in the lily-of-the-valley (see page 54). Pipe in some grasses and leaves at the bottom.

3 Using a no. 43 rope nozzle and white royal icing, add a running bead round the base.

**Design 30:** Chrysanthemum (round)

1 Take a round cutter a little smaller than the cake and gently emboss the paste on top of the cake with the circle. Drop a line on top of this with a no. 1 nozzle.

2 Use the same bag of icing to pipe a cross in the centre of the cake, then pipe another cross to make 8 lines.

3 Pipe a chrysanthemum in the middle with no. 1.5 nozzle (following the same method as for a dahlia, see page 75). Add a few leaves coming from the centre and slightly bigger leaves on the outside line.

4 Pipe a running bead round the base with a no. 43 nozzle then over pipe with a no. 2 nozzle.

Templates for more mini cake designs are given on pages 310 to 311.

# Templates

Oval cake-top
decoration

Freestanding designs for cake tops

Design for cake-top
decoration (round)

Congratulations

Congratulations

Congratulations

Greetings

Greetings

Noel

Christmas

NOEL

Greetings

Design ideas for lettering

NOEL

Best Wishes

Noel  Noel

Best  NOEL

Wishes

Happy Christmas

With Love

Design ideas for lettering

To my Valentine

With Love

Happy Valentine's Day

To My Valentine

EASTER

To My Valentine

EASTER

Design ideas for lettering

ABCDEFG
HIJKLMNOP
QRSTUVWXYZ

abcdefghijklmn
opqrstuuwxyz

Congratulations

Alphabet templates

ABCDEFG
HIJKLM
NOPQRST
UVWXYZ

abcdefghijklmn
opqrstuvwxyz

Alphabet templates

abcdefghijklmn
opqrstuvwxyz
ABCDEFGHIJK
LMNOPQRSTU
VWXYZ

abcdefghijklm
nopqrstuvwxyz
ABCDEFGHIJK
LMNOPQRSTU
VWXYZ

Alphabet templates

Run-out numerals, double-sided

Run-out numerals

Run-out plaques

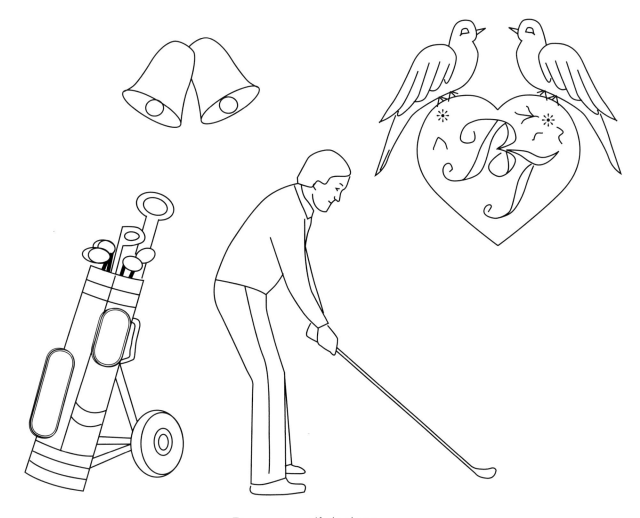

Run-out motif designs

Gazebo

Side panel

Doors

Roof piece

Outline for tulle
backing

Flower stand:
make 1 large
(for base) and 2
small

Solid base (large
and small hexagons)
and guideline for
roof assembly

Curved fillet

Corner run-out pieces

Collar design for Golfer Cake

Brush embroidery design for cake top

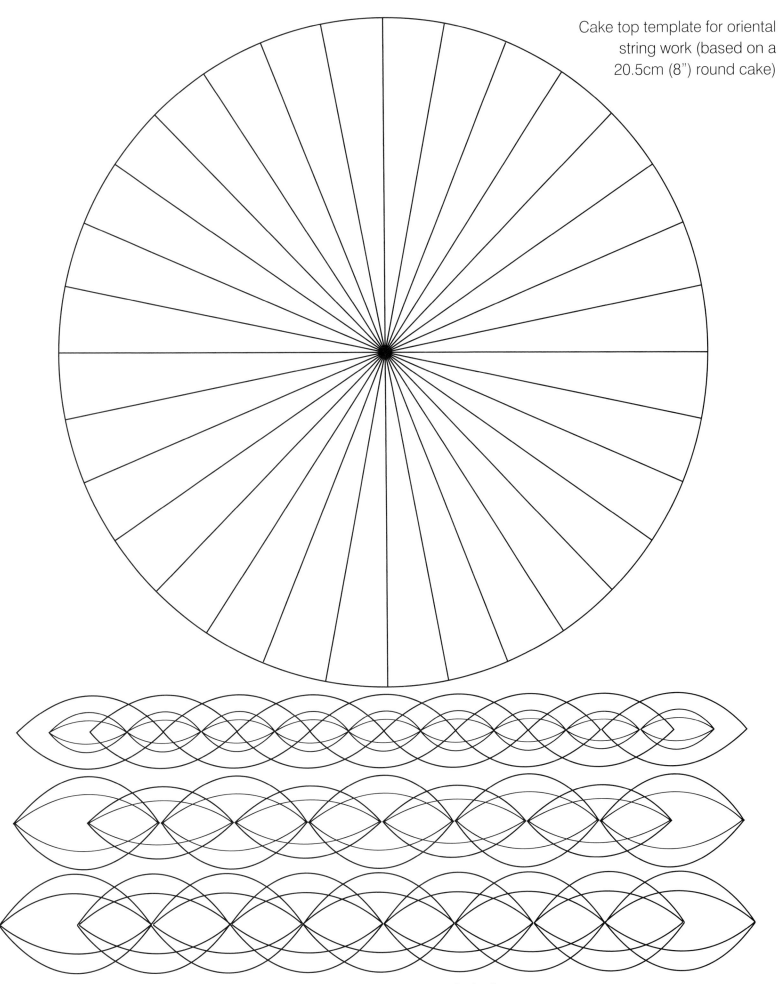

Cake top template for oriental string work (based on a 20.5cm (8") round cake)

Examples of oriental string work designs

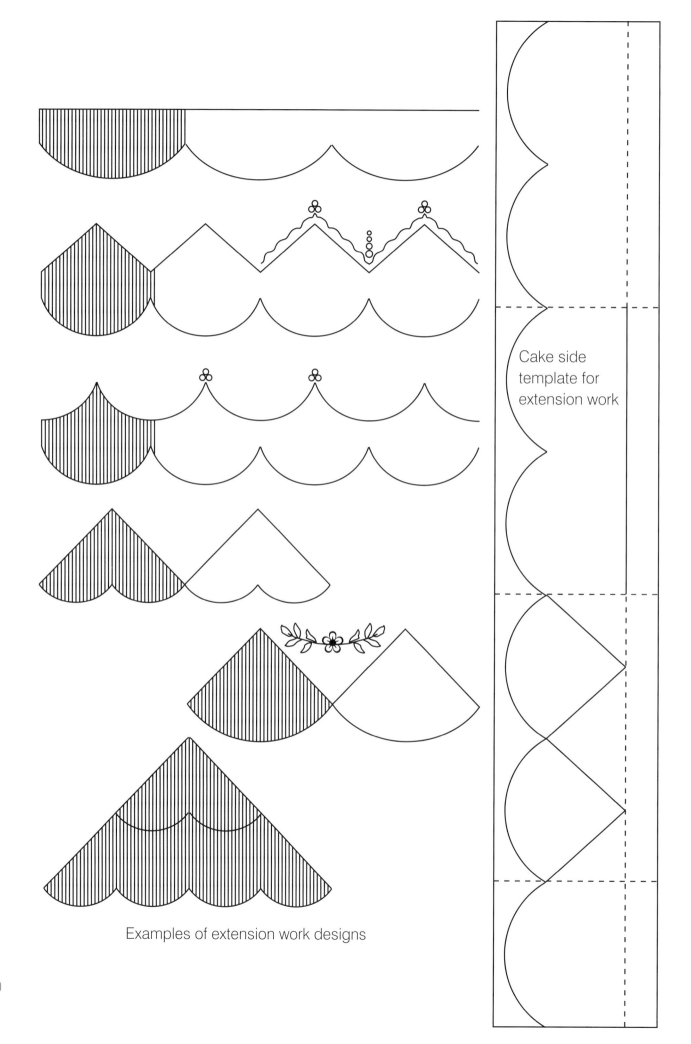

Examples of extension work designs

Cake side template for extension work

Cake top designs

**NOEL**

Cake top design

Gazebo platform

Gazebo top

Gazebo base

Gazebo for Hexagonal Wedding Cake

Side panel

Doors

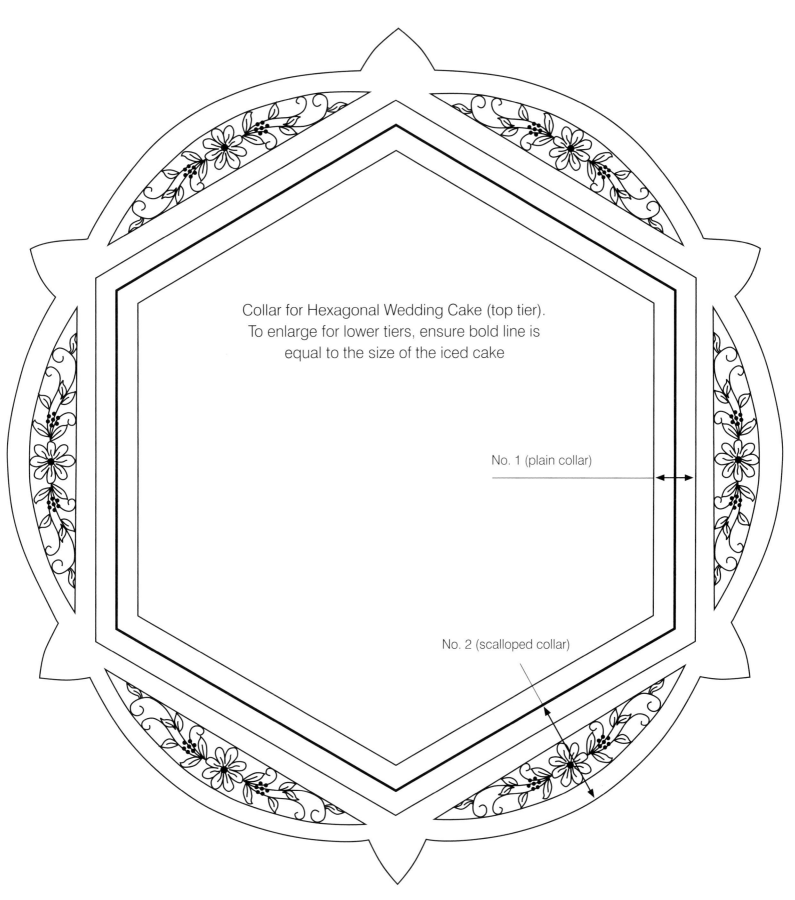

Collar for Hexagonal Wedding Cake (top tier).
To enlarge for lower tiers, ensure bold line is
equal to the size of the iced cake

No. 1 (plain collar)

No. 2 (scalloped collar)

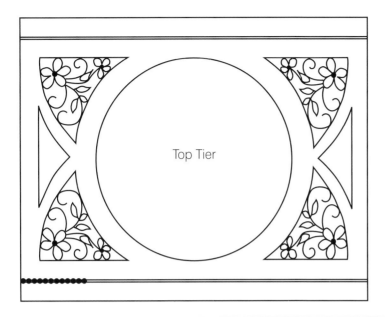

Top Tier

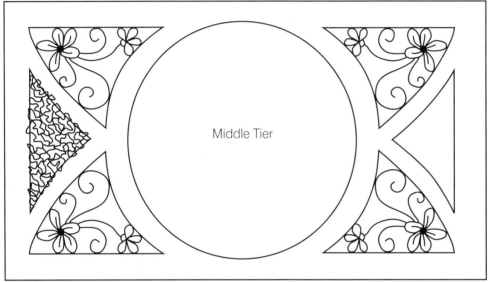

Middle Tier

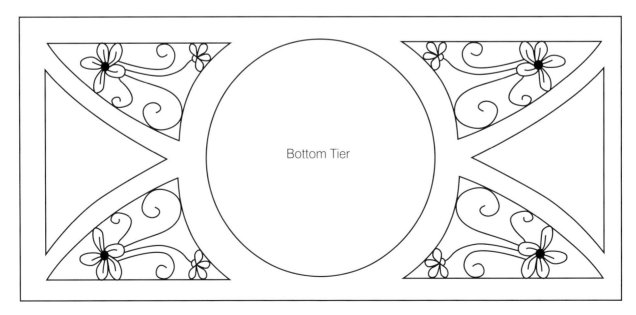

Bottom Tier

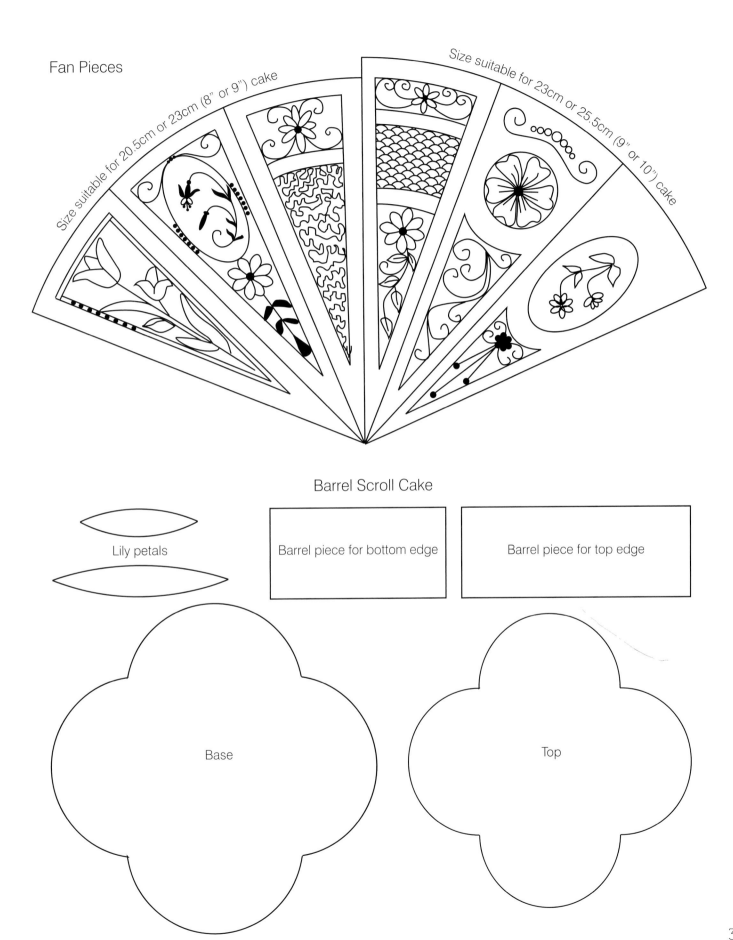

Fan Pieces

Size suitable for 20.5cm or 23cm (8" or 9") cake

Size suitable for 23cm or 25.5cm (9" or 10") cake

Barrel Scroll Cake

Lily petals

Barrel piece for bottom edge

Barrel piece for top edge

Base

Top

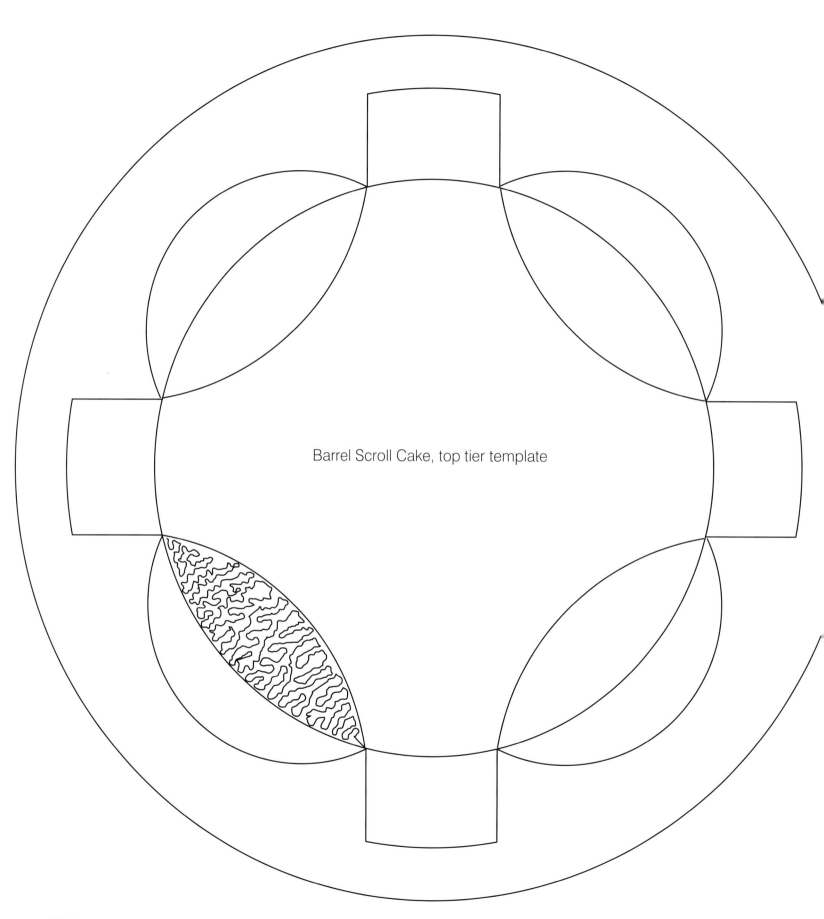

Barrel Scroll Cake, top tier template

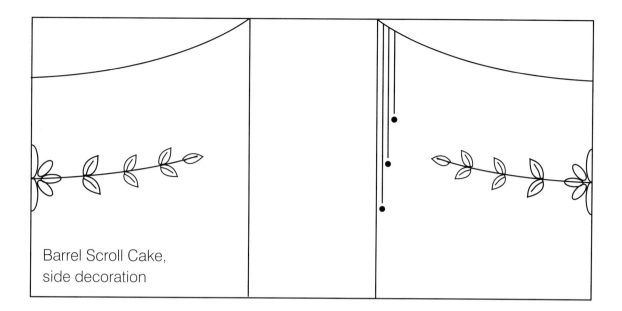

Barrel Scroll Cake,
side decoration

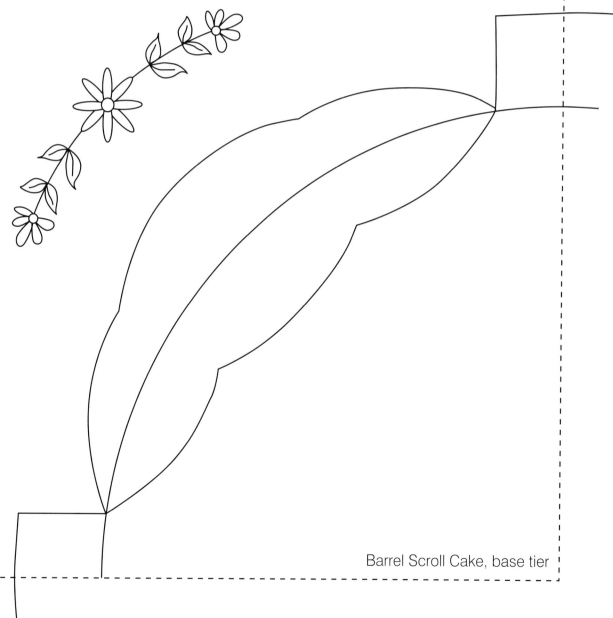

Barrel Scroll Cake, base tier

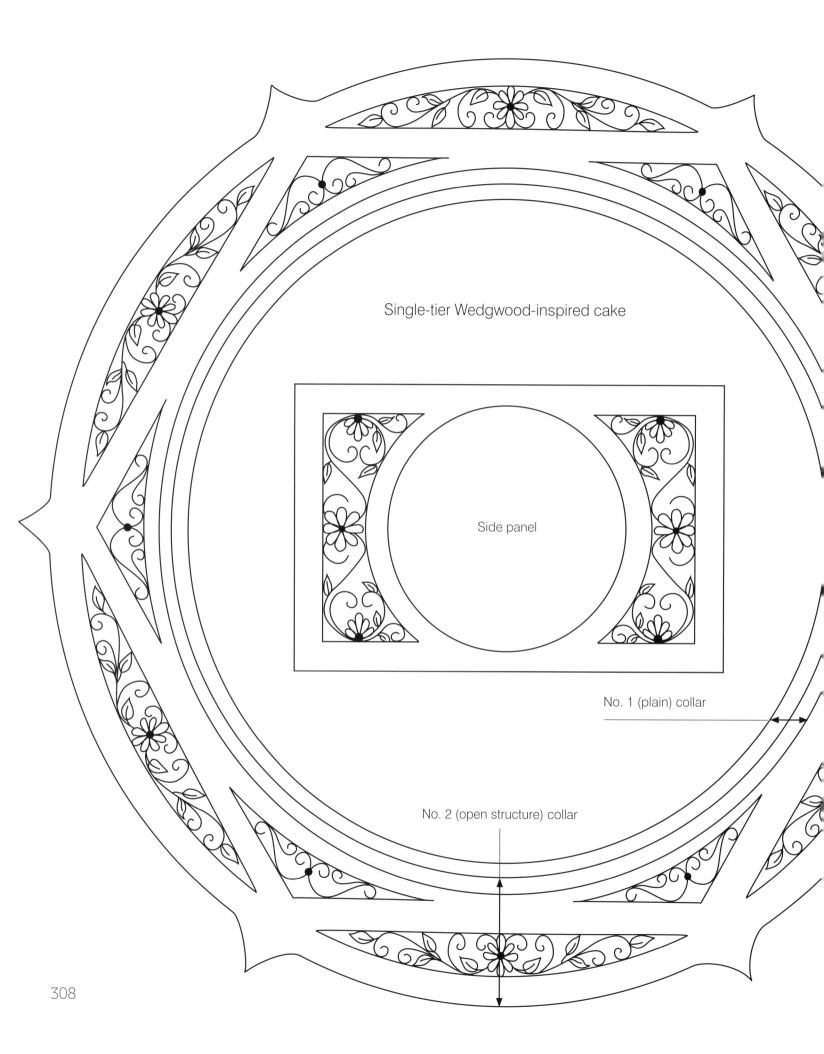

Single-tier Wedgwood-inspired cake

Side panel

No. 1 (plain) collar

No. 2 (open structure) collar

Cherubs for Wedgwood-inspired cake

Upright scroll piece for Christening Cake

Alternative upright scroll piece for Christening Cake

Cradle pieces for Christening Cake

Base x 1

Sides x 2

Front x 1

Back x 1

Rocker x 4

Scroll pieces for Victoriana Cake

Mini cake designs

Mini cake designs

# Troubleshooting

As with any technique where skill is involved, you may find that you come across problems with the decoration or the cake itself. There are a few 'tricks of the trade' that you can use to rectify some of the most common problems in baking and cake decorating.

## Cakes

| Problem | Cause | Solution |
|---|---|---|
| Fruit has sunk to the bottom of the cake. | This can be down to a fault in the recipe: not enough flour or egg; too much liquid, sugar or baking powder (if used in sponge or Madeira mixes); too much liquid in the fruit (e.g. syrup not removed from cherries). Alternatively, it may be caused by over-creaming the mixture or the oven not being hot enough. | Check you have followed the recipe carefully and adjust where needed. |
| Cake is small and sides have shrunk away from the tin. There may also be a raw streak at the bottom of the cake. | There may be too much liquid, not enough egg or baking powder, or the flour may be too soft. | Adjust the recipe. |
| Cake has collapsed in the centre and has a dark crumb and crust. | Too much baking powder in recipe. | Reduce the amount of baking powder used. |
| Large holes in cake and coarse, crumbly texture. | There may be excess baking powder (if used), not enough egg to fat or weak flour in the recipe. The mixture may not be creamed thoroughly. | Adjust the recipe. |
| There is a 'sad' (undercooked) streak under the top of the cake. | The cake may be under-baked or may have been knocked before baking. The oven may be too hot. | Check whether the cake is baked by pushing it gently with your fingertip: it should spring back up. Check the temperature of your oven. |

| Problem | Cause | Solution |
|---------|-------|----------|
| No fruit on top of the cake | The bowl has been scraped when transferring the mixture to the tin. | Never scrape the bowl; simply pour the mixture into the tin. |
| Cake lacks volume and there are white spots on the top. | Too much sugar used in recipe. | Reduce the amount of sugar slightly. |
| There are long holes in the cake. | The fat and sugar may not have been creamed properly or the eggs may have curdled. | Make sure the fat and sugar are light and fluffy or add a little flour to eliminate curdling. |
| The cake has scaling on the surface. | Ingredients have been over-mixed. | Always complete the last stage of mixing by hand. |
| Cake lacks volume and has a 'cauliflower' top. | The oven may be too hot or may not generate enough steam during baking. The flour may be too strong, the eggs over-mixed or not enough sugar. | Adjust the recipe or oven temperature. |
| Crumb is too tender and cake will not cut well or keep. | Too much fat in relation to egg which causes the mixture to feel very greasy. | Reduce the amount of butter used or increase the amount of egg. |
| Cake tastes bitter. | Sugar in the fruit has caramelized (burnt), causing the fruit to blow. | Reduce the temperature of the oven and make sure there is enough protection on the top, bottom and sides so that the cake doesn't get too hot. |
| Cake has gone mouldy. | 1. Marzipan or sugarpaste has been rolled out on cornflour which can cause mould spores to form.<br><br>2. Cake has been stuck to the board with royal icing. | 1. When rolling out marzipan or sugarpaste, only use icing sugar.<br><br>2. Use boiled apricot jam to stick the cake to the board if necessary (e.g. for oriental string work). |
| Apricot glaze does not stick the marzipan to the cake. | Water has been added to the glaze to thin it down | When marzipanning a cake, use boiled apricot jam because it is neutral in flavour and colour and high in natural pectins. As soon as it comes to the boil, put it onto the cake with a palette knife. |

| Problem | Cause | Solution |
|---|---|---|
| Grease coming through royal icing coating on a cake | Overworking the marzipan will cause the almonds to release oil. The oil will soak into the royal icing, making greasy marks on the side or top of a cake. | Warm approximately 450g (1lb) of marzipan in the microwave on a low (defrost) setting for 2 or 3 minutes. It will then be easier to roll out, lessening the chance of overworking the oil. If you already have this problem, put some egg white through a sieve and use a small brush or clean cloth to wipe the egg white over the cake where the grease has come through. Allow to dry for 30 minutes then repeat. You can now re-coat the cake without the risk of the grease showing through for a period of 8 to 10 days (the egg white forms a membrane). |
| Brown staining showing through royal icing coating on a cake. | 1. The marzipan is too thin and the colour from the fruit is bleeding into the icing. | 1. Use spacers to ensure that the marzipan is rolled evenly. When marzipanning the cake, the top should be approximately 7mm (¼") thick and the sides should be approximately 4mm (⅛"). |
|  | 2. There is too much alcohol in the cake. If the cake has been saturated in alcohol it will seep out of the bottom. | 2. After baking a fruit cake, allow it to 'rest' out of the oven for approximately 3 hours. Brush or spray some alcohol onto the cake surface. This should be sufficient if the cake has been baked properly (it will not need 'feeding' thereafter). |
| Yellow staining showing through royal icing coating on a cake. | Very yellow marzipan that is used on top of a very moist cake. The marzipan contains almonds, glucose and sugar; the sugar and glucose makes it hygroscopic, i.e. it will absorb the liquid from the cake. This causes it to become wet, then the royal icing (which contains glycerine) will soak up the yellow colour causing blotches. | Make sure the cake is not too moist (see above). The proportion of marzipan required for a wedding cake is half the weight of a cake. If the cake weighs 4.5kg (10lb), you will need approximately 2.25kg (5lb) of marzipan and 2.25kg (5lb) of royal icing to decorate the cake. |

# Icing

| Problem | Cause | Solution |
|---------|-------|----------|
| Icing is brittle and too hard (also known as 'flinting'). | There is no glycerine in the icing itself. | Add at least 5ml (1tsp) of glycerine per 450g (1lb) of royal icing for coating cakes. |
| Icing comes away from marzipan when cake is cut. | The marzipan has been left too long before the cake is iced. | Ideally, a marzipanned cake shouldn't be left for longer than 2 to 3 days in a dry atmosphere. For a single-tiered cake you can marzipan and ice it the same day. |
| Icing comes away from itself (also known as 'slating'). | Different consistencies of icing being used for each coating on a cake (different levels of glycerine). If the second coat does not contain as much glycerine, it dries quicker and harder (the same principle as washing a wall before plastering). | Carefully measure the ingredients when making icing. Ideally you would make all the icing for a cake in one go. |
| Cracks in the sugarpaste coating. | There is too much icing sugar on the surface of the sugarpaste. | It is very important to use a non-stick rolling pin. Make sure that you dust underneath the sugarpaste with icing sugar and do not mix extra icing sugar into the sugarpaste unless it is very sticky. You can avoid the problem of stickiness by adding a tiny amount of white vegetable fat to the sugarpaste to eliminate any stickiness. When you are bringing the sugarpaste down the sides of a cake, lift the paste and use your hand to gently ease it down. Polish the sugarpaste surface using a smoother or a pad of sugarpaste wrapped in cling film to eliminate any cracks. |

| Problem | Cause | Solution |
| --- | --- | --- |
| Icing won't hold its shape on shells, drop line work, oriental string work. | 1. There is fat/grease present on your equipment which breaks down the structure of the egg white so the icing will not hold its shape.<br><br>2. The icing has not been freshly beaten.<br><br>3. Egg yolks are present (these contain fats, see 1 above). | 1. When making royal icing, keep all equipment clean and free from fat/grease.<br><br>2. Always beat the icing before use, particularly if it has been left overnight.<br><br>3. Discard any contaminated icing and make a fresh batch, taking care not to allow any yolk into the mixture. |
| Difficulty in achieving sharpness around the edges of the letters and numerals. | Royal icing is too stiff. | Rub down (paddle) the icing slightly on the side of the bowl to remove some of the air and to help the icing 'settle down' on the cake surface. If you are still having this problem, use an artist's brush to neaten the edges of the lettering. |
| Icing made from fresh egg whites is weak in structure. | Fresh egg white is not as strong as powdered albumen (dried egg white). | Add some acid, such as citric acid (lemon juice); you will need 5 to 7 drops to 1lb icing sugar and 3fl oz of fresh egg white. Alternatively, add 4 to 5 drops of acetic acid (white vinegar). This will help to toughen and strengthen the albumen and give body to the royal icing. |
| Run-outs have a strong taste. | Animal fat, such as lard, has been used to grease cellophane. | Always use white vegetable fat where grease is required. Animal fat has a distinctive taste and the cake would not be suitable for vegetarians if it was used. |
| Icing for drop line work is too 'short' (breaks easily). | Icing has been left in a warm atmosphere, causing the air in the icing to expand. | Always re-beat icing before use, particularly if it has been left overnight. |

| Problem | Cause | Solution |
|---|---|---|
| Icing is bubbly and breaks when piped. | Icing has been over-beaten. | Place the bowl of icing into a basin of warm water with a warm cloth over the top. Leave for approximately 30 minutes: the air will expand and break down the air bubbles. Slowly beat it back to off-peak consistency before use. |
| Drop lines won't fall straight onto greased cellophane. | Rubbing the cellophane too much during greasing will create static. | Throw away the cellophane and cut a new piece. Grease lightly, taking care not to rub it too much. |
| Run-outs are dull. | Icing has taken too long to dry. | Always place run-outs under a desk lamp to speed up the drying process. This will result in a good shiny surface. |

# Glossary

### Apricot glaze

Apricot jam that has been boiled and sieved. This is used for putting onto fruit cakes before covering with marzipan as it has a neutral flavour and colour, is high in natural pectins and helps the marzipan stick to the cake. Do not use low-sugar jam as it will not keep as long.

### Brush embroidery

Using a paintbrush to emulate the effect of embroidery (see pages 168 to 175).

### Complementary colour scheme

Using colours that are opposite on the colour wheel, e.g. yellow and purple, to create impact in a design.

### Dowelling

Cakes with more than one tier must be supported with food-grade dowelling rods to prevent the upper tiers from sinking. Instructions for how to dowel a cake are given on pages 46 to 47.

### Drop line work

Lifting the icing up to extend it for work such as lettering, scrolls and extension work.

### Extension icing

Royal icing made from extra fine icing sugar that has been passed through a very fine sieve at least twice before use. This makes it suitable for extension work.

### Extension work

A form of drop line work that consists of lines extended either down from the sides of the cake onto a board or onto a piped bridge.

### Filigree

Filigree is a little like crazy paving in that it has no straight lines at all.

It is piped with the nozzle resting on the surface of the cake. In some cases lines must touch, e.g. in collar work, so the work doesn't drop out. When piping filigree work, use slightly rubbed-down icing.

### Flooding (in/out)

The process of filling in an outline with run-out icing. Also known as 'running in' and 'running out'.

### Glaze Cleaner (IPA)

Used for cleaning brushes after painting and glazing. After cleaning, wash the brushes out with warm water and washing-up liquid.

### Glycerides

Esters of glycerine (or glycerol) which are sometimes used in food colourings.

### Glycerine

A sweet-tasting, syrupy liquid which is mainly used in icing for coating cakes and for large scrolls piped directly onto the cake. It is added to icing so that, when it is dry, it does not become brittle or hard but remains soft enough to cut and eat. Glycerine is a humectant (i.e. absorbs moisture from the air).

### Glycerol

Another term for glycerine.

### Guttering

Using a curved former (similar to a piece of house guttering) to make off-pieces with a radius curve. The consistency of royal icing made for this purpose is sometimes known as 'guttering icing'.

### Harmonious colour scheme

Colours harmonise with one another when they are next to or close to each other on the colour wheel, e.g. orange and yellow.

### Lace work

Fine piping to emulate the patterns in lace. You can also pipe on top of real lace to make gazebos, fans, etc. as long as this is removed before the cake is eaten.

### Monochromatic colour scheme

Tints and shades of one colour. A tint is when white is added to a colour, a shade is when black is added.

### Off-pieces

Off-pieces are designs which are piped off the cake and are allowed to dry before being positioned on the cake. This is necessary for run-out work and is also useful for pressure piped motifs as it means you can practice piping away from the cake. It also means that you can prepare decorations well in advance which is particularly useful if you are working on a large project such as a wedding cake. When the designs are dry, they must be stored carefully in a cool, dry place.

### Oriental string work

Delicate line work that is piped onto the side of the cake so that it is freestanding. Also known as string work.

### Pull-up

A teardrop, either pointing up or down, often piped using a rope nozzle. Mainly used in scroll work but also used in pressure piping for making long petals.

### Pressure piping

Though all piped royal icing work is done using pressure, the phrase 'pressure piping' is used when piping figures, flowers, etc. onto a cake or plaque. Using the basic shapes for in pressure piping are

round, oval, pear, crescent, S scroll and reverse S scroll; these 6 shapes form the basis of all natural forms.

### Rope action

Rotating the nozzle to create a scroll that looks like a rope. You will find it easier to work clockwise if you are right-handed and anticlockwise if you are left-handed. When piping a reverse scroll it should be piped in the opposite direction.

### Running beads

A series of bulbs or 'pearls' which are piped in a line, either to hide a join, neaten an edge or add decoration. Hold the piping bag at 45° to the cake, squeeze to make a bulb, stop piping and 'lay down' the tip (i.e. touch the cake). Move along slightly and repeat around the cake.

### Rubbing down (paddling)

Take some royal icing on a palette knife and use a back-and-forth motion to rub it onto a clean work surface. To ensure the icing has enough flow after it has been rubbed down (paddled), scoop it up onto a palette knife and tap the knife on the edge of the table. If the icing appears shiny and wet, it is ready to use.

### Scratch piping

Pressure piping whilst keeping the tip of the nozzle on the cake.

### Tulle

Mainly used for off-pieces to make cradles, fans, gazebos, filigree churches and other cake top decorations. Adds strength by holding the icing in suspension. Always use rubbed-down icing for tulle work and remove it from the cake before serving.

# Index

# Suppliers

## Shops

### UK

**Squires Kitchen Sugarcraft (SK)**
Squires House
3 Waverley Lane
Farnham
Surrey
GU9 8BB
Tel: 0845 22 55 67 1/2 (from UK)
+44 (0)1252 711749 (from overseas)
E-mail: customer@squires-shop.com
Websites: www.squires-shop.com
www.squiresschool.co.uk

**Terri Simmons**
Cakes by Design
4 Bishopstone Road
Bishopstone
Seaford
East Sussex
BN25 2UB
Tel: 01323 490912 / 07714 231992
E-mail: terri@cakesbydesign.co.uk
Website: www.cakesbydesign.co.uk

**Jane Asher Party Cakes**
24 Cale Street
London
SW3 3QU
Tel: 020 7584 6177
Fax: 020 7584 6179
E-mail: info@janeasher.com
Website: www.jane-asher.co.uk

### Sweden

**Tårtdecor**
Bultgatan 14
442 40 KUNGÄLV
Svierge
Tel: +46 303 514 70
E-mail: info@tartdecor.se
Website: www.tartdecor.se

## Manufacturers and Distributors

### UK

**Confectionery Supplies**
Unit 11A, B and C
Foley Trading Estate
Hereford
HR1 2SF
Tel: +44 (0)1432 371 451/+44 (0)29 2037 2161 (mail order)
Email: kclements@btinternet.com
Website: www.confectionerysupplies.co.uk

**Culpitt Ltd.**
Jubilee Industrial Estate
Ashington
Northumberland
NE63 8UQ
Tel: +44 (0)1670 814 545
Email: info@culpitt.com
Website: www.culpitt.com

**decor4cakes Ltd.**
Telford Road
Clacton-on-Sea
Essex
CO15 4LP
Tel: 01255 687744
Fax: 01255 687745

**Food Packaging & Cakeboards Limited**
Unit 11 Farrington Road
Rossendale Road Industrial Estate
Burnley
Lancashire
BB11 5SW
Tel: 01282 423142
Email: sales@fpcb.co.uk

**Guy, Paul & Co. Ltd.**
Unit 10, The Business Centre
Corinium Industrial Estate
Raans Road
Amersham
Buckinghamshire
HP6 6FB
Tel: 01494 432121
E-mail: sales@guypaul.co.uk
Website: www.guypaul.co.uk

**Renshaw**
Crown Street
Liverpool
L8 7RF
E-mail: enquiries@renshaw-nbf.co.uk
Website: www.renshaw-nbf.co.uk
Manufacturers of Regalice and marzipan.

**Squires Group**
Squires House
3 Waverley Lane
Farnham
Surrey
GU9 8BB
Tel: 0845 22 55 67 1/2 (from UK)
+44 (0)1252 711749 (from overseas)
E-mail: info@squires-group.co.uk
Websites: www.squires-group.co.uk
www.cakesandsugarcraft.co.uk
www.squires-exhibition.co.uk

### Greece

**Sugar World – Aliprantis Ltd.**
M. Attikis 57
Ano Glyfada
16562
Athens
Greece
Tel: +30 210 9603114
Email: info@sugarworld.gr
Website: www.sugarworld.gr

### Nigeria

**Kogsy Merchandise**
12 Segun Gbelee Street
Omobe Estate Ph1
Ikeja
Lagos
Nigeria
Tel: +234 8022241682
Website: www.kogsycakeandsugarcraft.com

### Poland

**tortownia.pl**
ul. Chyrowska 4/6/8
03-569
Warszawa
Poland
Tel: +48 22 203 61 08
Email: kontakt@towtownia.pl
Website: www.tortownia.pl

## Classes, Colleges and Guilds

### UK

**Squires Kitchen International School of Sugarcraft and Cake Decorating**
Squires House
3 Waverley Lane
Farnham
Surrey
GU9 8BB
Tel: 0845 22 55 67 1/2 (from UK)
+44 (0)1252 711749 (from overseas)
E-mail: school@squires-group.co.uk
Website: www.squiresschool.co.uk

**The British Sugarcraft Guild**
Wellington House
Messeter Place
London
SE9 5DP
Tel: 020 8859 6943
Email: nationaloffice@bsguk.org
Website: www.bsguk.org

**Eastleigh College**
Chestnut Avenue
Eastleigh
SO50 5FS
Tel: 023 8091 1000 (Switchboard) 023 8091 1299 (Enrolment)
E-mail: goplaces@eastleigh.ac.uk
Website: www.eastleigh.ac.uk

**Frances McNaughton**
Frankly Sweet
Tel: 07850 105605
Email: frances.mcnaughton@gmail.com
Website: www.franklysweet.co.uk

**Scattercake**
26 Newland Street
Eynsham
Witney
Oxford
OX29 4JZ
Tel: 01865 464264
E-mail: annierelph@aol.com
Website: www.scattercake.co.uk

### Malaysia

**International Centre of Cake Atristry**
Wisma ICCA
1, Jalan PJU 5/15
Dataran Sunway, Kota Damansara
47810 Petaling Jaya
Selangor
Malaysia
Tel: 03-6140 8835
Email: inquiry@2decoratecakes.com
Website: www.2decoratecakes.com

abcdefghijk

Congratulations